Women and Suicide

Drawing on feminist theory, as well as theory surrounding the correlation between poverty and suicide, this study explores the increased rate of suicide among women in western Iran. Based on empirical research, including interviews with women from the Kurdish region of the country, the author considers the marginalisation of Kurdish populations in Iran, the suppression of their rights, and violence against women in its various forms. With attention to family violence, such as direct physical or sexual assault, psychological bullying, or through practices such as forced marriage or honour killings, the author also considers the political nature of such violence, as certain violent practices are enshrined in the Iranian constitution and legitimised in jurisprudential practice. A study of gendered violence and its effects, Women and Suicide in Iran will be of interest to scholars working in the fields of Sociology, Criminology, and Middle Eastern Studies with interests in violence, gender, and suicide.

S. Behnaz Hosseini is a Visiting research fellow in Centre for Studies in Religion & Society, University of Victoria in Canada and an Honorary Fellow in the Center for Research on Gender and Women at the University of Wisconsin College.

Routledge Research in Gender and Society

Trauma Transmission and Sexual Violence
Reconciliation and Peacebuilding in Post-Conflict Settings
Nena Močnik

Men, Masculinities and Intimate Partner Violence
Edited by Lucas Gottzén, Margunn Bjørnholt, and Floretta Boonzaier

Political Invisibility and Mobilization
Women against State Violence in Argentina, Yugoslavia, and Liberia
Selina Gallo-Cruz

Multiple Gender Cultures, Sociology, and Plural Modernities
Re-reading Social Constructions of Gender across the Globe in a Decolonial Perspective
Edited by Heidemarie Winkel and Angelika Poferl

Women of Faith and the Quest for Spiritual Authenticity
Comparative Perspectives from Malaysia and Britain
Sara Ashencaen Crabtree

The Genealogy of Modern Feminist Thinking
Feminist Thought as Historical Present
Ingeborg W. Owesen

Women and Suicide in Iran
Law, Marriage and Honour-Killing
S. Behnaz Hosseini

For more information about this series, please visit: https://www.routledge.com/Routledge-Research-in-Gender-and-Society/book-series/SE0271

Women and Suicide in Iran
Law, Marriage and Honour-Killing

S. Behnaz Hosseini

LONDON AND NEW YORK

First published 2022
by Routledge
2 Park Square, Milton Park, Abingdon, Oxon OX14 4RN

and by Routledge
605 Third Avenue, New York, NY 10158

Routledge is an imprint of the Taylor & Francis Group, an informa business

© 2022 S. Behnaz Hosseini

The right of S. Behnaz Hosseini to be identified as author of this work has been asserted by her in accordance with sections 77 and 78 of the Copyright, Designs and Patents Act 1988.

All rights reserved. No part of this book may be reprinted or reproduced or utilised in any form or by any electronic, mechanical, or other means, now known or hereafter invented, including photocopying and recording, or in any information storage or retrieval system, without permission in writing from the publishers.

Trademark notice: Product or corporate names may be trademarks or registered trademarks, and are used only for identification and explanation without intent to infringe.

British Library Cataloguing-in-Publication Data
A catalogue record for this book is available from the British Library

Library of Congress Cataloging-in-Publication Data
Names: Hosseini, S. Behnaz, author.
Title: Women and suicide in Iran : law, marriage and honour-killing / S. Behnaz Hosseini.
Description: Abingdon, Oxon ; New York, NY : Routledge Books, 2022. |
Series: Routledge research in gender and society | Includes bibliographical references and index.
Identifiers: LCCN 2021018128 (print) | LCCN 2021018129 (ebook) | ISBN 9781032073347 (hbk) | ISBN 9781032077253 (pbk) | ISBN 9781003208501 (ebk)
Subjects: LCSH: Suicide--Iran. | Women--Suicidal behavior. | Women--Violence against.
Classification: LCC HV6548.I7 H67 2022 (print) | LCC HV6548.I7 (ebook) | DDC 362.28082--dc23
LC record available at https://lccn.loc.gov/2021018128
LC ebook record available at https://lccn.loc.gov/2021018129

ISBN: 978-1-032-07334-7 (hbk)
ISBN: 978-1-032-07725-3 (pbk)
ISBN: 978-1-003-20850-1 (ebk)

DOI: 10.4324/9781003208501

Typeset in Times New Roman
by MPS Limited, Dehradun

Contents

	Acknowledgements	vi
	Preface	vii
1	Traditional society and violence against women	1
2	Honour killings and the rule of Islamic law	27
3	Child marriage and its consequences: poverty, addiction, and divorce	63
4	Marriage and life after divorce: caught between tradition, poverty, and suicide	88
	References	117
	Index	132

Acknowledgements

This book is based on research conducted on the Kurdish women in Iran between 2017 and 2020. I am grateful to a number of friends and colleagues for encouraging me to start this work, persevere with it, and finally publish it. In Iran, I thank Saedeh Dehnavi for academic support and fieldwork in Kurdistan. I visited Iran in 2017 and interviewed people in most of the cities in the Kurdish region. I am so grateful to the women and families who agreed to share their stories with me, and I hope I will help to list each of their voices.

In the Oxford and during my fellowship at FRSG group in Anthropology department at Oxford University, I am grateful to my professors, Philip Kreger and Soraya Tremayne, for their advice and support during the finalization of this project. I am also grateful to my colleague Ourania Roditi, who has read and commented on several chapters.

Completion of this book has been a lonely and painstaking process. The acute sensitivity of the subject, lack of sufficient resources, hesitancy and fear of the people during interview, and misinformation and false rumours emanating from Iranian officials and their opponents made it more difficult.

My research was funded by a small grant with JIWS in the USA.

I would like to thank ÖH Sonderprojekt for their support with publication.

Preface

In 2017 I was requested by the Dutch Immigration and Naturalisation Service (IND) to give an expert report on a sensitive case: namely, whether there was any reasonable justification for a 16-year-old girl not to report an honour crime to the Iranian authorities, that is, an attempt on her life by her father. While the Dutch Immigration Service did not dispute that a crime was committed against my client and her now dead sister, she was denied asylum in the Netherlands. The IND stated that, while it understood the difficulty women have when going to the police to report domestic violence in countries such as Iran, it is not impossible to do so. This crime was so heinous—the client was heavily burnt and her sister killed—that the IND found it incomprehensible that she did not go to the police.

That girl is now a 22-year-old woman. She is Kurdish-Iranian from the city of Sarpol-e Zahab in Kermanshah, and she and her family belong to the Ahl-e Ḥaqq (Yarsan) religion. She was born in 1997 and the crime was committed on 30 or 31 October 2013, when she was just 16. A paternal uncle of my client had proposed to her father that the girl should marry his son (my client's cousin). Although her father agreed, the young girl refused because the groom-to-be was too old, and she was in love with somebody else. She did not, however, tell her father about her boyfriend, a student she knew from school.

The two had been showing interest in each other for a few months but had never spoken, then he approached her and she agreed to spend some time with him. In October 2013 my client and her boyfriend were kissing in a car near a park, and they were seen by her father. When she got home, her father confronted her and beat her. He made it clear that he wanted her to marry her cousin. My client was locked in her room and forbidden from attending school. After a few days, her father dragged her outside, doused her in petrol, and tried to set her on fire. Her sister Nasrin, who tried to intervene, caught fire as well and later died in the hospital. My client managed to escape. She found a bucket of dirty water in a neighbour's courtyard to put out the flames, and the neighbour drove her to the hospital where she was treated for severe burns. She stayed in the hospital for about two months, not knowing that her sister had died, as the hospital staff and her maternal uncle kept that information from her. During her time in the hospital, her paternal uncle (the father of the cousin she was supposed to marry) visited her and threatened to kill her if she went to the police.

Two months later, her maternal uncle took her home. His family nursed my client, who was still very ill and bedridden for many months, unable to even go to the bathroom. She stayed with her uncle for two years as he took care of her. One year on, my client was still unable to go to school, so her uncle arranged for a teacher to come to the house a few times a week. After two years, he told my client that her father had been threatening him, demanding that he should throw her out of his house. Her uncle said that she would never be safe in Iran and arranged for her to immigrate illegally to Europe, paying for this journey. That is the story of how she came to be in the Netherlands.

My report to the IND stated how uncommon it is for women to contact the police for fear of tarnishing the family's reputation and bringing dishonour. In this particular case, nobody tried to seek justice and/or protection from the Iranian authorities. As there have been cases where Iranian courts convicted fathers on the grounds of violence/attempted murder against their daughters, the IND argued that there was no reason for the client not to press charges against her father. Another point they took into account was that my client stayed in Iran for two years after the assault. As a result, the IND stated that she had ample opportunity to seek justice and protection against her father and his brother from the Iranian authorities. The IND also claimed that it would have been expected of my client to at least attempt to report this crime with the help of her maternal uncle, who took care of her.

In conclusion, it is undeniable that she could have asked her uncle to go to the police on her behalf. The IND did not accept my client's explanation that it was not culturally permissible for her uncle to press charges against his brother-in-law. Apparently, her father had come to the house while she was ill and tried to take her away and kill her; however, she was not aware of this visit. My client was extremely anxious due to the fact that the IND did not believe her explanation that, based on the prevailing cultural norms and customs in her country, filing criminal charges against her father was simply not an option.

My recommendations reflected my client's opinion: that she was eligible for asylum as, based on Islamic law and the prevailing social norms, it had not been feasible or realistic to file criminal charges against her father. Although my client was eventually granted asylum, this example illustrates the challenges that thousands of refugee women face when authorities in potential host countries cannot understand the particular circumstances prevailing in these women's countries of origin. This extraordinary story prompted me to write a book on the different aspects of gender-based violence that women around the world are subjected to. Since many of these violent crimes lead to death and the majority go unreported, I came to see this publication as an effort to make women's voices heard and provide the world with much-needed information and understanding about the help they so desperately need.

1 Traditional society and violence against women

This publication aims to break new ground in discussing the painful and difficult subject of gender violence—in its many different manifestations—in Iranian Kurdistan. The topic has lain dormant, at least until quite recently, and in fact has never been fully addressed. The fieldwork for the present study was conducted by the author in Iranian Kurdistan in 2018. Although my analysis of concepts such as honour, shame, patriarchy, and gender-based violence relate to women throughout the country, some aspects of honour-based violence (HBV) affect Iranian Kurds more severely than other communities in Iran.

Iran is the second-largest country in the Middle East, the 17th largest in the world, and with 87 million inhabitants, the 17th most populous. Its ethnic makeup is complex, and there are large socio-economic differences among the country's regions. Iranian Kurdistan includes the provinces of West Azerbaijan, Kurdistan, Kermanshah, Ilam, and Hamadan, and borders Iraq and Turkey. There is also a significant Kurdish population in the North Khorasan Province in north-eastern Iran.

The Kurds themselves generally consider Iranian Kurdistan (eastern Kurdistan) to be one of the four parts of Greater Kurdistan, a roughly defined geo-cultural historical region where the Kurdish people make up the majority of the population. Greater Kurdistan is also comprised of parts of southeastern Turkey (northern Kurdistan), northern Syria (western Kurdistan), and northern Iraq (southern Kurdistan). The majority of the 4.5 million Iranian Kurds are Sunni Muslims and are settled across the borders of Iran, Iraq, Turkey, and Syria (Koohi-Kamali, 2003). An additional four million Kurds are estimated to live in Iraq, 10–12 million in Turkey, and 600,000 in Syria (Eickelman, 1998: 203).

The capital of Kurdistan Province in Iran is Sanandaj. With a population of 414,069, it is the 23rd-largest city in Iran and the second-largest Kurdish city. Sanandaj was founded about 200 years ago, yet, in its short existence, it has grown to become the centre of Kurdish culture. Today, the population of Sanandaj is mainly Kurdish; it used to have an Armenian minority which gradually emigrated from the city. According to the latest census by the Iranian Statistical Centre in 2011, Kurdistan Province had almost 1.5 million

DOI: 10.4324/9781003208501-1

inhabitants. Urban residents made up 66% of the total, while the rest lived in rural areas.

According to a labour force survey published by the Statistics Centre of Iran in 2018, the unemployment rate in Iran for 2017 was 12.1% in total: 10.2% for men and 19.8% for women. The percentage of unemployment in urban centres and in the countryside was 13.4% and 8.2%, respectively, while the unemployment rate for the regions of Kermanshah and North Khorasan was 21.6% and 9.7% (Statistical Centre of Iran, 2017–2018). In the Kurdish region of Iran, unemployment triggers a sense of vulnerability and causes individuals to fear for their future. Unemployment also creates a sense of loneliness and alienation due to meagre social support and non-existent government support such as social benefits, cash transfers, or loans. There is a large inequality gap between the Kurdish region and other regions, especially in the big cities.

Runciman (1966) points out that individuals perceive basic inequalities by comparing their position with the same "reference group" in the same category to understand their relative deprivation gap. For the whole community, however, other indicators of inequality are effective. A good overall measure of one's standard of living in a society is the cost of food (Runciman, 1966). As incomes rise, the total percentage of income spent on food decreases, and the share of non-food items, such as education, health, housing, etc., grows. The lower the food costs in a society, the higher the society's standard of living. In accordance with the Iranian Household Budget Survey from 1985 to 2017, the amount of income spent on food in urban Kurdistan was about 50% that of urban Iran, generally, while the share of food in the villages was very similar to villages in other areas. This was probably due to the general gap in living standards between rural and urban areas. According to the Statistical Centre of Iran, by 2017, the percentage allocated by households to food, in both rural and urban areas, was 37.2%, up by 13.9% compared to 2016.[1]

After centuries of monarchic rule by bilingual Turkic- and Persian-speaking dynasties, and despite the multilingual, multi-ethnic diversity of the population, Persian nationalists under Reza Shah, who was in power from 1925 to 1941, declared that Iran could only have one national language and one national culture. Intensifying the nexus between language, culture, and race, they spread Persian Aryanism as a scientific fact, creating a nationalist discourse or, more precisely, a set of identitarian narratives on culture that would shape not only Iranian politics but also social science research, the writing of history, and public debate for the century to come. It is convenient here to use two (admittedly simplistic) labels to describe the mindsets: "nationalists" and "ethnicists". The nationalists claimed to represent a reified Iranian nation, which the ethnicists argued is based on one ethnic group; the ethnicists sometimes referred to ethnic groups as nations without citizenship, in other words, those of Kurdish ethnicity were not citizens of Iran (Saleh, 2013: 204). Under Reza Shah, Kurds were no longer allowed to wear their traditional attire, a source of national pride. Kurds did not discard their attire, but rather kept it hidden, and the tribespeople in the mountains never really abandoned it at all (Roosevelt, 1947: 251).

The Kurdish regions in Iran enjoyed semi-autonomy until the late 1800s, but Kurdish claims for self-determination were suppressed by Reza Shah in the 1930s (Ghanea-Hercock, 2003: 12–16). In the aftermath of World War I, a major blow to the Kurdish quest for emancipation came when the 1920 Treaty of Sevres and later the 1923 Treaty of Lausanne quashed their dreams of being an independent state. The idea of Kurdish freedom returned during the occupation of Iran by Allied forces in 1941. As the Iranian army retreated and crumbled, much of its weaponry fell into Kurdish hands, while at the same time, many of the exiled Kurdish leaders were freed and were ready to return to their communities. The Soviet occupation of the area also emboldened the local Kurdish population. The indirect reliance of the Soviets on Kurdish tribes for the preservation of security in the region meant that the occupying power hesitated to subdue hopes for an independent statehood. In the end, the Soviets, who were not particularly trusted by the Kurds due to their history of brutality against them at the end of World War I, extended an official invitation to 31 local significant Kurdish chiefs to visit the Soviet Union (Eagleton, 1963: 14–16).

Soon afterwards, in the town of Mahabad in western Iran, a committee called the Society for the Revival of Kurdistan was formed, chaired by Qazi Muhammad. With Soviet support, on 22 January 1946, the short-lived Republic of Mahabad was established (Ansari, 2003: 88) and the Kurdish nationalists gained a foothold in Iran. Nevertheless, on 15 December of the same year, the Republic collapsed. This was mainly due to lack of tangible Soviet support and the opposition displayed by the tribes. Their opposition was heavily influenced by economic motives; for example, the tribesmen were severely affected by the loss of tobacco trade between them and the rest of the country, which was suspended following the Soviet presence (Roosevelt, 1947: 265). There was a heavy presence of government security forces in the Kurdish areas, and the activities of Kurdish separatist groups, such as the Iranian Kurdish Democratic Party, were closely monitored (Koohi-Kamali, 2003). Put somewhere else, the Kurds realised, following the withdrawal of the occupying army, how great their dependence had been on the Soviets economically and militarily. Finally, under pressure from the Western powers, including the United States, Iranian forces entered Mahabad, burnt Kurdish books, closed the printing presses, banned the language, and executed insurgents including Qazi Muhammad himself (McDowall, 2004: 245).

Introduction

The 1978–1979 Islamic Revolution in Iran, which led to the overthrow of Shah Mohammad Reza Pahlavi, ended with the approval in December 1979 of a new theocratic constitution and the declaration of Sayyid Ruhollah

Musavi Khomeini, known in the West as Ayatollah Khomeini, as supreme leader of Iran.

The Kurds participated in the revolution of 1979 and presented demands for a federal democratic state, the recognition of the Kurdish language, and the use of said language in education and publications. Several anti-regime demonstrations took place in the main Kurdish cities of Mahabad, Paveh, Kermanshah, Marivan, and Sanadaj (Maghsodi, 2001: 297). After the Kurds were denied a seat in the Assembly of Experts, which convened in 1979 to draw up the new constitution, Ayatollah Khomeini warned the Kurdish leaders that any attempts to undermine Iran's territorial integrity would be crushed, and he sent the Revolutionary Guards to north-east Iran to tackle the Kurdish insurgency (Zabih, 1982: 85). Despite Khomeini's warnings, in 1979, the Kurdish Democratic Party of Iran (founded in 1945) rebelled and demanded full self-determination, which the regime in Tehran perceived as an attempt at anti-Persian separatism (Hiro, 2013: 152). In response, Khomeini issued a Jihad and a Fatwa against the Iranian Kurds in the same year, declared its leaders enemies of the state, and initiated a military campaign against them. The hostilities continued well into 1980. Despite heavy casualties, the Kurdish leaders evaded capture and retreated to the mountains. The military campaign against the Kurds ended with hundreds of deaths and the banning of the Democratic Party of Iranian Kurdistan. Oppression persisted through the 1980s. Widespread poverty and starvation, killings, and executions were common while Khomeini's Jihad was still in effect. The 1979 rebellion eventually ended in 1982 with 10,000 Kurds killed and 200,000 displaced. The repression continued with killings, executions, and imprisonments, which, together with a lack of economic rejuvenation, further impoverished the region (Vali, 1998, 2003, 2014, 2015).

Unsurprisingly, the situation of the Kurds in Iran resurfaced during the Iran–Iraq War. Suffering and death were widespread, and Kurdistan underwent further social and economic destruction. In fact, by appealing to the patriotism of Iranians, the Islamic government consolidated its power over liberal voices in the country. The outbreak of the war occurred only shortly after the revolution, which in a way precipitated the "concentration and centralisation of power and the evolution of the instrument of oppression" (Saleh, 2013: 34). A wholesale oppression of the Kurdish people then began. According to Human Rights Watch, in addition to the destruction of many Kurdish villages, a large segment of the Kurdish population was displaced, and vast areas were contaminated with landmines (Human Rights Watch, 2019). It is estimated that 16 million landmines were laid during the Iran–Iraq War and are still located along the western border of Iran.[2]

On 28–29 June 1987, during the Iran–Iraq War, and although the city of Sardasht in West Azerbaijan Province on Iran's border with Iraq was not considered a military target, Saddam Hussein attacked it with what is believed to be mustard gas. This city, where Kurds were the dominant ethnicity, ranked first in deaths from suicide in 1991. After the war, although there was some minimal reconstruction work done by the local business sector, the region continued to suffer from stark underdevelopment (Vali, 2020). Even now, after all these years, many of the survivors suffer from respiratory problems, while a large number of people suffer from long-term psychological and mental health problems as the result of the attack (Shaddox, 2007).

In the late 1990s and early 2000s, Kurds supported the reformist Mohammad Khatami for president and enjoyed a short-lived, although not far-reaching, freedom to express themselves. A Kurdish party was established, which entered the Iranian Parliament in 1997. Newspapers and magazines started to be published in the Kurdish language; cultural and literary organisations were set up; and the first Shiite Kurd, Abdollah Ramazanzadeh, was appointed as governor of Iranian Kurdistan. However, these reforms did not last, as Khatami was unable to stand firm against the hardliners in his party. Their main concern was that Khatami's "realpolitik", which sought to both reinforce and reconcile patriotism and national pride in the country's rich heritage with a recognition of Iran's ethnic and cultural diversity, would undermine the regime's "political legitimacy" and the values of the Islamic Revolution (Saleh, 2013: 49–50).

The Kurds boycotted the 2005 elections, when the hardliner Mahmoud Ahmadinejad was elected president. One of the main issues for the Iranian Kurds was the establishment of the Kurdistan Regional Government in Iraq, which was legally declared an autonomous governing body within the state of Iraq in 2005, following the Iraq War in 2003. The protests that broke out were, once again, violently suppressed by the Iranian security forces. Kurdish disillusionment with Iranian politics continued even when the moderate Hassan Rouhani was elected in 2013 and again in 2017 (Gunter, 2020: 62–63). Discrimination in the areas of housing, employment, and political rights alongside arbitrary arrests, persecutions, and torture persisted, while Kurdish parents were even prohibited from giving Kurdish names to their children. As unemployment dramatically increased, many local youths left for other cities seeking jobs.

The desperate financial situation and the lack of viable options have given rise to the phenomenon of Kulbari. A Kolbar is a man or woman who is employed to carry goods on their back across the borders. Kolbars bypass customs and travel through mountainous roads under harsh conditions. The urgency to address this phenomenon has become more acute, with one Iranian non-governmental organisation (NGO), the Hengaw, stating that in 2018, 231 Kolbars were killed or severely injured (Gunter, 2020: 67). During the second week of June 2020 alone, two Kolbars were shot and wounded as they were crossing the border areas of Bāneh and Sardasht in the provinces of Kurdistan and West Azerbaijan (Kurdistan Human Rights Network, 2020). There are no reliable statistics about the number of Kurdish girls without fathers nor about widows and wives whose husbands have disappeared or were imprisoned or killed. This practice unearths many issues, such as the harshness of the working conditions, the risks involved, and that these men and women are often targeted by the border guards, who suspect them of smuggling drugs and other contraband.

Permanent reopening of border crossings, achieving sustainable development, and guaranteeing security for Kolbars' passage are some of the hot topics these days in the border provinces of the country, since these issues affect the lives of thousands. In 2019, for some unknown reason, the passage of Kolbars in the border provinces of the country, and in particular in Kurdistan, was blocked. It did not reopen until the representatives of the border towns of Bāneh, Marivan, Sarababad, and Saghez brought the issue to the Islamic Consultative Assembly and provincial authorities. For a period of one month, the passports required to pass the crossing were temporarily returned, pending a decision by the Ministry of Interior on a more permanent solution. (Border guards and economic activists believe that Kulbari borders should reopen and remain permanently open.) Although this line of work is exceptionally dangerous since people have to walk among mountain cliffs and minefields, it makes up significant economic activity, and it still is the main job opportunity in the area. According to statistics, 60,000 Kurds are working as Kolbars, smuggling goods through the Kulbari passages in the province, which contributes to the poverty and social damage in these border areas. This could cause further damage to the economy of the country. In the context of opening and managing the Kulbari passages in the country's border provinces, strategic plans and approaches are required in order to take advantage of these passages in a way that leads to sustainable development and security for everybody involved. Of course, the reopening of these passages will lead to a greater dependency on the central authorities, since they are, after all, responsible for border control. It should be noted that Kurdistan Province has four border stretches in the city of Bāneh and Marivan through these Kulbari passages.

Throughout their history, Kurds have been denied the right to nationhood, and as a result they have been subjected to systematic violence within the territories they inhabited (Khayati, 2008: 68–69). In the case of Iran, Kurds have been subjected to "systematic and sophisticated violence", and their quest for democracy has been labelled as separatist, threatening the territorial integrity of the country. Military operations in the region have resulted in additional violence and have forced thousands of Kurds to flee (Khayati, 2008: 68–69). Given that Iranian Kurds, alongside Baluchis, are the only non-Persian and non-Shia communities in the country, they have suffered severely from widespread discrimination, deprivation, and unequal access to economic opportunities (Saleh, 2013: 123). As a result, Kurdish regions remain socially and economically destitute: the poorest and most undeveloped regions in Iran with the highest rates of unemployment (Kaviani Rad, 2007: 103–114). Because of the state's discriminatory policies against the Kurds, the economic opportunities in these areas do not measure up to those in other parts of Iran. These regions are also the least educated areas in the country (Mohammadpour & Soleimani, 2020). Yet, the Kurdish opposition is arguably the most organised and militant opposition against the Iranian regime (Vali, 1998: 88).

Indeed, the Kurds' history of separatist campaigns, their strong cross-border connections and networks, their control of large land areas and populations, and their opposition to the Persianisation project make them the single strongest threat to Iran's territorial unity (Sanasarian, 2000: 14). Persianisation, the policy of assimilation into the dominant culture, has been mainly channelled through cultural and linguistic oppression and encouragement of the Kurdish population to disperse throughout Iran, which has had the intended result of altering the country's demography. Like other ethnic groups, Kurds define themselves (Sheyholislami, 2011) in terms of a collective pan-Kurdish identity, encompassing ethnic origin; spoken language; and religion, culture, and traditions irrespective of where they live. Economic underdevelopment, discrimination in the job market, rising crime, assault on cultural and religious symbols, and exposure to different conflicting messages are only a few of the factors that have contributed to a sense of alienation from the central regime in Tehran (Saleh, 2013). Nevertheless, Iran has a rich ethnic and cultural profile, and the identity of different ethnic groups remains quite distinctive. For the various ethnic groups to coexist harmoniously, a sense of "complementarity" with regard to "some of their characteristic cultural features" should be present (Barth, 1969: XX). Instead, in the case of Iran, and as Alam Saleh (2013) argues, the different ethnic identities have become politicised: interlinked with the ethnic and cultural context. Sepehr Zabih (1982: 85) also believes that the issues of ethnicity and religion among the Kurds are clearly politicised. At times, the religious minorities in Iran have been dragged into conflict through internal political developments in the country, and a large group of them have joined the Kurdish movement against the central government in response to Iranian nationalist ideologies. However, as previously mentioned, the Kurds are a largely heterogeneous group, encompassing tribes, clans, and communities that lack any concrete vision of national unity, and although the vast majority of them are Sunni Muslim, their linguistic, cultural, and geographical variations can be stark. A common factor is that their existence has mainly been marked by widespread oppression and a constant quest for nationhood (Griffiths, 2002). Interestingly enough, they have never been capable of putting forward a comprehensive roadmap leading to a unified state addressing the needs of all Kurds across frontiers. In contrast, they have pursued a rather localised nationalistic agenda, which differs considerably from country to country and is expressed in a multitude of political formations (Khayati, 2008: 66–67). Yet, like all ethnic groups in Iran, the Kurds also feel culturally close to fellow Kurds across borders (Saleh, 2013).

The general state of human rights in Iran has consistently drawn criticism from local and international prominent figures, governments, and organisations in recent decades. On 9 December 2019, a petition signed by Amnesty International, Human Rights Watch, the International Federation of Human

Rights, and many more civil society organisations appealed to the UN Member States to condemn the human rights violations perpetrated by the Iranian regime, namely, the unlawful arrest and the use of extreme force against civilians during the protests of November 2019 (Radio Farda, 2019), which took place in response to increased fuel prices announced by the government on 15 November. According to information provided by Amnesty, on 16 November, a thousand people were arrested during the protests, while the spokesperson of the Iranian Parliamentary Committee for National Security and Foreign Policy, on 26 November, maintained that up to 7,000 had been arrested (Amnesty International, 2019). Soon afterwards, during his regular statement before the 40th session of the Human Rights Council, the special rapporteur on the situation of human rights in the Islamic Republic of Iran, Mr. Javaid Rehman, also condemned the unlawful arrests taking place across the country, including the arrests of many journalists. He also voiced his concern about the disproportionate number of arrests and convictions involving members of minority communities (Rehman, 2019). According to the World Report produced by Human Rights Watch, during 2019, 217 people were executed, numerous human rights advocates were unlawfully imprisoned, and the right to a fair trial took another blow when the supreme leader, Ayatollah Ali Khamenei, appointed Ebrahim Raeesi, who had ordered the execution of several thousand political prisoners in 1988, to lead Iran's judicial branch (Human Rights Watch, 2020).

Since then, the Kurdish region of Iran has become militarised, and the Iranian government closely monitors the Kurds through regular checkpoints. The government also monitors them through the use of mobile phones and telecommunications, as well as social media. Based on information provided by the United Nations Human Rights Council, according to certain regulations introduced in 2017, monitoring includes private accounts and national search engines. Phone calls and social media are monitored by a 45,000-strong body established by the Iranian Revolutionary Guard Corps; prime suspects include a wide spectrum of civilians, such as academics, intellectuals, and activists. It is believed that a separate section of this body is stationed in the Kurdish dominated areas (Danish Immigration Service, 2020: 20–21).

An example of family and married life among Kurds in the region of Khorasan

In the region of Khorasan, many Kurds have lived as nomads for a century (although some have chosen to settle), and their livelihoods depend on finding pastures to feed their livestock. All the Kurdish nomads live in the areas from Khorasan to the centre of Quchan. They live in the highlands and villages of Chenaran, Quchan, Shirvan, Bojnurd, Mane and Samalqan, Asfarayn, Neyshabour, Kalat, and Dargaz, and in the middle of July they reach the northern hills around these cities and villages. Relocating to Aban in October, they move to Kalat and Maraveh Tappeh in the provinces of Golestan and

Sarakhs. Their way of life—always on the move and semi-self-sufficient—has solidified the role and significance of women in the nomadic community. In addition to their traditional roles of wives and mothers in large families, they also take care of the livestock, provide accommodation, defend the community in the absence of men, prepare food, and make clothes. These women are the true guardians and the main protectors of the folklore, traditions, and crafts (McGregor, 2013: 35).

The position of a woman in the Kurdish nomadic community in Kerman, Khorasan, is at the centre of life; however, they are still considered inferior to men. The man is the head of the family and the chief decision maker. He makes many decisions, from important changes to simple, logistical issues, such as the time spent on chopping wood. In the past, due to the lack of birth control, nomadic women had many children, usually between six and 12, some of whom died before birth or in childhood. However, two decades ago, the implementation of a population control programme in Iran improved access to contraceptives. This has steadily reduced the number of offspring, so that young families have no more than two to three children. Previously, it was normal for girls to be married by the age of 20, but usually they were married from the age of 16. Others who had to help out their families got married later, sometimes after reaching 35. Nowadays, because of the girls' reduced workload, the average age of marriage among the female nomads has dropped to 13 years. Many families accept this tradition due to the fear of abandonment; for example, a girl may find her own husband at a later age. He may not be a friend of the family and may live miles away, so, to be safe, parents find their daughters a husband at an early age to ensure the girls will stay close.

In the past, many marriages were planned by the girl's parents and brothers, and in many cases, the daughter's or the son's wishes were not taken into account. Many marriages were planned from birth and, prioritising the family over the children that were to be married, the families chose the future spouses while their children were still small. The children were informed of who their spouse would be by the time they had reached maturity. A dowry for the bride was provided, which was the amount of the bride's gold (Samadzadeh, 2015: 15). The engagement period was very long, and sometimes, the groom had to work for a couple of years for his wife's father. If a couple wanted to marry and their families prevented the marriage, they would flee, usually with someone's help. This was usually the girl's mother. She would help the runaway couple to get married at the earliest opportunity so that they wouldn't be forced to come home. Among the Kurds, serious violence rarely occurred towards the girl and boy who had run away, and they would usually be accepted after their marriage (Motavalli Haghighi, 2010: 58).

In an interview in North Khorasan, my informant, who was 35 years old and an expert on the Kurdish culture in North Khorasan, explained:

In the past, the stealing of girls was both a common place and in their favour. If a man wanted a girl, and the girl did not object, they did not run away; on the contrary, when convenient, the man alone, or with the help of several tribal men, attempted to rape her. Of course, the rape was not always forced on the girl, but her family were left with no other option than to marry her. Of course, there were times that the girl did not want to be kidnapped and resisted until she became pregnant of her kidnapper.

The tragedy of this kidnapping and the return of the girl became one of the most beautiful, traditional Kurdish folk songs in Kermanshah. At present, among the tribes and villages, if the two lovers choose to run away because their families oppose their union, they tend to formalise their relationship. In this case, the man goes back to his house so that the necessary arrangements can be made. Some families are happy with the bride, while other families even organise a wedding party and help to create a stable life for the couple. The relationship between the couple is mainly focused on ensuring the household peace and they only tend to the house and take care of the children. In the past, there had been widespread abuse and there have also been cases, where wives were beaten up even by their brother-in-law, but today things have become more subtle and the extent of physical violence has been revealed (Interview with Goli, researcher for a cultural heritage organization in North Khorasan, Shadkam, 2017).

As this quote illustrates, girls get married earlier. The girl runs away and may be raped by the boy and his friends until she gets pregnant: this is now a beautiful folksong. The mothers help them run away and then they all come back to a big celebration. So much of the subtle violence that is so common in this culture takes root in the institution of marriage.

Violence against women

Iranian women are subjected to many types of violence, the consequences of which are exacerbated by specific cultural traditions and laws. Married women are frightened of the prospect of separation or divorce, the difficulties associated with living a single life, losing custody rights, or being unable to visit their children following divorce (Amin, 2000). Together with child/early marriages and honour-based violence (HBV), these are considered the main manifestation of the widespread discrimination and violence to which women are subjected on a daily basis in Iran. Over the last two decades, and owing to the growing international awareness of these issues, there has been increasing resistance to this form of violence, and change has begun to take place in terms of both social attitudes and policy changes. In recent years, national and international initiatives concerning honour-based violence have been developed, often as a result of women's activism and the work of human rights organisations (Idriss, 2011). These initiatives have begun the long process of both challenging the practice of HBV and putting in place culturally specific strategies and measures to support victims.

However, societies do not change overnight. A recent positive example can be found in the latest piece of legislation introduced by the Iranian Guardians Council on 7 June 2020 on the protection of children from violence. Unfortunately, this response came a decade too late. The reason for this law was the widespread outcry surrounding the beheading of a 14-year-old girl by her father because she ran away from a marriage he had arranged between her and a family member (Esfandiari, 2020).

Families in Iran are frequently based on arranged or forced marriages, sometimes involving underage girls. Research shows that, in Iran, violence against women is widespread, manifesting itself in different forms, ranging from direct physical and sexual assault to indirect psychological violence and economic discrimination (Tizro, 2012). In its most extreme form, the violence is reflected in the number of abused or murdered wives, honour killings, and the suicides of young girls suffering violence within their marriages. Violence against women, especially in situations where women feel unable to seek justice, let alone obtain it through the legal system, is under-researched, and gaps in existing approaches to understand it have become increasingly evident in recent years.

As previously mentioned, social attitudes have slowly begun to change in Iran. However, in the rural areas of the country, due to the current economic conditions, men often struggle to find work in order to recreate their previously secure role as breadwinners—a development they perceive as humiliating (Mohammadpour & Soleimani, 2020). The repercussions, such as poverty, child marriage, forced marriage, suicide, and addiction, disproportionately affect women and girls who face many barriers—social, political, cultural, and economic—in their struggle to improve their situation and, in addition, frequently have to bear the brunt of male frustration.

Many women are forced to marry at an early age because their own families are financially stretched, and having one less mouth to feed is a relief. The majority of these women are divorced within a few years or commit suicide because of the intolerable pressure and abuse imposed upon them by their husbands and members of his family. Others, after or during the divorce proceedings, will be subjected to the unending suspicion of sexual infidelity by their husbands or families and may even be killed by them to restore the husband's family honour. In her 1989 book *Misogynies*, Joan Smith argued that the discrimination, denigration, and violence that women suffer are not historical accidents but are manifestations of misogynistic attitudes and behaviour. She writes: "Misogyny wears many guises, reveals itself in different forms which are dictated by class, wealth, education, race, religion, and other factors" (Smith, 1989: 11).

According to Dobash et al. (2005: 45), certain types of animosity can be aroused within the kind of hierarchical and inequitable marriages that occur so frequently in Iran, including suspicion, shame, and diminishing self-esteem. The asymmetrical dynamics involved in such a marriage undermines the quality of the relationship and causes tension and violence (Wilkinson, 2005; Daly & Willson, 1988). For a man, this can take the form of sexual jealousy or an expectation that his wife will obey him and act as his domestic servant. For a woman, such attitudes can lead to a desperate desire to leave the marital relationship. Indeed, many of the beatings and murders of women by their husbands (or their husbands' families) result from jealousy. Adultery, it seems, must be tolerated by women but will not be tolerated by men.

Sometimes, this mistrust—the fact that husbands are overly suspicious of their wives of committing adultery if they do not behave in a certain way—may be considered acceptable among the Kurdish community (Campbell, 1992: 242). For example, if a husband asks his wife to behave in a certain way, he encourages her to be obedient and will be unhappy if she fails to obey him. Dobash et al. (2005) explain that women are perceived to be the property of men and that, in Iranian culture, this perception is an established, societal norm.

Mohamadi believes that patriarchy merely reflects and accommodates the female need that leads normal women to marry domineering men. According to this theory, a woman likes to marry a stronger man and allocates the function of heading the household to the man, as she prefers him to run the social order. In her very nature and the core of her being, she has no wish to rule or manage. Mohamadi continues that her weaker mind and her fragile nerves find such work demanding and wearing. Instead of making decisions and acting as a director, she prefers to be the person who does as she is told and functions as her husband requires her to. Instead of opposing and confronting the man and contesting his decisions and commands, she prefers to be his subject, follow him, and act as he commands (Qaeni, 1994: 47). Qaeni (1994) argues that such descriptive verses should not be seen as legally binding injunctions: patriarchy was the prevailing system before Islam, so Islam accepted it as part of customs and practices and incorporated it into its teachings, but this was included because it was the prevailing practice rather than a religious duty. In a radical reconstruction of the faith, from this axiom, Qaeni concludes that the assertion that men are heads of the household is merely a reflection of things as they stood at the inception of the faith and that nothing in the text of the Qur'an demands that the situation should continue forever. This religion does not appoint the man as head of household, rather it was the common practice and so it was followed. There are no religious injunctions to follow such a pattern as a matter of duty; there is merely a desire not to disturb the existing order. It is possible for people to alter their practices in certain societies over time. In such cases, because the edicts of religious laws had been issued to meet the needs of the time and the times have changed, so should the religious laws, or their relevance disappears (Qaeni, 1994).

Men and their families have endless ways to impose control over women's lives. The feeling of a lack of control over one's life is known to be a contributing factor to depression, while socially determined gender roles and responsibilities are considered far more likely to place women, rather than men, in situations where they may feel this lack of autonomy. Autonomy is connected with an individual's well-being and the ability to make informed and rational decisions in pursuit of one's personal goals and interests. Women often perform unpaid labour and are under-appreciated for their household work and childcare. They experience social and financial dependence, which, coupled with ongoing gender-based discrimination legitimised by the laws and policies of the Islamic Republic, can lead to negative self-esteem, which is, in other words, tantamount to feeling unlovable, rejected, and inadequate. Sometimes, those affected by the ongoing oppression, mistreatment, and discrimination may feel as if suicide is the only way out of a hopeless situation where nothing appears as if it is going to change. A large number of women are affected by anxiety connected to this ongoing situation, developing trauma-related disorders, which also lead to suicide. Social factors, such as family pressure upon women, is another reason why many of these women are desperate and try to attempt suicide. Domestic violence and forced and child marriages, coupled with poverty and market discrimination, severely hamper women's autonomy and contribute to helplessness, depression, and, ultimately, to an increased number of suicide attempts.

Violence against women in its various forms, within and outside the home, continues to be a widespread violation of human rights. Furthermore, these women's limited access to education prevents them from developing their decision-making abilities and limits their capacity to express their concerns and seek justice. The opportunities that women have to learn about their rights and to defend them are constrained by the political, bureaucratic, and cultural context in Iran. The Iranian state does not consistently and effectively uphold and enforce women's human rights. In all societies, to a greater or lesser degree, women and girls are subjected to physical, sexual, and psychological abuse that cuts across the lines of income, class, and culture. The low social and economic status of women can be both a cause and a consequence of violence against women. This is a pronounced problem in the Kurdish regions. Perpetrators are rarely investigated or charged by the police, and women are not protected against aggressive husbands or other male relatives. The issue of control over women and men's mentality towards them is a thorny issue in Islam and in Islamic society and will be subsequently explored; however, it is worth noting that because men's control over women is deeply embedded in the social structure, it is considered perfectly normal.

Honour killings

Honour killings refer to the murder of women and sometimes men under the pretext of restoring or safeguarding the lost honour of a family. Honour is a notion derived from ancient Greek culture and covers a multitude of meanings: dignity, reputation, socially accepted, chastity, holiness, and integrity (Safilios-Rothschild, 1969: 598).

The concept of honour is not gender specific and has a neutral meaning (Qadir Shah, 2002). Every society ascribes its own meaning to the word according to its socio-economic and cultural practices. Patriarchal societies manipulate and contort it to make honour the sole responsibility of males and defend the notion that men are the sole possessors and defenders of honour. The cultural practices and traditions that have shaped societal moral values are highly biased against women as evidenced by the widespread discrimination and violence against them. In Kurdistan, women accused of besmirching the family name are murdered to restore the honour of the family. Such killings are morally and ethically justified because they are based on the cultural and patriarchal perception of ownership of women—a woman is considered the repository of family honour, while the man is the sole source of authority who will dictate when this honour has been tarnished and how it can be restored.

What makes the situation even more complicated and worrying is that honour crimes are sometimes committed with the connivance of female members of the family. Almost counterintuitively, killing in the name of honour occurs in a family system where members are closely tied to each other in bonds of affection, compassion, and love. This is a strange, yet unique combination where affection and brutality coexist in conflict as well as unity. Given the absence of hard statistical evidence, it is difficult to quantify the full scale of the problem. Yet, according to a report drafted by the Home Office (U.K.), 340 instances of honour killings occurred between 2016 and 2017 in Iran, mostly in the regions of Kurdistan and Khuzestan. Moreover, it is reasonable to expect that the number of honour killings has increased in the past few years, as the rationale for justifying this inhumane practice has broadened. For example, women and men who committed adultery used to be killed in the name of restoring the family honour, but now, women are murdered for a number of indiscriminate reasons ranging from being the victim of rape to refusing a marriage proposal.

It is of the utmost importance to clarify that not all violence against women in the family is honour related, nor are all murders of girls and women honour killings. What differentiates honour-related violence and murder from ordinary family violence is that the deed is often decided by the family as a whole, and it is premeditated. The perpetrator, often a close male relative of the victim, is chosen on the basis of given criteria and is treated with respect and pride by the family. Restoring the family's honour and washing away the shame is seen as a social obligation and the right of the offended group, that is, the family and relatives. The misdeed is often met with understanding and silent acceptance by the local community, the village, or the ethnic group. Both men and women are subject to honour killings, but most victims are women.

Instances of honour-related violence and honour killings are well documented in many countries, such as Pakistan, Kurdish communities in Turkey and Iraq, the Palestinian population, and in immigrant communities in a number of European countries (Salih, 2013; Julios, 2016).

Research methodology in Iranian Kurdistan and the challenges encountered

This study aims to examine the factors underlying different aspects of violence against women in Iranian Kurdistan. In particular, I have identified the concept of honour, which plays a pivotal role in regulating social relations in the region. It is well known that scholarly research on honour crimes among the Kurdish-Iranian communities emphasises the connection between honour and culture. I chose this particular topic because child marriages and honour crimes against women remain a widespread and sensitive phenomenon in the Kurdistan region of Iran in spite of legislation being adopted on domestic violence and increasing collaboration between state and civil society to combat it. Nowadays, murders in the name of honour are considered even more brutal, degrading, and inhumane than 20 years ago. Yet, they are not addressed and recognised as honour crimes by civil society or state institutions. Journalists and NGOs working on women's issues report cases of honour crimes as domestic violence or murders motivated by honour. No critical arguments are provided to explain the meaning of honour and honour crimes in Iran. The question therefore arises as to why certain people feel the need to legitimise such murders in the name of culture and tradition.

A significant part of my research sheds light on people's perceptions of what constitutes honour and specifically on how the concepts of honour and honour-based violence are inextricably linked with culture and customs inherited from the past. Iranian Kurdistan is a socially conservative and male-dominated society. The family structure is based on patriarchal principles; for example, the hierarchy of family members is determined by gender and age. Men have dominance over women and elders have dominance over youths. The relationship between individuals of different genders is based on the genders being inherently different but compatible. Traditionally, Muslims see men and women as being equal but distinct from each other. Duties and rights within a family and marriage are gender based, which is very clearly reflected in Islamic and Iranian family statutes. This has implications for the police and courts' handling of women, women's legal position, women's positions in society, the number of honour killings carried out, and the extent to which women who are victims of violence can seek help.

The research methodology I employed in this study is based on both qualitative and feminist approaches. Data were collected through face-to-face, semi-structured interviews and were analysed using the conventional thematic analysis approach. For a limited number of instances pertaining to female suicide and due to the scarcity of available information and the unavailability of witnesses or peers wishing to come forward, I researched and analysed certain cases I found on reputable websites online. Thematic analysis is the most common way of dealing with data in qualitative research as detailed by Snow et al. (2005) and Silverman (2005). It uses analytical induction to classify data into concepts and categories as they emerge through an interpretive process, or, in other words, themes come from the data and are supported by data (Charmaz, 2006; Conrad et al., 1993). I used thematic analysis of the data in order to examine the diversity among the personal narratives of my informants more closely. I also focused and interpreted all the secondary information they provided, such as family and personal relations, including who was involved in the smuggling of goods, in order to construct a coding frame, followed by a step-by-step procedure of qualitative text reduction (Mayring, 1983: 37).

In the process of data collection, observation and deep interviewing methods were used. Twenty-one women between the ages of 17 and 36 years were interviewed. In some cases, I interviewed men or the family members of girls or women who were killed by their husbands, brothers, or fathers. On different occasions, I interviewed relatives or neighbours if the murderers themselves had been killed. In this case, the number of interviews I conducted is higher than the number mentioned in this study. For my interviews, I employed the method of oral history, which usually covers the respondent's life story. It follows the life experience of individuals and aims to document the participant's subjective understanding and establish what an individual brings to a given situation or set of circumstances. In-depth interviewing allows the feminist researcher to access the voices of those who are marginalised in a society. Women, people of colour, LGBTQ+ people, and the poor are examples of marginalised groups. Finally, since I physically lived in the communities and observed them for a significant period, my research falls, in my opinion, within the category of ethnographic research.

The interviews were conducted in Persian and Kurdish. My primary target of subjects included women who had been subjected to domestic violence, married at a very young age, got divorced, and had personally experienced or had relatives who had been victims of honour killings. I made use of semi-structured interviews, as I expected that respondents would be flexible with their answers. This also allowed me to better understand the informants' perceptions and attitudes regarding honour crimes against women. All my informants were selected through the snowball method, by making use of my personal networks and contacts I had established with the NGOs working in the area. Due to the sensitivity of the topic I was dealing with, I had to take into account the concerns raised by some of the interviewees. For example, it was very difficult to confront the informants with questions about matters such as sexuality, as this issue is considered a taboo and people hesitate to talk about it. To bypass obstacles during the interviewing process, I occasionally had to resort to unstructured questions, and I believe I was fully in control of my research agenda. Often, I adjusted my questions depending on the responses I received, in order to delve deeper into uncomfortable topics.

Reinharz and Davidman (1992) argue that interviewing is one method used by feminist researchers to attempt to access women's hidden knowledge, and researchers can use it to gain insights into the world of their respondents. It is a method used by feminists in a range of social and natural science disciplines, from anthropology, where the researcher conducts fieldwork within a given culture, to sociology where the feminist researcher wants to gain an insight into the respondents' innate knowledge and feelings. We can see that the range of interviews conducted by feminists ranges from the unstructured, in-depth variety to much more specific sets of questions that fit into a survey format suitable for the lives of respondents living in a community or society. Feminist researchers bring a unique perspective to the practice of in-depth interviewing. This is because they are often cognisant of issues of power and authority that might affect the research process. These researchers are mindful that they must consider their own standpoint. Feminist researchers are able to discern how their own values and biases affect their research at all points along the research continuum and are particularly interested in issues of social justice and social change for women and other oppressed groups (Hesse-Biber, 2007).

My research started with a period of preliminary desk research to establish the situation of women living in the Kurdish regions. Using extensive primary and secondary materials, including internet-based resources, resources from the KHRP (Kurdish Human Rights Project), information from regional partners, and other specialist resources and publications, I drafted a background paper, presenting an informed analysis of the issues, which contributed to an understanding of the main challenges and aspects of violence confronted by women in the region on a daily basis. It also helped me prepare a detailed questionnaire to be used during the fieldwork. The research included an analysis of suicides among women in Iranian Kurdistan in order to gain a better understanding of the phenomenon. In the first phase of fieldwork, I visited Kermanshah, Kangavar, Ilam, Kohdasht, and Sanandaj between September 2017 and September 2018.

At a more practical level, when I started interviewing, I faced many obstacles and limitations. The interviewees were of different ages; most of them were Shia and only a few Sunni. The fieldwork took place in Kurdistan, which means that my ability to work was limited first by my gender, secondly by the respondents' background, and, last but not least, by governmental attitudes towards Kurdish people. As already explained, although my personal contacts and my Kurdish heritage facilitated my work, I had to limit the geographical scope of my fieldwork by staying in cities, some of which did not have hotels, meaning that I had to stay with local families. I faced another challenge when people realised the nature of my work. Although I attempted to keep a low profile and be discreet, this did make my research more difficult. I also visited the villages of Islamabad, Kermanshah, Asadabad, Ganghareh, and Ilam. In Kermanshah, I succeeded in speaking with a women's lawyer. Yet, the deputy governor of Kermanshah and the welfare officer provided me with no additional information. The hospitals and psychology clinics that I had hoped would help me, or at least provide me with some basic information, did not, invoking patient confidentiality. In the data I collected, all the names have been changed to ensure the anonymity of the interviewees. Further, the relationship between the author and the interviewees was mostly based on personal contacts I cultivated with the local people, most of whom came to appreciate me as a woman of a similar age and ethnicity.

The Iranian authorities do not permit human rights groups such as Amnesty International or Human Rights Watch, foreign researchers, or journalists to travel to Iran on their own to obtain information about honour killings or other forms of violence against women. Many have struggled with this problem; for example, Landinfo's (2009) report on honour killings in Iran was considerably more influenced by general analyses based on the limited information and statistics available about Iran than on concrete detailed examples taken from a wide range of sources. As a result, the primary sources of available, open information came from representatives of civil society, the authorities, and media run by exiled Iranians. Further, it has to be noted that this research lacks official statistics of instances of violence against women and honour killing, despite having established reliable contacts with the local authority in Kurdistan. Estimates of the number of child marriages or suicides is limited to online Persian news. It was reported that in 2011 there were 960 child marriages, 220 child marriages in 2012, 176 in 2013, and 179 in 2014, however, the official statistics do not register unofficial religious marriages below the age of 13. According to the Iranian website Entekhab, every year between 500,000 and 600,000 child marriages take place in Iran. It is estimated that up to 400,000 girls are between 11 and 14 years old, while around 300 are under the age of nine (Stone, 2019).

During my fieldwork I strove to contact as many lawyers as possible to protect the anonymity of the clients/interviewees. This was not always particularly easy. At the beginning of my research, it took me hours to identify a lawyer who was willing to talk to me. It was my priority to set up an interview under prime conditions; at one point I even experienced a delay of roughly one month before the meeting was arranged. Eventually, the long-awaited interview turned out to be no more than a simple conversation, since the intelligence agency gave very limited information about several clients and postponed the remaining interviews. I also met with an education consultant, with whom communication proved equally ineffective, as he only provided me with very vague and ambiguous answers.

During the process of conducting research, I could not interview state officials, as meetings I requested were often turned down. The findings and subsequent recommendations were therefore based primarily, but not exclusively, on information obtained from interviews conducted with civil society representatives and women's NGOs. Most of the information on female suicides and attempted suicides collected was provided anecdotally. For example, I was told about several cases of women who had killed themselves or attempted suicide as a result of the violence and discrimination they experienced on a daily basis. Most of the information on suicides was provided through snowballing samples, such as when talking with neighbours, family members, and acquaintances. In most cases, it was difficult to interview families who had experienced an honour-related suicide. Therefore, I interviewed those who knew what had happened. The stigma attached to suicide survivors meant that gaining information directly from them was extremely difficult. This setback, coupled with the lack of accurate official governmental statistics regarding precise numbers of female suicides in the Kurdish regions, made the use of the questionnaire in the field largely redundant. I carefully monitored and evaluated the findings of the desk research and the results of the fieldwork in order to produce an interim report including preliminary recommendations and findings. The report concluded that, despite the lack of hard data to prove information on a rising female suicide rate, women living in the Kurdish regions are disadvantaged to a far greater extent than those living in the rest of the country.

As a feminist interviewer, I was interested in the subjugated knowledge of the diversity of women's realities that often lies hidden and unarticulated. I was asking questions and exploring issues that were of concern to women's lives, such as issues of social change and social justice for women and other oppressed groups. As a female interviewer I was aware of the nature of my relationship with those I interviewed, careful to make them understand my personal and research standpoint and what role I played in the interview process in terms of my power and authority. I organised my interviews with women with whom I shared the same language and culture; I was both an insider and an outsider. I belonged to the country where some of my informants lived, and I shared the same ethnicity as the women I interviewed. During the course of her fieldwork among Gullah women, Beoku-Betts (1994) found that her research was enhanced when she informed her participants that she too was raised in a rural community with similar cultural practices. This revelation of her social positionality and background helped her to make contacts and gain data that would not otherwise have been available. However, I am also a researcher who inhabits a social world different from my informants. While achieving "insider" status or becoming completely integrated into a field setting can enhance a researcher's access to key informants and information, it can also provoke issues of role conflict (Brannick and Coghlan, 2007: 70). The key to understanding appears to be in building relationships of trust with people to gain privileged insider status, for without that insider status, one learns less (Tope et al., 2005: 489).

In fact, my gender did not always work to my advantage: most people in Kurdistan could not comprehend how my family permitted me to travel alone, or how could I sit alone with men and ask questions. As Bucerius (2013: 27) explained:

Gender is a particularly salient characteristic when considering the differences between a researcher and her research participants. When I give talks at criminological conferences, for instance, most people's first question to me is often, "How could you do this research as a woman?" My gender sometimes facilitates my work, as most people try to help me and protect me as a lone woman. It is not surprising that being a woman at once facilitates access (it permitted me to serve as a relationship counsellor, for example) and also impedes it in other circumstances (I could not follow the young men into brothels and observe their interactions with sex workers, who were among their biggest cocaine clients).

Sometimes, being an insider is not enough to ensure effective communication, as being a middle-class female university researcher who lives outside Iran was perceived as incompatible with a 14-year-old married or divorced girl living in Iranian Kurdistan. In many cases, I tried to come up with useful advice and remind the interviewees that I was still connected with their own surroundings and experiences. Catherine Kohler Riessman (1987), who researched divorce narratives, found that just being a woman was not enough for her to understand the experiences of divorced women whose classes and ethnic backgrounds differed from hers. My shared cultural background proved instrumental in providing access to research participants and in reducing social distance at a critical stage of the research process. Undoubtedly, an insider has other advantages, as most of my informants only wanted to talk once they got to know me through people they already knew.

Reflexivity can be an important act that allows researchers to be aware of their positional ties, gender, race, ethnicity, class, and any other factors that might be important to the research process. Reflecting on differences allowed Riessman (1987), Edwards (1990), Beoku-Betts (1994), Weiss (1994), and Weston (2004) to negotiate their differences and similarities with their respondents in order to gain access and obtain data that would not have been available to them otherwise. They were also able to gain new insights into their data from the perspective of difference.

To me, personally, the feminist reflexive researcher's perspective begins with an understanding of the importance of one's own values and attitudes in relation to the research process. Our beliefs, backgrounds, and feelings are parts of the process of knowledge construction (Mann and Kelley, 1997: 392). My position as a woman gave me this chance to overcome the impact of difference in the interview process, and my age and race helped to gain insider status during the interview process. This also helped me to secure cooperation and establish a rapport with the respondents so that they were eventually certain that I could understand them well, as in most cases they finished their sentences with "You know what I mean…".

Book structure

The publication is divided into four chapters. In the introductory chapter, I start with bringing forward the main concepts that will come up throughout the rest of the book, namely, honour killings, violence against women, and suicide. Further, I introduce certain methodological issues, problems, and ethical dilemmas I encountered during my fieldwork. I also address the religious, cultural, and traditional values that underpin the societal fabric in Iranian Kurdistan—manhood, honour, and patriarchy—and how these are all related to the different aspects of violence against women. Last but not least, I use this introductory chapter that is my first chapter to share with my readers my inmost and frank incentive that provided the foundation of this publication, namely, my willingness to make women's voices heard and, through personal narratives, provide the world with information and understanding about the help they so desperately need. In the introduction, I discuss the methodological issues, problems, and ethical dilemmas I encountered in my study. I also provide a very brief contemporary historical overview of the region and analysis of the socio-economic context. In particular, I discuss the patriarchal structure and the traditional norms and values that underpin the Kurdish society. Particular emphasis is paid to the manifestations of different forms of violence that women experience in the region. Additionally, I present the concept of honour, how it has come to be associated with women and, in this way, I demonstrate how honour crimes are entwined with the cultural traditions and customs of Kurdish society. This chapter concludes with a brief reference to my empirical research, the challenges that I faced whilst embarking upon my research, and the methodology I utilized and will be make use of throughout the book.

In the second chapter, based on the personal narratives I have collected, one of the main themes raised was that of criminal injustice and discrimination against women. In order to better elaborate on these concepts, this chapter discusses the current laws, which are applicable to cases of honour killings. It also presents an analysis of the Iranian legal system and criminal jurisprudence as well as a critical analysis of the most recent amendments made to the criminal law with regards to honour killings. In this chapter, I also discuss the state's obligation to amend the constitution in accordance with international human rights treaties and customary international law in view of protecting human rights and in particular the rights of women. Finally, this chapter addresses the state's obligation to investigate and eradicate the manifestations of the different aspects of violence committed against women by agents of the state or private actors which is often justified in terms of traditional cultural norms and values.

In the third chapter, I focus on child marriages and how these are connected to poverty and the prevailing socio-economic and cultural status quo. Building upon literature on child marriages and the Iranian legal framework, I identify the main factors that perpetuate child marriage in Kurdish society and under Islamic law. Further, I provide a general overview of the status of women in society by demonstrating, through my research, how prevailing economic underdevelopment and widespread poverty, as well as social norms and religious and cultural expectations encourage child marriage. Moreover, in this chapter I analyse the personal narratives that I collected during my fieldwork which illustrate the pattern of child marriage and its causes. I also attempt to map out child marriage in the region and present women's perceptions of this issue, as well as how it affects women's health and growth, personal and social development, family and community relations, and the progress of the wider society. Socio-economic conditions coupled with rigid, traditional preconceptions about the woman's role within and outside the family unit have created such an untenable and desperate situation for women that drives many of them to suicide. The chapter in particular focuses on widows and divorcees and, through a number of personal narratives, tells us the harrowing stories of desperation, hopelessness, and defiance.

The fourth chapter explores the positioning of women in society, firstly, through marriage and the formation of family, secondly vis-à-vis the job market. Discrimination, the search for employment, and the "feminisation" of poverty are only a few of the concepts introduced and debated against the background of modern Iran. In the fourth and final chapter, I revisit one of the key concepts that runs throughout this current publication, namely, patriarchy and how this is connected to the widespread violence against women. This chapter provides a cultural background to the concept of honour against the patriarchal and conservative structured society of Iranian Kurdistan, I also explore the values that underpin the Kurdish family and society and how these affect the role and position of women in society, in particular, and social relations in general. I also discuss the complex and manifold reasons for gender-based violence, which incorporate deeply rooted concepts and beliefs about honour and shame, control over female sexuality, modernity vs. conservatism, deeply entrenched patriarchy, and a profoundly flawed judicial system that is unable to provide protection and support. Finally, in this chapter I delve into the psychological aspects of suicide and the available treatments, and more importantly the known prevention strategies in this field.

Notes

1 https://www.amar.org.ir/Portals/1/yearbook/1396/2017/21.pdf. Accessed May 2018.
2 https://www.hrw.org/reports/1999/landmine/WEBME3.html International Campaign to Ban Landmines/Middle East - North Africa, non-signatories.

References

Amin, Avni. 2000. "Violence against Women. Sanandaj, Islamic Republic of Iran." *Women's Participation Research Center of Kurdistan Province* 9: 180–197.
Amnesty International. 2019. "Iran: Thousands Arbitrarily Detained and at Risk of Torture in Chilling Post-protest Crackdown." Accessed 17April2020. https://www.amnesty.org/en/latest/news/2019/12/iran-thousands-arbitrarily-detained-and-at-risk-of-torture-in-chilling-post-protest-crackdown/.

Ansari, Ali. 2003. *Modern Iran since 1921: The Pahlavis and After*. London: Longman (Pearson education series).
Barth, Fredrik. 1969. "Introduction." In *Ethnic Groups and Boundaries: The Social Organization of Culture Difference*, edited by Fredrik Barth, 9–38. London: Allen & Unwin.
Beoku-Betts, Josephine. 1994. "When Black Is Not Enough: Doing Field Research among Gullah Women." *NWSA Journal* 6, no. 3: 413–433. Accessed 12June2020. www.jstor.org/stable/4316353.
Brannick, Teresa, and David Coghlan. 2007. "In Defense of Being 'Native': The Case of Insider Academic Research." *Organizational Research Methods* 10, no. 1 (January): 59–74.
Bucerius, Sandra Meike. 2013. "Becoming a 'Trusted Outsider': Gender, Ethnicity, and Inequality in Ethnographic Research." *Journal of Contemporary Ethnography* 42, no. 6 (December): 690–721. DOI: 10.1177/0891241613497747.
Campbell, Jacquelyn. 1992. "Wife-Battering: Cultural Contexts Versus Western Social Sciences." In *Sanctions and Sanctuary: Cultural Perspectives on the Beating of Wives*, edited by Dorothy Counts, Judith K. Brown, and Jacquelyn C. Campbell, 229–249. Boulder, CO: Westview Press.
Charmaz, Kathy. 2006. *Constructing Grounded Theory: A Practical Guide Through Qualitative Analysis*. London: SAGE Publications.
Conrad, C., A. Neumann, J. G. Haworth, and P. Scott. 1993. *Qualitative Research in Higher Education: Experiencing Alternative Perspectives and Approaches*. Needham Heights, MA: Ginn Press.
Daly, M., and M., Wilson. 1988. *Homicide*. Hawthorne, NY: Aldine deGruyter.
Danish Immigration Service. 2020. *Iranian Kurds: Consequences of Political Activities in Iran and KRI*. Accessed 16April2020. https://www.ecoi.net/en/file/local/2024578/Report+on+Iranian+Kurds+Feb+2020.pdf.
Dobash, Russell, Rebecca Emerson Dobash, Margo Wilson, and Martin Daly. 2005. "The Myth of Sexual Symmetry in Marital Violence." In *Violence against Women*, edited by Raquel Kennedy Bergen and Claire M. Renzetti, 31–54. UK: Rowman & Littlefield.
Eagleton, William Jr. 1963. *The Kurdish Republic of 1946*. London: Oxford University Press.
Edwards, Rosalind. 1990. "Connecting Method and Epistemology: A White Woman Interviewing Black Women." *Women's Studies International Forum* 13, no. 5: 477–490.
Eickelman, Dale F. 1998. *The Middle East and Central Asia: An Anthropological Approach*. Upper Saddle River, NJ: Prentice Hall.
Esfandiari, Golnaz. 2020. "Iran Passes Child-Protection Law Following Gruesome Killing of Teenager." Radio Free Europe / Radio Liberty. Accessed 18November2020. https://www.rferl.org/a/iran-passes-child-protection-law-gruesome-killing-teenager-father/30660956.html.
Ghanea-Hercock, Nazila. 2003. "Ethnic and Religious Groups in the Islamic Republic of Iran: Policy Suggestions for the Integration of Minorities through Participation in Public Life." Paper presented at the United Nations Commission on Human Rights, Sub-commission on the Promotion and Protection of Human Rights, Working Group on Minorities. 9th session. Accessed 17April2018. https://

ap.ohchr.org/documents/E/SUBCOM/other/E-CN_4-SUB_2-AC_5–2003-WG_8.pdf.
Griffiths, Paul. 2002. "Juvenile Delinquency in Time." In *Becoming Delinquent: British and European Youth, 1650-1950*, edited by Pamela Cox and Heather Shore, 23–40. Dartmouth: Ashgate.
Gunter, Michael M. 2020. "Iran's Forgotten Kurds." *Journal of South Asian and Middle Eastern Studies* 43, no. 2: 54–67.
Hesse-Biber, Sharlene Nagy. 2007. "The Practice of Feminist In-Depth Interviewing." In *Feminist Research Practice*, edited by Sharlene Nagy Hesse-Biber and Patricia L. Leavy, 110–148. Thousand Oaks, CA: SAGE Publications, Inc. 10.4135/9781412984270.n5.
Hiro, Dilip. 2013. *Iran under the Ayatollahs*. London: Routledge.
Human Rights Watch. 2019. "Iran: Events of 2018." *World Report 2019*. Accessed 21March2020. https://www.hrw.org/world-report/2019/country-chapters/iran#.
Human Rights Watch. 2020. "Iran: Events of 2019." *World Report 2020*. Accessed 17April2020. https://www.hrw.org/world-report/2020/country-chapters/iran#be6679.
Idriss, Mohammad Mazher. 2011. "Honour, Violence, Women and Islam—An Introduction." In *Honour, Violence, Women and Islam*, edited by Mohammad Mazher Idriss and Tahir Abbas, 1–15. Abingdon, Oxon; New York: Routledge.
Julios, Christina. 2016. *Forced Marriage and "Honour" Killings in Britain: Private Lives, Community Crimes and Public Policy Perspectives*. UK: Routledge.
Kaviani Rad, Morad. 2007. "Political Regionalism in Iran: The Case of Iranian Baluchestan." *Strategic Studies Quarterly* 10, no. 35: 89–101.
Khayati, Khalid. 2008. *From Victim Diaspora to Transborder Citizenship? Diaspora Formation and Transnational Relations among Kurds in France and Sweden*. Linköping, Sweden: Linköping University.
Koohi-Kamali, Farideh. 2003. *The Political Development of the Kurds in Iran: Pastoral Nationalism*. New York: Palgrave-Macmillan.
Kurdistan Human Rights Network. 2020. "Two Kurdish Porters Wounded in the Border Areas of Baneh and Sardasht." Accessed 17April2020. http://kurdistanhumanrights.net/en/two-kurdish-porters-wounded-in-the-border-areas-of-baneh-and-sardasht/.
Landinfo. 2009. *Honour Killings in Iran*. Accessed 20January2018. https://landinfo.no/asset/960/1/960_1.pdf.
Maghsodi, M. 2001. *Tahavolate Quomi dar Iran*. Tehran: Institute of National Studies.
Mann, Susan A., and Lori R. Kelley. 1997. "Standing at the Crossroads of Modernist Thought: Collins, Smith, and the New Feminist Epistemologies." *Gender and Society* 11, no. 4 (August): 391–408.
Mayring, Philipp. 1983. *Qualitative Inhaltsanalyse: Grundlagen und Techniken*. Basel: Beltz.
McDowall, David. 2004. *A Modern History of the Kurds*. 3rd ed. London: I.B. Tauris.
McGregor, Heather Elizabeth. 2013. "Situating Nunavut Education With Indigenous Education in Canada." *Canadian Journal of Education/Revue Canadienne De l'éducation* 36, no. 2: 87–118.

Mohammadpour, Ahmad, and Kamal Soleimani. 2020. "'Minoritisation' of the Other: The Iranian Ethno-theocratic State's Assimilatory Strategies." *Postcolonial Studies* 24, no. 1: 40–62. DOI: 10.1080/13688790.2020.1746157.

Motavalli Haghighi, Yousef. 2010. "A Reflection on the Causes and How to Immigrate to Khorasan." *Specialized Journal of Jurisprudence and History of Civilization* 6, no. 21: 591–672.

Qadir Shah, Hassam. 2002. *There Is No "Honour" in Killing: Don't Let Them Get Away with Murder*. Lahore: Shirkat Gah Women's Resource Centre.

Qaeni, Mohsen. 1994. "Kotak zadan yeki az asar ryasat mard" [Beating is a symptom of the supremacy of man]. *Zanan* 18, no. 18 (June-July): 36–45.

Radio Farda. 2019. "Rights Organizations Urge UN Members To Condemn Iran Human Rights Violations." Accessed 17April2018. https://en.radiofarda.com/a/rights-organizations-urge-un-members-to-condemn-iran-human-rights-violations/30318461.html.

Rehman, Javaid. 2019. "Statement by Mr. Javaid Rehman, Special Rapporteur on the situation of human rights in the Islamic Republic of Iran at the 40th session of the Human Rights Council." Accessed 17April2018. https://www.ohchr.org/en/NewsEvents/Pages/DisplayNews.aspx?NewsID=24340&LangID=E.

Reinharz, Shulamit, and Lynn Davidman. 1992. *Feminist Methods in Social Research*. New York: Oxford University Press.

Riessman, Catherine Kohler. 1987. "When Gender Is Not Enough: Women Interviewing Women." *Gender & Society* 1, no. 2 (June): 172–207.

Roosevelt, Archie Jr. 1947. "The Kurdish Republic of Mahabad." *Middle East Journal* 1, no. 3: 247–269.

Runciman, W. G. 1966. *Relative Deprivation and Social Justice: A Study of Attitudes to Social Inequality in Twentieth-century England*. Berkeley: University of California Press.

Safilios-Rothschild, Constantina. 1969. "'Honour' Crimes in Contemporary Greece." *British Journal of Sociology* 20: 205–218.

Saleh, Alam. 2013. *Ethnic Identity and the State in Iran*. New York: Palgrave Macmillan

Salih, Ruba. 2013. "From Bare Lives to Political Agents: Palestinian Refugees as Avant-Garde." *Refugee Survey Quarterly* 32, no. 2: 66–91.

Samadzadeh, Hassan. 2015. *The Book of the Kurdish Nomadic Community of Khalkhal (Kormanj)*. Tehran: Nokhbegan Publications.

Sanasarian, Eliz. 2000. *Religious Minorities in Iran*. Cambridge Middle East Studies. Cambridge: Cambridge University Press.

Shaddox, Colleen. 2007. "Years after Gas Attack, the Horror Lingers in an Iranian Town, EPH Alumna Finds." *Yale Medicine Magazine* (Winter): 6. Accessed 20March2017. https://medicine.yale.edu/news/yale-medicine-magazine/years-after-gas-attack-the-horror-lingers-in/.

Sheyholislami, Jaffer. 2011. "Kurdish Identity." In *Kurdish Identity, Discourse, and New Media*. The Palgrave Macmillan Series in International Political Communication. New York: Palgrave Macmillan. DOI: 10.1057/9780230119307_3.

Silverman, David. 2005. *Doing Qualitative Research: A Practical Handbook*. London: SAGE Publications.

Smith, Joan. 1989. *Misogynies*. London: Faber and Faber.

Snow, David, Leon Anderson, John Lofland, and Lyn H. Lofland. 2005. *Analysing Social Settings: A Guide to Qualitative Observation and Analysis*. UK: Wadsworth Publishing.

Statistical Centre of Iran. *Statistical Yearbook (2017–2018)*. Accessed 18 March 2018. https://www.amar.org.ir/english/Iran-Statistical-Yearbook/Statistical-Yearbook-2017-2018.

Stone, Taraneh. 2019. "Child Brides in Iran: Tradition, Poverty and Resisting Change." *BBC Monitoring*. Accessed 21March2018. https://monitoring.bbc.co.uk/product/c200rxfl.

Tizro, Zahra. 2012. *Domestic Violence in Iran: Women, Marriage and Islam*. United Kingdom: Routledge.

Tope, Daniel, Lindsey Joyce Chamberlain, Martha Crowley, and Randy Hodson. 2005. "The Benefits of Being There: Evidence from the Literature on Work." *Journal of Contemporary Ethnography* 34, no. 4 (August): 470–493.

Vali, Abbas. 1998. "The Kurds and Their 'Others': Fragmented Identity and Fragmented Politics." *Comparative Studies of South Asia, Africa and the Middle East* 18, no. 2 (August): 82–95.

Vali, Abbas. 2003. *Essays on the Origins of Kurdish Nationalism*. Costa Mesa, CA: Mazda.

Vali, Abbas. 2014. *Kurds and the State in Iran: The Making of Kurdish Identity*. London: I.B. Tauris.

Vali, Abbas. 2015. *Modernity and the Stateless: The Kurdish Question in Iran*. London: I.B. Tauris.

Vali, Abbas. 2020. *The Forgotten Years of Kurdish Nationalism in Iran*. UK: Palgrave Macmillan.

Weiss, Robert Stuart. 1994. *Learning from Strangers: The Art and Method of Qualitative Interview Studies*. New York: Free Press.

Weston, Kath. 2004. "Fieldwork in Lesbian and Gay Communities." In *Feminist Perspectives on Social Research*, edited by Sharlene Nagy Hesse-Biber and Michelle L. Yaiser, 198–205. New York: Oxford University Press.

Wilkinson, Richard G. 2005. *The Impact of Inequality: How to Make Sick Societies Healthier*. London: Routledge.

Zabih, Sepehr. 1982. *Iran since the Revolution*. Baltimore and London: Johns Hopkins University Press.

2 Honour killings and the rule of Islamic law

Introduction

This chapter provides an overview of the criminal justice system in Iran and the bias against the protection of women's rights in the country. The judicial interpretations of the amendments made to criminal law after the Islamic revolution (i.e., *Qisas* and *Diyat* law) are included, as are the changes in the criminal justice system with respect to women. This chapter analyses the case law in instances of honour killing to determine whether it is based on substantive law or driven by customary law and includes further analysis of the rules of interpretation used by judges. Additionally, the chapter explores how the perpetrators usually manage to get away with the heinous crimes involved in honour killings and why the police, and the justice system in general, fail to protect the basic rights of women in the country.

Further, this chapter provides a cultural background of the notion of honour in the patriarchal society of Iran. It discusses the substantive and procedural laws applicable in cases of honour killings and the rights guaranteed by the Iranian Constitution to women as citizens of Iran. To support the arguments related to criminal injustices suffered by and discrimination against women, the chapter analyses the criminal law applicable in cases of honour killing and the amendments that have been made to it. It includes a critical analysis of the most recent amendments to criminal law with regard to honour crimes and discusses the responsibility of the state to protect human rights, in particular the rights of women, as well as its obligation to investigate and eradicate cultural violence against women by state agents or private actors.

Following an analysis of the legal framework and the basic values underpinning Iranian society, this chapter evaluates the geographical region of Iranian Kurdistan, which is the focus of this publication. The concepts of honour and society, tribalism, patriarchy, and conservatism are introduced and debated. Personal narratives provide a perfect illustration of how pervasive gender inequality and the deeply entrenched patriarchal mentality contribute to increased violence against women and more specifically to honour-based violence and crimes.

DOI: 10.4324/9781003208501-2

Some opening remarks on honour killings

Adultery committed by a married woman is considered the most serious offence and can lead to honour killings, which are often based on unconfirmed suspicions and rumours and, in the most conservative communities, can be sparked by very minor acts, such as talking to an unknown man in a public place. No comprehensive statistics are available on the subject, but Iran's police occasionally publish information about cases and the number of honour killings known to the police. The subject received much more media attention in 2008, when the police found out about 50 honour killings in the space of seven months. According to police statistics, a total of 340 honour killings, in which the victims were women, took place in Iran between March 2011 and March 2012. Most of the murders were committed in Kurdistan and Khuzestan (Bakhtiarnejad 2009: 16, 35, 53, 176; Etemaad et al., 2019; Landinfo, 2009; Nayyeri and Iran Human Rights Documentation Center IHRDC, 2013: 12).

The killing of women is a heinous act of violence; however, the killer is not a fugitive from the law. On the contrary, he walks freely in society, proud of his deed, having secured the blessing of the victim's family and the appreciation of the community. In recent years, attention to this phenomenon, which is not specific to one country or region in particular, has increased, and, according to the United Nations, honour killings occur almost all over the world (Boyer, 1998). According to statistics published by the United Nations Population Fund, the number of honour crimes, that is, the official number of female deaths at the hands of their close relatives, quintuples every year (Tripathi & Yadav, 2004: 65).

Of course, the prevalence of this phenomenon varies considerably. Historical records show that honour killings have occurred in various civilisations throughout history, such as ancient Rome and Greece (Campbell, 1964; Safilios-Rothschild, 1969: 597; Syngellakis & Lazaridis, 1995). Honour killings occur more frequently in Asian countries (Asano-Tamanoi, 1987; Baroja, 1966; Bell, 1979; Bourdieu, 1966; Burkholder, 1998), and the highest number of honour killings are recorded in Pakistan, Bangladesh, Indonesia, Jordan, and Turkey (Casimir & Jung, 2009). This phenomenon is not associated with one religion or faith in particular, although it does tend to occur in countries with a Muslim majority population (Abu Zayd, 1988; Al-Khayyat, 1990; Antoun, 1976; Chakravarti, 2005). In India, honour killings are also widespread. Basu (2013), who conducted extensive research in this field, attributes them to the prevailing caste system, intra-group marriage, the prohibition of marriage outside the group, economic poverty, cultural poverty, lack of social mobility, and very rigid traditional beliefs.

At the individual level, relationships and community have the greatest impact on women's experiences of violence (Fulu & Kerr-Wilson, 2015); however, honour-based violence is not a novel idea. Wyatt-Brown (1982) states that in the southern state of Mississippi, honour was one of the main features of original 19th-century culture and was connected to the contemporary societal structure, norms, privileges, family, and community. Honour guided social behaviour and reinforced patriarchy and was also reflected in the legal system, which included rituals of shaming and violence, such as lynching (Shalinsky, 1986). Despite the strides made by modern civilisation, honour—as a state of mind and a social privilege—is still very much alive and present. In the past, there was little awareness of honour-based violence, as family and friends, the immediate community, or high-level officials in government circles and the media were not willing to discuss the issue (Akbari & Tetreault, 2014). Today, the voices of victims are heard in the media, in courts of law, at community gatherings, and in academic circles. We live in different times, where women have a significant presence in the political, social, and cultural scenes—a presence that is based on empowerment, communication, and self-determination.

There are various social, economic, legal, and cultural factors behind honour-based violence. Reviewing these factors fully requires extensive research and study. In general, the patriarchal customs and culture of a traditional society, the media, the rule of law, immigration, and the overall level of education should be considered as variables (Sev'er & Yurdakul, 2001: 964). Although women and girls are the main victims of honour-based violence, men are not immune from it, even in patriarchal societies. Families and relatives, who take over the role of judge and jury, sentence victims to death. In contrast, the murderer enjoys immunity on the basis that the slaying was "necessary", "inevitable", and "morally justifiable". In fact, their family and community, who encouraged them to perpetrate the crime in the first place, often protect the perpetrators, and they consider this a part of their tradition. Honour killings have survived the test of time, but they are a stain on the progress that human civilisation boasts to have achieved. Unconventional romance, betrayal, adultery, escape from home, and loss of virginity, among others, are all situations in which honour killings occur, with victims' behaviour being labelled as dishonourable, insane, scandalous, and impulsive. Sometimes, the spread of a rumour or a public announcement is sufficient for a web of infamy surrounding the alleged "dishonour" to smear the good name and respect of a family (Cohen, 1992; Dresch, 1989; Hasluck, 1967). According to researchers (Baker, Gregware, & Cassidy, 1999; Feldner, 2000; Tilly, 2003: 88; Kressel, 1981), honour killings are also connected with the politics of reputation: the public defence of perquisites, precedence, and honour in order to maintain a family's credibility in the eyes of other families and tribal patrons. These are all reasons that can be used to justify the killing of women at the hands of their loved ones for departing from the gender norms determined by society (Chakravarti, 2005). Thus, honour-based crimes and killings are a serious problem, particularly in the Kurdish region and the Kurdish diaspora in Europe (Alinia, 2013; Begikhani, 2005; Begikhani, Gill, & Hague, 2010; Mojab, 2001; Mojab & Abdo, 2004).

Family, society, and gender inequality

The punishment for sexual indiscretion is usually death. In a traditional society, death is the only way to eliminate the scandal and infamy created and to restore honour to the injured party. Eliminating the perpetrator is equivalent to saving the society from disgrace. Generally, the role of executioner is based on blood ties and family, such as brothers, fathers, sons, spouses, cousins, and female relatives willing to carry out the punishment (Vreede-de Stuers, 1968).

In Iran, the family structure is based on patriarchal principles, that is, family members are ranked according to gender and age. Napikoski (2020) uses the term "patriarchal principles" to describe a general structure in which men have power over women: a male-dominated power structure that runs through organised society and individual relationships. In Iran, men are ranked higher than women, and older family members are ranked higher than younger ones. In line with Muslim beliefs, the relationship between the genders is based on difference but complementarity, meaning that men and women are equal, but distinct. Duties and rights within a family and marriage are gender based, which is very clearly reflected in Islamic and Iranian family legislation. For example, "men have certain financial obligations in marriage: mahriye (dower payment), nafage (spousal support) and ojrat al-mesl (compensation for domestic work). In return, women are expected to abide by the principle of tamkin, or submission to their husband's will" (Ceasefire, 2019: 28). It is also important to remember that Iran is a large country with a complex ethnic composition and significant socio-economic and regional differences. Although Persian culture is dominant, there are many different minorities and cultures in the country. At a local and regional level, minority cultures are very powerful. This has consequences for the police and courts' attitudes towards women, women's legal and actual position in society, the number of honour killings carried out, and the extent to which women who are victims of violence can seek help. Men define the parameters of honour according to the moral values of their clan, based upon their personal perceptions and concepts of honour, or a combination of the two (DeSilva, 2000).

In these societies, women are monitored. For instance, the number of telephone calls and visits they may make outside of the home are limited. They are faced with threats of harassment against their children and have to cope with complaints to the police and the court about them and their relatives. Husbands are also allowed to abuse their wives and threaten them with divorce or remarriage (Warnock, 1990: 33). According to Mahdi (2014: 190), they deny their wives the right to financial independence, refuse divorce despite the woman's insistence, use coercion and physical violence, and insist on not using contraceptives and having unprotected sex, even if they suffer from a sexually transmitted or otherwise contagious disease. Although abuse and violence against women and children in the family are common in society, currently, no specific law protecting women against domestic violence in accordance with the requirements of the international legal framework has been adopted by the Islamic Republic of Iran.

In general, the most important aspect of an Iranian woman's life is the kind of family she was born into. If she is married, her husband's values and ideas will be of great, if not decisive, significance. In addition, class background, level of education, ethnic origin, religious affiliation, and residence all shape and define women's lives and the options they have in practical everyday life. For Kurdish girls in small towns and villages, getting married at a very young age is common and encouraged by Sharia (Girls Not Brides, 2020). On the other hand, women who grow up in cities receive a much higher level of education than women from rural communities. Many of them also work in the public and private sectors; they participate in political processes and are active in voluntary organisations, the arts, and the media. Numerous young, well-educated women live in central and urban districts, and their lives are considerably different to those of women living in more traditional clan societies and rural areas, who often live with a great deal of social pressure. Women from rural clans are generally less educated, have very little freedom of movement, have limited knowledge of their legal rights, have less influence in choosing a husband, and are at greater risk of being married off in their early teens. Due to the prevailing financial insecurity, when a Kurdish man loses his job, his wife is also hurt because the woman relies on her husband economically, mentally, and psychologically. This is the very same woman that he oppresses, but she cares for and worries about him. On the other hand, according to McDonald (2001: 143), a report stated that "this is partly due to the double oppression of Kurdish women and girls and the result of deep attitudes and practices rooted in Kurdish culture. And to some extent, this is due to the government's failure to promote and support women's and Kurdish Rights". Village communities are also smaller, and people are more familiar with each other's lives than they are in towns. In a setting where news travels fast, it is only a matter of time before the whole village finds out about an illicit relationship and demands restoration of the affected family's honour.

Kurdish women and the concept of honour

Before exploring honour-based violence (HBV), it is crucial to define and understand the concept of honour. Honour is often defined as a virtue or character trait associated with integrity, good moral character, and altruism, embodied by individuals who demonstrate these characteristics (Vandello & Cohen, 2003). According to the dictionary definition of the word "honour", it is not gender specific. As previously explained, the term "honour" is a fluid concept, is found in every society, and has various meanings in different texts and in different cultures; however, there is no commonly agreed definition (Afary, 2009; Brandon & Hafez, 2008; Martin, 2005: 112). In general, it relates not only to the respect and dignity that an individual enjoys and how that individual views society, but also to how society perceives said individual. In fact, every society has its own definition of "honour", in line with its socio-economic and cultural practices. Patriarchal societies, such as Iraq, Iran, and Pakistan, have manipulated and distorted its meaning to make honour the sole prerogative of men. They have arrived at the opinion that "men are the sole possessors and defenders of honour" (Ibrahim, 2005: 11). This customary practice has allowed patriarchal leaders to maintain social control over women and preserve their subordinate position in society. Another issue to consider is that a thorough search of the relevant literature did not yield any satisfactory information or explanation of the part that females play in honour killings. Researchers have attempted to argue that this important issue is entirely due to the patriarchy, the male-dominated power structure that underpins society and personal relations (Begikhani, 2005; Pervizat, 2011; Sev'er and Yurdakul, 2001; Siddiqui, 2005).

The dignity and honour of a person also reflect the behaviour of others, and, as a result, the pride and prestige we enjoy do not solely depend on our own conduct and accomplishments (Araji, 2000: 2; O'Doherty, 2017). Having honour is perceived as a positive thing and confers many advantages, in particular, trust and respect from others (Nisbett & Cohen, 1996). In many different conservative settings, the way a society or community views a person depends on, or is determined by, the general demeanour and conduct of the female relatives.

There is also a second definition of honour linked to status and reputation (Pitt-Rivers, 1966), which is based upon a person's ability, strength, and power to enforce their will and command respect from others (Nisbett & Cohen, 1996). So, rather than being a character trait, honour—according to this definition—is something that must be fought for. While this idea of honour is less common, particularly in modern industrialised Western nations (Bowman, 2007), it is held with some conviction by a substantial number of individuals throughout the world, and it is this particular focus on obtaining and defending honour that appears to be most associated with HBV (Bowman, 2007; Vandello & Cohen, 2003). It is clear from the evidence provided in this chapter that attitudes to honour discussed here are associated with violence-supporting attitudes, but it is unclear whether they are causally related. More research is needed to explore the impact that committing an act of HBV has on offenders and, in particular, how this affects their beliefs and attitudes toward HBV.

Holding attitudes and beliefs favourable to HBV may be one outcome of living in an honour-bound culture; however, this alone cannot explain why only certain individuals act on those beliefs. An intention to display a particular behaviour develops from the strength of the attitude in favour of it and is strongest where social pressure is greatest and where individuals believe that they have the ability and capacity (strong control beliefs) to carry out the behaviour (Ajzen, 1991, 2001, 2011). Beliefs, attitudes, and intentions are all internal mental states, and it is important to note that they are highly idiosyncratic (Ajzen, 1991, 2001, 2011). Once an intention has been set, whether behavioural or connected to decision-making, a major factor that limits or encourages its occurrence is the environment. The theory of planned behaviour (TPB) accounts for environmental effects in terms of the actual behavioural control that an individual has, that is, the extent to which they are actually able to control the environment in order to carry out an act (Ajzen, 2011). A high level of actual behavioural control exists where the environment is supportive of a particular intention, for example, the intended victim may be present, and weapons may be available with minimal risk of intervention from others. In the next section, a more detailed account of the proposed motivational model for HBV will be presented in order to highlight its utility in considering the interaction between multiple causal factors.

The socialisation of honour-related norms influences some individuals towards developing behavioural beliefs that stress the importance of honour, reputation, and toughness and make them more inclined to use violence, issue threats, or exercise control strategies in response to challenges to their or their family's honour (Nisbett & Cohen, 1996; Vandello & Cohen, 2008). Given the ubiquity of honour concerns within honour-bound cultures, an individual from such a culture is likely to hold normative beliefs that are supportive of HBV, largely because of a reasonable assumption that others would consider honour important and would accept the use of violence to defend it. Note that this is not the same as claiming that everyone in an honour-bound culture would be supportive of HBV, rather, it highlights the idea that the beliefs of the individual are of great importance when examining this issue, no matter how abhorrent one may find them. Following the tenets of the TPB, an individual with normative beliefs of this kind will experience social pressure to behave in ways that favour violence in response to honour challenges. Research has supported such normative beliefs within honour cultures (Nisbett & Cohen, 1996; Vandello et al., 2008).

In an honour culture, cultural conditions may serve to heighten behavioural control beliefs towards carrying out HBV. For example, in honour cultures, male heads of families have significant power over subordinates, such as spouses and children (Baker, Gregware, & Cassidy, 1999). This power often extends to control over many of the resources used by these subordinates, such as food, accommodation, and socialisation opportunities (Bowman, 2007). Moreover, this power may enable the family heads to call upon others to aid them in their activities, including HBV, and those called upon may feel duty-bound to do so (Cohen, 1992). Indeed, the research literature indicates that HBV often involves several family members (Baker, Gregware, & Cassidy, 1999) and may involve younger, more subordinate family members, particularly young males who are encouraged or forced to carry out the violence (Baker, Gregware, & Cassidy, 1999; Mora, 2009). In these circumstances, the head of the family, who has been dishonoured by the behaviour of a subordinate, is likely to believe that he has the capacity to carry out HBV (strong behavioural control beliefs) because of his effective control over the target's environment, making it easy for him to gain access to the victim. Similarly, HBV is most likely to occur in honour cultures where there are few, if any, legal sanctions against it and weak or non-existent law enforcement responses (Kulczycki & Windle, 2012).

"Honour" in Iran has been defined as "a woman, a woman's body, sexuality, and the control over women" (Farahani, 2017: 102–110). This is also true for a man's sisters and mother, the other women in his family, and women in his close circle. The male is responsible for watching over and overseeing the conduct of all of these women. Under such an understanding, women are not only under the control of their fathers, brothers, and husbands, but all men in their close circle. When the responsibility of these males widens, the pressure on the women is increased. For the most part, a male relative (usually a father, brother, or husband) kills a woman for engaging in, or being suspected of, committing illegal sexual relations (Abu-Odeh, 1996; Nanes, 2003), even though the grounds for any accusations that are made may be spurious and no more than rumour. Intrinsic to this way of thinking is the belief that the value of women exists not only as a result of their position as wife, mother, or sister, but also as the embodiment of the honour of the community of men around her. Based on their reproductive capacities, women are forced to take on the role of keepers and transmitters of traditions and group values and thus are reduced to simply vessels to continue on the culture.

Honour killings have existed for centuries throughout the greater Middle East and Asia, and they are present to a great degree within the Kurdish community (Yildiz & Taysi, 2007: 55). The concept of honour among the Kurdish community came from tribal life and its lawlessness, which derived from a time when there was no centralised government in place and tribal customs ruled the clans in order to regulate the affairs of daily life. Many of these tribal customs, such as honour killings, may have prevailed throughout the years because there was no other avenue for resolving differences among the people. During those times, only the elders and tribal chiefs had the authority to negotiate. When the concept of modern government came into being, individuals consented, explicit or tacitly, to surrendering their rights to that government.

Triandis (1989) concluded that the rate of honour killing among tribes is much higher, and women are murdered in the most extreme ways due to men's distrust of them. These murders are upheld and condoned by tribal elders. According to Treyandis, factors such as violence, distrust of women, patriarchal culture, and the violent structure of tribal life influence the frequency of honour killings. For Van den Haag & Conrad (1983), the closeness among people in a nomadic environment, traditional relations, patriarchal rule, revenge, and aggression are among the causes of an increased number of killings. Further, Abdi (2003) argues that in the nomadic regions of Iran, most collective conflict occurs due to sexual and honour-related affairs. Honour killings among the tribes are common, and the traditional structure, cultural backwardness, low educational level, and traditional system are among the factors contributing to these killings. Other cultural, social, and legal variables that are instrumental in the high number of honour killings are customs and traditional norms, patriarchal culture, and individuals' level of education (Gerrard, 1994: 76).

According to Elias & Scotson (2008), the advent of government liberated the people from the old system and the cultural norms imposed upon them. Instead of the people having to solve their own problems inside the community and the tribe, the government developed a security system and created a set of rules designed to resolve all disagreements among people in the communities. This implies that such tribal practices are no longer acceptable and are, in most cases, illegal. The tribal practices pass from generation to generation. These particular processes of civilisation are inseparable from the worldwide process of civilisation, but they differ conceptually from tribe to tribe and from nation to nation—in short, from survival unit to survival unit—in line with the evolution of their own distinct destinies. The courses of a particular process of civilisation are different from one another and, as such, have particular shapes or patterns. One of their most tangible expressions is in the common social habits of the individuals who, together, form a particular survival unit, for example, a tribe or state (Elias & Scotson, 2008: 3–5). Elias and Scotson saw his primary task as attempting to regain, within a limited area, the lost perception of the long-term psychical process of civilisation, a process involving changes in behaviour and feelings extending over many generations. These traditions did not pay attention to individuals at that time; all importance fell on the rightfulness of the clan and the tribe. But today, based on national and international legal framework and human rights law, such traditions are a violation of human rights and are mostly illegal under these laws. Nevertheless, the unwritten laws within the society reflect a mix of traditions.

The Kurds exist in a political and cultural space in which their group identity is perpetually challenged by outside forces. As a result, their honour mentality remains highly relevant. Ava Homa (2016) mentions that Kurdish women, in particular, have experienced various forms of discrimination: the national chauvinism of the nations that rule them, the male chauvinism of their own nation, the mistreatment of Islamic groups, and continuous war. Middle Eastern and Western studies show how statelessness has led Kurdish women to be ignored and deprived. Kurdish women take on the burden of embodying the culture and tradition of a nation that is denied a right to autonomy by the policies of the states in which they live. Those of a traditional mindset challenge concepts such as autonomy, gender equality, and sexual freedom, as they are viewed as foreign concepts aimed at stripping Kurdish women—and, by proxy, the Kurdish people—of their honour, culture, and tradition. This way of thinking has resulted in both honour killings and suicides in order to rectify a perceived insult to the honour of the family. These insults are sometimes the result of women attempting to exercise their own choices over an aspect of their life, such as education, employment, or choice of spouse. In other cases, they are the result of incidents such as the rape of a woman by state security forces. Although it is widely understood that honour killings remain a major problem in the Kurdish community, as do other issues of violence against women, there are few data available concerning the extent to which honour killings are practised within the Kurdish community, partly as a result of the reluctance to discuss this subject (Landinfo, 2009: 6).[1]

The practice of honour killing was rare in pre-modern Iran and usually confined to the Kurdish and Arab peripheries of the nation (Gilsenan, 1996; Laffin, 1975). However, the post-1979 Islamist state established a new type of honour killing, one that was adjudicated and enforced by the state, rather than by the father, the brother, or the community (Afary, 2009). Habibzadeh mentioned that during the first three years of post-revolutionary Iran, the Islamic criminal code did not include a clause to sanction a husband killing his wife (Habibzadeh & Babi, 1999: 89–90). Under this code, purity and honour involved more than the expectation of virginity for girls and fidelity for wives; a woman's conduct should completely preclude any doubts about her honour (Keddie, 1991: 9). In the Iranian culture, honour is also synonymous with notions such as infallibility, mystery, mastery, and knowledge of the very essence of the word "honour" itself.

Matters of honour can ultimately result in multiple acts of violence (against dishonour, the people involved, and even non-affiliated entities). The culmination of this violence is often murder, taking the lives of people who have been involved in an honourless deed, for example, an illegitimate affair or a runaway attempt, and certain members of the family and/or the tribe are assigned to carry out the murder. This intensifies the question as to whether the judiciary is competent to make a judgement on honour-based violent crimes within a traditional, patriarchal society with weak rule of law and a weak judicial system. In almost all of the killings, the perpetrator believes that the murder of a girl or a woman is permissible because she has acted in a way that is unconventional or illegitimate.

The real cleavage, the fundamental power struggle, in Iran as in other Muslim contexts, is between democracy and despotism, and this is often obscured by religious politics and the instrumentalisation of religion. Thus, it is essential to demystify religious politics, to challenge those who attempt to invoke religious authority to justify autocratic rule, and to win the power games by seeking justification in religious scriptures. It is only then that the intimate and intricate links between patriarchy and despotism can be revealed and challenged sustainably (Hamzić & Mir-Hosseini, 2010: 112).

Islamic law and honour killings

The judiciary, an official conflict resolution mechanism, plays an important role in defining violence against women and designing various tools to deal with the issue. In Iran, the law is divided into public law and private law (Ebadi, 2002). The public or general law governs the relations between the government and the people, while private law covers relations between private entities. The most important branch of private law is civil law, which regulates the interaction of individuals based on their membership of the community. One of the most important branches of public law is criminal law (in Iran, this branch is called the Islamic Panel). The cases referred to the judicial system are resolved in accordance with this set of rules.

Orthodox jurisprudence is a powerful force for shaping the minds and lives of ordinary people in Islamic countries (Marini & Masugi, 2005). Orthodox jurisprudence is the legal discourse of Islamic civilisation (Coulson, 1969), and traditional theories are published mainly by orthodox jurisprudence and its related institutions and structures. There are two distinct elements in the formulation of Islamic law: divine revelation and human reasoning on the part of jurists. Orthodox jurisprudence, in its historical evolution and its response to the challenges of time and space, brings together a set of features and attributes. It has a monopoly on the production of religious knowledge and jurisprudential rulings. With this structure of power and knowledge, orthodox jurisprudence allows for the interpretation of religious sources with its own biases and uses this discursive tool to take an uncompromising stance. The sacred text, language, and methodology can only be understood through the professional activities and terminology of religious scholars (Tizro, 2014: 2).

Obviously, the legal rights of Iranian women are regulated by Islamic law and its principles. Only a man can legally be the head of a family, or, as it is officially stated, "the position of the head of the family is the exclusive right of the husband" (Civil Code of the Islamic Republic of Iran, 2015: art. 1105). A husband has more rights than his wife in marriage and in the event of divorce. Unless otherwise specified in the marriage contract, the husband can refuse to let his wife take a job or leave the house without his consent, and to be issued a passport and permitted to travel abroad, a married Iranian woman must have her husband's written permission. A husband has an unconditional duty to support his wife, while his wife has a duty to live together with her husband. Rape within marriage is not a punishable offence, and the concept barely exists within the civil code, as it is deemed a husband's right to have sexual relations with his wife as and when he pleases. Simply stating wide-ranging generalisations, however, fails to describe the full picture regarding the position of women in Iran, as social standing and living conditions can vary enormously from region to region and from social class to social class.

Unless there is a fully transparent and accountable legal framework, as well as law enforcement agencies that work at both the central and the community levels to deter potential criminals and punish convicted criminals, it is not entirely possible to eradicate crime, the reasons for it, or the conditions that generate it in society. In fact, as some lawyers argue, criminal law is not the only or the best instrument with which the community can defend itself. Indisputably, punishing perpetrators should be the ultimate tool to which a society can resort; however, criminal law plays a more important role in the case of honour killings because, unlike ordinary crimes, which are widely condemned by society, these crimes are culturally and socially acceptable and can even have popular support. In summation, if the applicable legal framework does not explicitly address these crimes, there will be no other available mechanisms to prevent them. As things currently stand, the current applicable laws do not properly confront honour killings, and Islamic law is not fully equipped to deal with them. Without negating the basic Islamic religious ideals and values that the society adheres to, these laws need to be revised and substantially reformed so that they punish the perpetrators of honour killings and act as a deterrent by addressing and eliminating the deeply embedded structures that provide the impetus for these crimes to occur.

The rule of law is the foundation of a responsible government, requiring that settled and just laws are administered fairly without fear and favour in order to further the rule of law. Such laws must offer protection to all individuals and their rights, especially those who are minorities or otherwise at a disadvantage. Although the state is obliged to establish a society in accordance with the injunctions of Islam, personal bias comes into play and moral standards are overlooked when decisions are being made about the rights and liberties of women within Islamic society. This is against the teachings of Islam because the Qur'an, inter alia, establishes that personal likes or dislikes must not influence the administration of justice. The administration of justice depends on the actors involved in the penal system—the police, the prosecutors, and the judges—for its effectiveness. Women will turn to the police and judicial institutions for justice; however, police are generally corrupt—as noted by Azadi (2020)—and, given that the majority of police officers are men, they are not generally supportive of women—the main victims of honour-based violence.

There are many cases of women who are mutilated and killed by male relatives because they are suspected of having an illicit relationship or of adultery. Of the cases that actually are reported, few are thoroughly investigated by the police, and those accused are often acquitted under the mitigating circumstances of the grave and sudden provocation that was allegedly caused by the victim's dishonourable act. Even when the state does not inflict violence on women directly, it often supports or condones an exploitative family structure through various laws and behavioural rules that legitimise the authority of male members over the lives of female members, whose rights are not upheld.

In cases of honour killings, judges have even pronounced dead women to be immoral on the pretext of protecting family honour. Courts have praised the actions of "honourable" men who avenged family honour, and every loophole possible has been utilised to condone these murders and exonerate the men who have committed them. Judges have encouraged this customary practice whereby men take the law in their own hands; however, judges do not act in a vacuum. Cultural norms, religious beliefs, and political pressure all influence judicial decisions. Against this background, it is often the case that judges do not follow the rule of law but pronounce decisions that infringe upon human rights. An example is the case of invalidating the marriage of a woman who weds without her guardian's (*wali*'s) consent by declaring the marriage illegal.

Religion is often used to protect the perpetrator from being convicted of the crime and to present him as a hero and saviour of the family honour. In cases where the courts referred to *hadith* (the sayings of prophets) and were guided by the injunctions of Islam, the judges stated that murder committed on account of *ğeyrat* (honour, the tendency to control female members of the family or clan and to protect them from sexual attention) was not the same as *qatl 'amd* (intentional murder). They also said that people with such pure and simple intentions deserved to be pardoned, not punished. To assert whether these honour crimes emanate from Islamic scriptures or reflect a customary practice, we look into the relevant provisions of Islamic law and their interpretation in light of verses of the Qur'an, especially those related to women (Ali, 2002). There are specific regulations under Islamic law regarding what is required from a man if his wife is accused of adultery when no clear proof of the deed can be provided (Awde, 2000). We must bear in mind that, although the Qur'an disapproves of promiscuity, in honour killings, the key distinction, or rather the principal difference, is that the victim is supposedly carrying out illegitimate acts.

Before we begin our analysis, it is important to clarify a few key concepts: *Zina* is an Islamic legal term referring to unlawful sexual intercourse and includes adultery, pre-marital sex, prostitution, bestiality, and rape. *Zina* laws are a part of a complex system of norms and laws regulating sexuality in ways that serve the patriarchy. Furthermore, in Islamic law, *Ta'azir* refers to punishment for offences where the degree and type are not specified in the Sharia and are left to the discretion of the judge (*Qadi*) or ruler of the state. Imprisonment under *Ta'azir* does not deter potential perpetrators; on the contrary, the realisation that there is a legal vacuum makes them bolder and more confident in committing this act.

Ta'azir is one of three major types of punishments or sanctions under Sharia Islamic law, together with *Hadd* and the *Qisas*. The punishments foreseen for these offences vary; for example, in the case of *Hadd* they may vary from public lashing and stoning to amputation and crucifixion, while for the *Qisas*, the death penalty is a common sentence. The *Hadd* offences, which are included in the Qur'an or Hadith (i.e., are defined by God), include, among others, illicit sex, rape, and alcohol consumption. *Qisas*, which is synonymous with the "eye for an eye" style of retribution, allows equal retaliation in cases of intentional bodily harm. *Ta'azir* can be in the form of imprisonment, fines, or flogging (it should be less than the punishment reserved for *Hadd*). *Diya* is the financial compensation paid to the victim of crime. The literal translation of the word is *blood money* or *ransom*, and it is mentioned in the Qur'an, verse 4:92 (Pickthall, 2017):

> *It is not for a believer to kill a believer unless (it be) by mistake. He who hath killed a believer by mistake must set free a believing slave, and pay the blood-money to the family of the slain, unless they remit it as a charity. If he (the victim) be of a people hostile unto you, and he is a believer, then (the penance is) to set free a believing slave. And if he cometh of a folk between whom and you there is a covenant, then the blood-money must be paid unto his folk and (also) a believing slave must be set free. And whoso hath not the wherewithal must fast two consecutive months.*

It is up to the family to decide whether the payment of blood money and imprisonment are a sufficient punishment, or whether the perpetrator is to be executed. According to a female Iranian lawyer, the acceptance of blood money in murder cases usually means that the perpetrator will be sentenced to between three and 15 years' imprisonment.

Honour killings are investigated as murder, and the perpetrator can be tried by a court. However, the punishment that the perpetrator receives depends on who the perpetrator is and the degree to which they will be able to "justify" the act to the court (cf. *Islamic legislation and conception of the law* in Kar, 2008). According to law, a father's punishment for killing his child is not based on *Qisas*, the retaliation principle, but rather executed through the payment of blood money to the child's mother or relatives. Payment varies based on a complicated system of values and is defined by law. Other family members who do this, such as brothers, uncles, or mothers, risk being charged with murder, but the practice is such that they are not executed if the family, for a number of different reasons, wishes to spare their lives. A husband is allowed to kill his wife (and her sexual partner) without incurring any form of criminal prosecution if he has witnessed her being unfaithful.[2] If the woman's family protests and there is no evidence that the murder was "justified", the husband usually only risks being sentenced to pay blood money; it is left to the judge to decide.

The Islamic Penal Code of Iran does, however, specify that a father who kills his child shall not be convicted on the basis of the retaliation principle (Iran: Islamic Penal Code, 1991: art. 220). If the father is also convicted of abusing the child prior to killing them, he will be sentenced to approximately one year's imprisonment or, if applicable, fined and/or a given number of lashes. Article 220 applies irrespective of the child's age and legal status. A person charged with murder might make reference to the victim's immoral behaviour in an attempt to avoid punishment, citing that the killing was just and necessary in order to protect the perpetrator and Muslim society (Iran: Islamic Penal Code, 1991: art. 295). This provision can be invoked by everybody, for example, men who have committed honour killings or killed prostitutes and women who claim to have killed in self-defence. In such cases, the perpetrator may avoid the death penalty and will be entitled to a considerable reduction of their sentence. It is up to the judge to decide whether the killing was "justified" or carried out in self-defence and how great the reduction to the sentence should be.

In the past, Article 179 of the 1926 Iranian criminal code[3] was seen as directly contributing to an increase in the number of honour killings. This article stipulates that if a wife is discovered committing adultery by her father, husband, or brother, then they are all allowed to kill her without being prosecuted. On the other hand, if the roles are reversed, the husband is caught in the act of unfaithfulness and the woman attempts to take revenge on her husband, she may be punished with lengthy imprisonment. Before the revolution, murder was an offence that carried the death penalty, but family members or the chief of the tribe could have carried out the penalty, or, depending on the circumstances, the punishment would be reduced to life imprisonment. After the revolution, the death penalty was based on *Qisas*. Until 1991, but also nowadays, in certain remote areas among tribal communities, the fate of both the victim and the perpetrator are decided by the Council of Elders, who have the power to impose the death penalty or to acquit the accused. However, a law was passed that year which foresaw imprisonment sentences of between three and ten years, even if the perpetrator had been convicted solely for disturbing public order. In cases where the perpetrator had killed his wife or daughter, the council's final decision on his sentence or acquittal would be taken based on deliberations about similar cases. Among the tribes and the traditional communities of Kermanshah and Kurdistan, a mere suspicion, such as the suspicion of the loss of virginity, was considered a fully justifiable reason for killing women and girls. If no action was taken, it affected the dignity of the family. Usually, it was up to the Council of Elders to make the decision to kill a woman or a girl, and the council was responsible for choosing who would carry out the killing as well as preparing them mentally and psychologically for the act. This act was not seen as a homicide, and the killer was subsequently released without punishment. It is also worth re-emphasising that the killer would be convinced that he did the right thing, which was a belief that passed from generation to generation where killers evaded punishment.

Iran's new penal code, adopted in 2013, was severely criticised on many accounts. The reasons for this included the link it draws between criminal responsibility and puberty or maturity and the fact that it relies mostly on Sharia and *Fatwas* instead of legal sources, perpetuates the use of torture and inhumane punishments, and upholds a number of discriminatory practices against women. Article 630 of the Iranian Penal Code states that a husband is permitted to murder his wife and her lover if he catches them together. However, if it is obvious that his wife did not consent to this, he is only permitted to kill her rapist. Additionally, a paragraph was added to the penal code to emphasise that the husband is exempt from *Qisas* law (meaning that he will not be punished as harshly as he acted in retaliation) (Home Office, 2019, p. 24).

This article can be interpreted as a general rule; in reality, it is very rare that these conditions will be all met at the time of the honour killing. There are three ways of approaching Article 630: according to one interpretation, prescribing such a decree is a legitimate defence of religious beliefs and honour. The second reading is based on the maintenance and safeguarding of the ethics, opinion, and security of the society. Finally, the spiritual incitement of the murderer, departure from the natural state, and impossibility of making the right decisions are reasons for committing such an act. From a generic point of view, Article 630 encourages people to kill instead of showing restraint. Most jurists believe that although the husband has not really committed a sin by killing his wife, he should be able to prove adultery beforehand. In other words, although a man has a legal right to kill his wife and her lover if he catches them in the act of adultery, cases in which the provision is applied in practice are rare. The reason is that, according to Sharia law, the man would need to have four witnesses to the act, which is almost impossible to achieve in practice (Haley & Yusuf, 1999: 967; Afary, 2009). Certain scholars, such as Abolqasem Khoei, have also asserted that so many people commit honour killings without fear of harsh punishment because of this law (Sadeghi, 2009).

Article 220 of the criminal code is related to the murder of a child by a father or ancestor of the father. According to the article and contrary to other cases of murder, the father or grandfather of the victim is not condemned under *Qisas* but should only pay blood money and be subject to *Ta'azir*. Although Article 220 is apparently not linked to honour killings, it can have a role in influencing this debate, and it is very crucial to consider because, according to research, it is fathers who commit two-thirds of honour killings. Certain experts believe that the legislature has extended the provisions of Article 220, for reasons of jurisprudence, to include the execution of the father because of domestic violence cases, including honour killings. However, according to some jurists, this ruling can be limited to cases where, for example, the killing of the child by the father was not based on reasonable grounds. According to the current conditions, this needs to be corrected, for example, by the addition of a note to this article that would increase the *Ta'azir* punishment for the father and exclude him from the qualifications required by Article 220 of the criminal code. At this point, it is interesting to note Article 147 regarding criminal responsibility: "The age of maturity of girls and boys, are, respectively, a full nine and fifteen lunar years" (Iran: Islamic Penal Code, 1991). Therefore, if a girl aged nine and a boy aged 15 commit a crime, they will be treated as adults. This automatically exposes children to a totally new set of rules and expectations within a society, making them dependent on whether a judge determines that the child understood the nature of the crime and should be subject to severe punishment or even death.

The permission for murder if the victim is *Madhur-al-Dam* (a person whose *blood is void* [Aranchi & Ebadpour, 2017]) is mentioned in Article 226 and is usually reserved for a person who insults the prophet, in cases of legitimate defence, or when the murder is committed in accordance with Sharia. It is within the jurisdiction of the judiciary to enforce the punishment, and this type of retaliation is the heritage of the pre-Islamic Arabs. With the advent of Islam, if anyone sinned and deserved death, they were tried by the Imam or the Caliph, as it was believed that they delivered justice on earth on "God's authority". The application of Note 2 in Article 295 refers to the case where the slain person did not deserve to be murdered, but the perpetrator killed them by believing in *Madhur-al-Dam* or *Qisas* and was able to prove it to the court. In that case, it would be a deliberate murder, and a perpetrator should be punished. It is important to reiterate that in all honour killings, the murderer believes in the martyrdom of the victim and, therefore, this can easily be used to provide justification to the murderer for committing the act.

One of the important issues in the subject of honour killings is whether, and to what extent, the potential murderers are familiar with the legal framework that applies in the country. Typically, ordinary people are not well informed about the content of these laws, which creates a de facto tendency to kill more women. For example, the general public is aware of Article 630 of the Iranian Penal Code, although they may not be fully familiar with all of the details and exceptions it includes. But, for the ordinary people who live under this law, it is the fact that the law allows for the murder of women that is at the forefront of their minds. It is therefore imperative for the adopted legal framework to have a preventive and deterrent aspect; laws should be clearly outlined and not leave room for multiple or conflicting interpretations. However, a revised legal framework alone is not enough to combat honour crimes because, in the prevailing cultural and social norms, this type of killing will always find moral justification. Still, if there were a very definite and clear punishment for a perpetrator of an honour crime, this might deter a potential murderer. In short, and in particular concerning the tribal populations, improving the legal framework by omitting the clauses where the perpetrators are exempted from punishment could reduce the frequency of honour killings. People should expect an appropriate punishment for the act they have committed. The language has to be clear and straightforward so that it does not leave any margin for misunderstanding, misinterpretation, or loopholes. It must not create the false impression or, indeed, the hope that there is way to be exempt from punishment.

According to the law of the Islamic Republic, laws and regulations on any matter cannot conflict with Islamic law. The punishment for retaliation is based on Sharia. Despite repeated calls by human rights activists and organisations recommending its replacement with other punishments, its removal would be contrary to Islamic law. Despite the emphasis of the Qur'an on the imposition of *Qisas*, more than 35 verses also call on people to prevent such perpetrators from committing murder. Under Iran's Islamic penal code, a father faces a maximum jail sentence of ten years if convicted of murder because fathers are considered guardians and, unlike mothers, are exempt from capital punishment for murdering their children. In the current political system, men not only have tradition on their side, but also the law. All the important decisions in women's lives are made by their fathers or husbands, even after death. As previously mentioned, Iran's Islamic code of criminal law enshrines the principle of retribution, meaning that if a girl or woman is the victim of a crime, her father or husband decides whether the perpetrator is punished—frequently with the death sentence—or pardoned. Honour is a woman's most important asset, and, in many cases, the father or grandfather enlists a brother or cousin of the "dishonoured" girl to carry out the murder. After the crime has been committed, he takes responsibility himself or pardons the killer.

> *In most honour killings, there are no complaints by the plaintiff or guardian, and the murderer is quickly released at the agreement of both parties. According to Article 43 of the Islamic Penal Code, if a father is involved in the murder of his child with others, the killer will be sentenced to retaliation in order to prevent the blood of the victim from being trampled. The Penal Code, in particular Article 301, effectively reduces punitive measures for fathers and other family members who murder or physically harm children, including in domestic violence or "honour killings" (Rights of the Child in Iran, 2015).*

The judicial procedure in these cases also recognises the right of retribution for relatives, and this leads to a larger number of honour killings. From the moral perspective, the position of the relatives having a final say in a killing is no different from that of the killer's; however, they will not be punished and they will also be given the right to decide on the retribution required. Given that pardoning the murderer is an integral part of honour killing cases, it is necessary to consider the issue of alternative punishments or retribution. According to Article 612 of the criminal code,

> *anyone who has committed a deliberate murder and for any reason is not a retribution, the court commits the perpetrator to three to ten years imprisonment if his action disrupts the order and security of the society or the commerce of the perpetrators or others.*

There is no willful murder that does not disturb the security of the community; thus, these conditions are present in all murder cases. The length of imprisonment depends on the court, the circumstances of the crime, and the person who committed the crime; therefore, the judge must examine the case more thoroughly before giving a ruling. As the judge is open to virtually any ruling in determining the term of imprisonment, in addition to Article 612, he may also grant the accused conditional release on the basis of Article 38 of the criminal code, after a period of imprisonment. These reduced sentences are very common among convicted honour killers.

Finally, it is also worth mentioning Article 301, which reads as follows:

> *The murder of a person is to cause retaliation, if the victim is not permitted to be killed under Sharia, and if he/she deserves to be murdered, the killer must prove that he/she is entitled to carry out his/her murder in accordance with the rules of the Court.*

The mention of whether he/she is permitted to be killed according to Sharia is ambiguous, as the "legislator has not specified who is the reference source of the identification of Madhur-al-Dam (literal translation: whose blood may be shed with immunity)" (Aranchi & Ebadpour, 2017: 2128). The clear message is that killing another person as a form of retaliation is permissible. Of course, Articles 302 and 303 become obsolete when they are subjected to Note 2 of Article 295 of the Islamic Penal Code, which stipulates that if a person believes in retribution or that the victim is Madhur-al-Dam, this must be proven in court. This is important because this assumes that the killing of another person is permissible. This defect has not been eliminated from the law.

In Islamic jurisprudence, the term *Bayanah* means clear and undeniable proof, and it includes all kind of evidence. It has been used by jurists, especially in matters relating to litigation and disputes involving only two parties. In other words, there have to be two testimonies, and if there are more or less, they are not considered valid. Also, the claimants must be male, and a woman's testimony is not considered valid, except in certain cases. Further, if the applicant is not able to present a religious certificate to defend his testimony, he can prove his claim by introducing a male witness or two women. This principle requires that the victim was not killed because of adultery and the deed was done in order to deliver justice (Jebari, 2018: 109). According to Sharia, honour killings are a righteous act and they are dictated by the will of God (Akbari & Tetreault, 2014).

The criminal laws of a society are the expression of the most important values and norms of that society in terms of how power should be organised and controlled and what kind of social behaviour is acceptable and punishable by the law (Shoro, 2019: 31). The punishment is imposed by the judiciary. The legislature usually embodies and incorporates certain customs and traditions of a society. The gravity of the crime may be viewed differently in different societies; this is obviously due to many factors that need to be thoroughly investigated and identified. The role that laws and regulations of a society have in terms of the amount and type of crimes committed cannot be easily conveyed (Vago, 2015: 232). In fact, the laws and regulations that are employed in the fight against crime and delinquency in the community, in particular criminal law, contradict basic Islamic principles with regards to various crimes, for example, assassinations and honour killings. Therefore, these rules play an important role in preventing people from committing various crimes (Pradel, 1991).

Patriarchy in Kurdish society

In recent years, attention has been paid to the social dimensions of honour killings and society's response. There has been increasing criticism in Iran of honour killings. This reveals not only a growing awareness of their brutal nature but also a gradual change in the cultural and social values underpinning modern Iranian society. Naturally, in provinces such as Iranian Kurdistan, with its strong tribal traditions, a low educational level and the prevalence of particular cultural norms, such as inter-family marriages, the likelihood of such murders is greater. Yet, in such societies it is just as important to educate women so that they develop a kind of psychological–emotional ownership of themselves to overcome gender-based discrimination more easily. However, this process starts from within the woman herself. It involves her becoming self-aware and socially aware so that she is able to challenge the traditional autocratic values that support and perpetuate gender discrimination. And it is gender discrimination together with gender inequality that are to a large extent to blame for the occurrence of the one of the most notable human rights violations.

Gender-based violence

Violence against women in Iran stems from deep-rooted notions of gender inequality (Chamlou, 2016; Kazemzadeh, 2002), which leads to many different kinds of gender-based abuse that causes physical, sexual, or psychological harm to women in their private or public lives. Examples of abuse include intimidation, coercion, and deprivation of liberty. A perpetrator can be the victim's husband, father, family member, friend, or a stranger. Religion, culture, economic factors, politics, and legislation all contribute to perpetuating violence against women (Ennaji & Sadiqi, 2011: 1). According to one survey, 20% of marriages in the 21st century have been between cousins and 20% between distant relatives. The liberal Gilan Province in the north of the country has had the fewest inter-family marriages, while the conservative Sistan and Baluchestan provinces near the Pakistani border, where the average age of marriage for women is just 16, has recorded the majority of inter-family marriages (Bahramitash & Kazemipour, 2006).

Three women in Marivan, one in Sanandaj, and two men in Piranshahr were victims of honour killings in 2017, and on International Women's Day, a girl was killed by her father. In my interview with a civil rights activist in Marivan, she told me that honour killing is a tradition that has no boundaries. She also narrated the story of a woman named Saffron who was separated and was planning to remarry, but the groom's family did not approve. Parvin Zabihi, a civil rights activist residing in Marivan, said:

> *This woman, Saffron, escaped with her boyfriend and they went together to his house. The father of the man told Saffron's father that he found her*

and choked her. He took her corpse to the village and announced to everyone that "I've destroyed this disgraced corpse."

Zabihi continued:

> Saffron's father had long been under the pressure of public opinion. The villagers blamed him for his daughter's behaviour, who already had five children with her husband. Marivan is a Muslim region that is transitioning from tradition to modernism. People still accept these murders. Many also encourage the family to commit these killings. If the father of the child is the killer, the mother will not ask for punishment because she will lose her man as well. Then, in the case of husbands, wives, who are not the killers themselves, are usually provoked to be killed by others. Many of these husbands after the death of their wives are more likely to receive blood money to finance their grievances (Shojai, 2013).

According to the theory of power control, even in patriarchal families, mothers play a central role in the upbringing of their children. Such a family, where the father figure is employed and the mother stays at home, imposes more control over the female children than the male children. This unbalanced instrumental relationship is part of the function of internal social control and is a distinctive feature in mastering control over girls in patriarchal families, as men take advantage of the gender gap to use their power over women (Hagan, Simpson, & Gillis, 1987). On the other hand, control within egalitarian families is more evenly distributed, and girls are not oppressed. There is a far greater chance of boys from patriarchal families displaying delinquent behaviour; the theory of power control asserts that gender differences result from unbalanced and patriarchal family structures rather than from more balanced and egalitarian family class structures. These differences can be removed when variables associated with unbalanced, patriarchal relations are reversed.

I have argued that a predominantly male pattern of delinquency results from the class structure of modern patriarchal families. This patriarchal family structure is historically rooted in the separation of family from work that Weber, Gerth, & Mills (1946) saw as crucial to the rationalisation of modern industrial capitalism. In these families, an instrument–object relationship takes the form of fathers, with mothers controlling their daughters more than their sons. This relationship plays a key role in the social reproduction of a gender division between family and work, or in other words, between the sphere of domestic labour and consumption and the sphere of labour power and direct production. My argument is that the instrument–object relationship that characterises the parent–daughter relationship in patriarchal families tends to prepare daughters for a "cult of domesticity" that makes their involvement in delinquency comparatively unlikely. For example, girls are socialised in a manner designed to prepare them for the kind of domestic life where their husbands are employed in positions of control and influence (a form of economic authority) and the girls are either unemployed or employed in positions without authority.

Though family honour rests upon the behaviour of family members, women provide a convenient scapegoat in the face of subjective qualifications, such as "public morality", decency, and religion, which enforce morality and chastity on women. Honour-based violence is directly related to the notion of men being the guardians of women's chastity, which serves as a justification for the killing of women at men's hands. In Iran, religion is broadly used to support and promote social prejudices against women (Mir-Hosseini, 2000; Derayeh, 2006), however, it must be acknowledged that the collective and ritual honour killing is not a tradition among Persians, or in Persian-dominated areas (O'Doherty, 2017: 28). Traditionally, Iranian communities do not exert social pressure on men to abuse or kill female relatives who break the code of honour. Although conservative voices sanction men's violent outbursts and aggression towards women, there is no traditional expectation among Persians that this must be done in order to restore the family's honour. Honour killings in Iran have not been systematically mapped; official and verifiable statistics on the scope of honour killings are not available, nor can any reliable conclusions be reached from unofficial statistics. The available sources suggest that honour killings primarily occur among tribal peoples such as the Kurds, Lori, Arabs, Baluchs, and Turkish-speaking tribes (Landinfo, 2009).

These tribal groups are considered to be more socially conservative than the Persians, and discrimination against women in attitude and practice is deeply rooted in their tribal culture. The majority of these groups are Sunni Muslims who live in the socio-economically least developed and geographically most isolated areas of the country. The Kurdish population lives in north-western Iran; more than two million ethnic Kurds live in Khorasan Province and are descended from those deported there in the 17th century from the northern part of Kurdistan in Turkey by Shah Abbas. These arrivals did not cease until well into the 18th century (Manuello, 2014). The population of the Ilam province is also almost exclusively Kurdish, and a considerable Kurdish minority lives in West Azerbaijan. The Lori live in Lorestan, and there are many Arab, Lori, and Turkish-speaking tribes in Khuzestan. Arab tribes live in southern Iran and in Baluchistan, and among Baluchs, honour crimes are widespread and are attributed to a variety of reasons: declining an arranged marriage proposal, being sexually assaulted, being sexually active, asking for a divorce, or being accused of "allegedly committing adultery" (Taheri, 2012: 35).

There are many examples of honour killings, all of which have one point in common: young girls are very conscious of their status and societal expectations when it comes to their relationship with the opposite sex. As a result, they try to hide their relationships or dissatisfaction with their partners because they are aware of the consequences if they do not.

Another example is the story of Atefeh, which is narrated by her sister in Ilam:

> *Atefeh was an 18-year-old girl killed by her father. She was arrested by the police after she was found in the presence of a boy on a street and her father killed her. My mother had intervened to save Atefeh's life and was stabbed with a knife. While in prison, my father even announced that if he was released, he would kill me too as I was 16 years old... When I returned home from school, no one opened the door for me. I called my home phone, but nobody answered. I told my cousin. He went to the gate and opened the door. We entered the house. It was horrifying. Blood was everywhere; in every corner of the house where Atefeh had attempted to save herself; finally, she had pulled herself close to the entrance door. My mother was in another corner, my dad was angry at the other side. With a kitchen knife in hand, he had stabbed Atefeh and injured my mother.*

Atefeh did not even have sex with the boy. Her friends and classmates originally suspected that she had committed suicide, but after a while they started to doubt this. Her mother still wears a black veil after three years of mourning the loss of her daughter. The father, who, in the meantime, had also killed Atefeh's boyfriend, was in prison for a very short period of time until the boy's parents legally confirmed that they were satisfied with the length of his punishment. They said he had no control over his actions because he suffered from diabetes and that made it difficult for him to stay in jail.

On the basis of the information available, there is nothing to suggest that the Iranian authorities actively try to combat honour killings. Receiving justice free from of gender discrimination is a fundamental right of every citizen, yet, judges, as part of the patriarchal establishment, are prejudiced against women and, as a result, their verdicts in cases of honour killings are influenced and shaped by the cultural and social expectations of society. Whenever women deviate from norms that are in line with the society's traditional values, the justice and security institutions fail to protect them and safeguard even their most basic human rights. In other words, judges do not deliver an impartial verdict in the cases of honour killing because they are also agents of the patriarchal society, and their sympathies lie with the murderer. As a result, the judges of a conservative society have not undermined the ability of governments, elites, and political groups to use secular and Islamic discourses that further reinforce these values. Colonial authorities left existing gender relations largely intact, as did middle-class reform and nationalist movements. While secular legal codes have been adopted in many countries, they have generally deferred to the religious authority matters of family or personal status laws. Colonial authorities and secular legal codes are nationalist, and Islamic discourses have used the ideals of Islamic ethics and cultural originality to maintain control and change the discourse.

Increasing economic and educational opportunities for women and the emergence of residential models of the nuclear family have destroyed the structures of the patriarchal family, for example, old forms of arranged marriages give way to elements of romantic attachment. The tradition of Muslim cultures considers the problems and violence in families to be a private and domestic issue, which is a common and widespread problem (Koggel, 2006). The court tends to justify the action of a perpetrator who has killed a woman to restore his honour and who, in other words, acted as a respected and honourable man (*Qeira't*, a man who possesses honour).

Instances of honour killings in Iran have also made worldwide news, leading to protests and outcries to criminalise crimes of this nature. One example was the story of Romina Ashrafi, 14, who was murdered by her father after trying to run away with her boyfriend, who was 34 years old. The police let her father take her back home, although she told the police that "she feared a violent reaction from him" (Associated Press, 2020). This international story led to the hashtag #RominaAshrafi trending on many social media platforms, with users worldwide calling for this practice to be outlawed.

The ideological roles relating to gender under Islam in the modern period have accompanied dramatic transformations, including the rise of modern state systems, Western colonial expansionism, and various reform and nationalist movements. Such complex processes have not significantly challenged the patriarchal values that underpin the sexual stratification. This is also the case in Iranian culture and society. The current religious and sociocultural situation means that many girls and women do not see the option of getting help from outside the family circle or from the authorities as a real alternative. The lack of awareness of their legal rights combined with strong family ties, fear of social shame and stigmatisation, threats, and financial dependence leads many girls and women to give in to their family's wishes, remain in unhappy marriages, or commit suicide.

The following is the story of a 15-year-old girl, Setareh, who was also the victim of her father's tyranny in Ilam. Her father forced her to marry her cousin, whom she did not like. She cried, begged, and went on a hunger strike, but her protests bore no results. At one point, while talking to her father, Setareh made an unintentional mistake and told him that she "married" the boy. Her father interpreted this statement to mean that she had already engaged in sexual relations with him, and he gave her no time to correct her sentence; he immediately attacked her and choked her. He did not receive any punishment and was released from custody.

A woman who is threatened with honour killing or subjected to other forms of violence must seek help on her own. The community around her will not come to her assistance unless she directly asks for help. Whether it is possible to ask for help depends on where the woman lives—in some parts of Iran, the physical and geographical conditions make fleeing impossible. The extent to which a woman can get help depends on a number of factors: the nature of the case, how old she is, where she lives, what she wants, and to what extent she is able to mobilise parts of her own family network to plead her case and negotiate in the conflict. Depending on the nature of the case, she can, for example, seek help from a women's network, provided that such a network exists where she lives and that she is aware of it, file a lawsuit in a family court, or report the matter to the police. If she goes to the police, the scope of the violence and threats will be decisive in determining whether she receives help and what kind of help she will be offered. She is responsible for presenting evidence that she is, in fact, threatened, or that her life is in danger, which, in certain cases, can be impossible to prove. The attitudes of the police or a local judge may have a decisive impact on her chances of being given real protection. The Western European model of a crisis centre or shelter for women exists in Iran, however, it is limited in function and thus not organised enough to operate a shelter. There are state institutions for single women, prostitutes, drug addicts, children, and young people who have run away from home, which are run by the national welfare organisation and offer protection, welfare services, and rehabilitation programmes of varying quality for a transitional period. The number of institutions that help women and victims of domestic violence, as well as their exact locations, are not currently known. The Iranian authorities are generally unwilling to provide the public with any type of information that may, directly or indirectly, generate criticism against Islamic law and the Republic.

One of the lawyers from Kermanshah confided the following:

> *The main reason for these killings was the lack of proper sexual relations between husband and wife, and the fact that women are forced to marry at a young age. When a woman loses her virginity, she also does not care about her husband, she easily loves another young person, and it ends only in one thing; death.*

Following our previous discussion, the starting point for various relief efforts under the auspices of public and private stakeholders is that social and family-related problems must be solved within the framework of accepted cultural and religious values. Certain attitudes, such as the idea that women neither can, nor should, live on their own because they need the protection of a husband and family, are deeply rooted in all social classes in Iranian culture. Both family courts and non-governmental organisations working in conflict mediation seek to reunite a girl or a woman with her family through mediation and written guarantees for her safety, or, if applicable, to have her marry in order to be protected and supported. In cases where this is not possible and the girl is over 18 years of age, civil society organisations can assist in finding her accommodation and work. Living alone with no family network is not seen as a real or acceptable alternative for an Iranian woman, and it may also be associated with danger.

Honour crimes in Iran have been imposed on women whose behaviour, actions, activities, or experiences have been defined as "un-Islamic". This might include political and social activism for things such as women's rights, attempts to access one's own rights, a relationship outside the family that is deemed to be improper, and being the victim of a physical or sexual assault, or the reason might simply be a way to restrict and regulate women's behaviour. The belief that a woman and her family bear the shame of a sexual assault committed by someone outside of her family is widely held; honour crimes are identified as a way of removing the perceived shame.

The results of a survey on the rate and extent of domestic violence cases against women reported by the Committee on the Elimination of Violence Against Women showed that 66% of the families, or 30% of the households, had experienced, at least once, some form of serious physical, domestic violence, and in 10% of households, violence had resulted in temporary or permanent injuries. If women want a divorce, their husbands often resort to violence when the men do not want to pay them the *Mahr*, which is the sum of money paid by the groom to the bride at the time of their marriage (Hajnasiri et al., 2016). The *Mahr* is not only limited to money but can also include furniture, land, or other goods, and it should be returned to the husband should the wife initiate divorce proceedings. If the husband initiates divorce proceedings, then the wife is entitled to keep all of the *Mahr*.

Violence against women in Iranian Kurdistan is intertwined with daily life. Several authors have discussed and analysed gender-based and sexual violence in Iraqi Kurdistan with reference to patriarchy, tribal culture, nationalism, militarism, and Islamism (Begikhani, 2005; Begikhani, Gill, & Hague, 2010; Mojab, 2001; Mojab & Abdo, 2004). In Iraqi Kurdistan, the official annual count of female homicide victims is around 100, the majority of which are assumed to be related to honour (Begikhani, Gill, & Hague, 2010: 46). More recently, Alinia (2013) provided an in-depth analysis of honour-based crimes, paying attention to the way that various power structures, such as ethnic and national oppression, economic marginalisation, patriarchy, religion, and tribal and kinship structures as well as displacement and militarisation of society intersect to produce a "hegemonic honour discourse". To those interlinked structures, Alinia also added the significance of the prevailing notion of masculinity in controlling women's bodies, their sexuality, and their honour. While Alinia moved away from the more generalised explanations pertaining to culture, religion, tribalism, and nation, Kanie (2015) provided a further nuanced and in-depth insight by pointing to shifts in social, political, and economic norms and values, resulting in a "normative disorientation", and the emergence of new forms of masculinities alongside the older hegemonic *peshmerga*[4] masculinities, all contributing to an increase in gender-based violence. In my own view, "normative disorientation" is an excellent analytical lens through which to explore the impact of more recent political, social, and economic changes, but I would also argue that an intersectional approach is key and that we need to be very specific in terms of the relevant intersecting oppressive structures, as Alinia (2013) suggested.

Nasrin, 38, is unemployed and labouring on agricultural land. She was 20 years old when she married. She said of her husband: "I was pleased with the fact that he was well-motivated and kind and satisfied. As much as he could, he could provide me with everything". A little while later, her husband began taking drugs and became addicted. This meant that he was not able to provide a stable enough income for them. They started arguing. She divorced him and later married an older man. These days are not good for her. It has been a whole year since she returned to her parental home. Being a divorced woman is not easy, as she had to pay additionally for her children's expenses. Furthermore, in order to retain custody of the children till the age of seven, she was required to forego all of her rights, her alimony, and her dowry.

A cheating husband is also a very painful experience for women in a traditional society, since a wife has no choice but to stay with him. In such a setting, women are never encouraged or supported by their families if they decide to leave their husbands. Narges, a 38-year-old woman who was well aware of her husband's cheating, said to me:

> I just doubted him in the beginning. I had been watching him for some time. He made a lot of phone-calls, which was suspicious, and he was outside the house for hours and for not good reason. The first time, I saw an SMS, I contacted that number and found out that she was a woman. But he was not only in contact with one woman; he was involved with many women. When I found out about the relationship, I just pretended I knew nothing about it; it was too late for me to divorce.

As previously mentioned, honour killings occur across the globe and are not necessarily linked to one particular religion; yet, they seem, at least nowadays, to be mostly prevalent in Muslim majority countries. One important factor affecting the number and extent of honour killings in a community is related to the applicable penal system. The type of punishment envisaged for perpetrators of honour killings and the familiarity of the community with the existing legal provisions are very powerful tools in deterring these heinous crimes. It is therefore not possible to tackle honour killings without adjusting the legal framework. Undoubtedly, in the Iranian context, one cannot alter the existing penal code without taking into consideration Islamic law or Sharia.

Conclusion: the way forward

As long as perversions of religious practice continue to be validated by religious and tribal leaders, women's freedom of movement and expression, as well as their basic rights, such as the right to live without violence, will always be under threat. As long as village, community, and religious leaders are left to maintain social control without educating men and women about women's human rights, there will be little improvement to the situation of women in Kurdistan in the near future. Although some of the information I gathered was anecdotal in nature, over the course of the two-week interview period I conducted, I encountered an excess of contributing factors to the widespread mentality associated with honour-based violence, including, but not limited to, a lack of protection for victims of domestic violence and an acknowledgement of mental and psychological problems experienced by a substantial part of the population within the patriarchal society. Other factors, such as family pressures, forced marriage, polygamy, lack of education, language barriers, financial insecurity, unemployment, generational conflict, forced prostitution, state violence, and weak application of the rule of law, compounded by the ongoing insecurity surrounding Iraqi Kurdistan have all made way for clan leaders to provide social structure independent of the regional leadership or political parties and for Islamic fundamentalism to spread. This leads to a lack of clarity in the laws governing Iran and Kurdistan specifically, a loss of hope and a sense that life will never improve, and feelings of shame and "dishonour".

In honour killings, the murderer himself is also a victim. To address and combat honour killings, one must consider all the elements that shape them, such as religion and tribal customs, prevailing cultural norms, and weak laws, which not only fail to deter killings, but provide prospective perpetrators with sufficient justification to commit them. The fight against honour killings will need to be based on close collaboration and targeted interventions among legislators, law enforcement agencies, community leaders, and public figures in order to overcome deeply entrenched cultural norms. This approach has to be based on the assumption that these killings have become institutionalised and are supported by local customs and unwritten moral codes to such an extent that it can be argued that the killer acted within his rights to restore honour and dignity to the family. Further research, mapping, and analysis of the variables contributing to honour killings, such as extreme cases of prejudice against women, the dominant patriarchal tradition, psychological disorders, and the role of religion and law in society, is necessary if tailor-made and culturally sensitive interventions are to be developed (Caulfield, Chambers, & Putnam, 2005; Findlay, 2003; Orywal, 1996).

The root causes of honour killings should be primarily looked for among the norms and values that are prevalent in society and the weak legal framework that allows male relatives to kill females when they deem it appropriate, without fear of prosecution. Societal values and relations clearly reflect men's dominance and control over women, which creates a social dynamic that women internalise and that eventually becomes an important part of their identity in a traditional society; if they refuse to conform, their life is in danger. Economic under-development and marginalisation contribute to the persistence of these archaic traditions, alongside prejudice and violence. Besides the need for a modernised legal framework, civil society must reach out and support women at risk, undertake public information campaigns on the need to strengthen the rule of law, and inform the wider public about the extent and brutality of honour killings. Rule of law means that a conviction should not be decided by the Council of Elders but by the competent court, and that a murderer must face justice. Of equal importance is combatting and overcoming gender stereotyping and, instead, instilling a gender identity that promotes an independent human identity.

The issue of honour killings has attracted international attention in recent years. It has become the focus of a heated debate among journalists, politicians, lawyers, human rights defenders (especially women's rights defenders), and political thinkers. Unfortunately, so far, the criticism of honour killings has mainly been limited to expressing aversion to them and indignation against them. Instead, the available resources should be mobilised to conduct further scientific research, provide reliable reporting and crime statistics, analyse their effect on the psychological development of females, and determine credible and realistic measures to eradicate this most heinous crime.

Administering effective punishment is one of the most decisive ways of delivering justice for honour killings. As previously mentioned, there are various laws and regulations in Iran that can be used to deter people from honour killings; however, the penal code does not directly criminalise incidents associated with honour-based violence. Perpetrators can be only prosecuted as ordinary homicides in accordance with the Islamic law. The practice of circumventing longer-term imprisonments has to be further addressed. Equally worrying is the practice of pardoning the killer. For a punishment to be effective, it has to be clear that there are no loopholes in the system so that the killer cannot escape punishment. It is also important to ensure that adequate protection measures are in place to deter further perpetrators from committing a crime, meaning that information campaigns should also be designed in order to disseminate information about the legal framework, gender discrimination, and the repercussions of honour killings to remote areas among traditional and tribal communities.

The most direct way to challenge longstanding and deeply rooted traditional beliefs is through community education programmes. This is a common methodology within public health settings, where the intention is often to increase awareness of various symptoms and change behaviour by encouraging the uptake of preventative and treatment options (Hardeman et al., 2005). The challenge, then, is to design anti-HBV education programmes that show would-be offenders that there are alternative responses, thereby pushing an individual towards different courses of action. An important consideration, which is emphasised in the literature on social influence (Cialdini, 2009), is that education programmes are most successful when the messages are presented by individuals who have credibility within their target group and are perceived as insiders—that is, they share similar cultural backgrounds and experiences with the target audience. Communicators might, therefore, include victims of HBV who can present their stories, or individuals from communities where HBV is an issue but who have anti-HBV attitudes. Similarly, others who wield community influence could be used, including community and religious leaders, or locally revered celebrities. To achieve this, education programmes could be aimed not only at the community, but also at professionals such as teachers, community workers, social workers, legal professionals, and law enforcement to enable them to recognise the signs and risks of HBV and to act upon their suspicions. Target-hardening is also engendered by having clear legislation against and a penalty for HBV, coupled with a law enforcement response that takes this form of offending seriously and investigates all allegations.

Notes

1 For detailed analysis of honour killings in Iran see S. Zarabadi, "Bā Ejāzeh-ye Khodam Nāmusam Rā Mikosham" [I kill my honour with my own permission], *Zanān* 109, Khordād 2004: 29–33; and S. Sadr, "Namuse-e zanan vabasteh be Yek mard" [Women's honour depending on a single man], *Zanān* 93, Abān 2002: 10–13.
2 Article 630 of the Iranian Penal Code: If a wife has been subjected to sexual assault/rape, the husband is only allowed to kill the offender without punishment.
3 The Persian language version of this code is available from the Majles website. http://rc.majlis.ir/fa/law/show/91023. Accessed 27 March 2018.
4 Military forces of the federal region of Iraqi Kurdistan.

References

Abdi, Kamyar. 2003. "The Early Development of Pastoralism in the Central Zagros Mountains." *Journal of World Prehistory* 17, no. 4 (December): 395–448.
Abu Zayd, Nasr. 1988. "The Perfect Man in the Qur'ân: Textual Analysis." *Journal of Osaka University of Foreign Studies* 73: 111–133.
Abu-Odeh, Lama. 1996. "Crimes of Honor and the Construction of Gender in Arab Societies." In *Feminism and Islam: Legal and Literary Perspectives*, edited by Mai Yamani and Andrew Allen, 141–193. New York: NYU Press.
Afary, Janet. 2009. *Sexual Politics in Modern Iran*. New York: Cambridge University Press.
Ajzen, Icek. 1991. "The Theory of Planned Behavior." *Organizational Behavior and Human Decision Processes* 50, no. 2: 179–211.
Ajzen, Icek. 2001. "Nature and Operation of Attitudes." *Annual Review of Psychology* 52, no. 1: 27–58.
Ajzen, Icek. 2011. "The Theory of Planned Behaviour: Reaction and Reflection." *Psychology and Health* 26, no. 9: 1113–1127.
Akbari, Daniel, and Paul Tetreault. 2014. *Honor Killing: A Professional's Guide to Sexual Relations and Ghayra Violence from the Islamic Sources*. USA: AuthorHouse.
Ali, Kecia. 2002. "Rethinking Women's Issues in Muslim Communities." In *Taking Back Islam: American Muslims Reclaim Their Faith*, edited by Michael Wolfe and Beliefnet. Emmaus, PA: Rodale Press.
Alinia, Minoo. 2013. *Honor and Violence against Women in Iraqi Kurdistan*. New York: Palgrave Macmillan.

Al-Khayyat, Sana. 1990. *Honour and Shame: Women in Modern Iraq*. London: Saqi Books.

Antoun, Richard T. 1976. "Anthropology." In *The Study of the Middle East: Research and Scholarship in the Humanities and Social Sciences*, edited by Leonard Binder, 137–228. New York: John Wiley & Sons.

Araji, Sharon K. 2000. "Crimes of Honor and Shame: Violence against Women in Non-Western and Western Societies." *The Red Feather Journal of Postmodern Criminology* 8: 1–12.

Aranchi, Mahboub J., and Latif Ebadpour. 2017. "Madhur-Al-Dam (A Person Whose Blood is Void) in Iran's Criminal Law with Emphasis on the Issued Verdicts by Judiciary Courts." *Quid* Special Issue, no. 1: 2126–2133.

Asano-Tamanoi, Mariko. 1987. "Shame, Family, and State in Catalonia and Japan." In *Honor and Shame and the Unity of the Mediterranean*, edited by David Gilmore, 104–120. Washington, DC: American Anthropological Association Special Publication, no. 22.

Associated Press. 28 May 2020. "Romina Ashrafi: Outcry in Iran over So-Called 'Honour Killing' of 14-Year-Old Girl." Accessed 24November2020. https://www.theguardian.com/world/2020/may/28/romina-ashrafi-outcry-in-iran-over-so-called-honour-killing-of-14-year-old-girl.

Awde, Nicholas, ed. 2000. *Women in Islam: An Anthology from the Qur'an and Hadith*. Translated by Nicholas Awde. New York: St. Martin's Press.

Azadi, Pooya. 2020. "The Structure of Corruption in Iran." Stanford Iran 2040 Project. Accessed 21April2020. https://iranian-studies.stanford.edu/sites/g/files/sbiybj6191/f/publications/the_structure_of_corruption_in_iran.pdf.

Bahramitash, Roksana, and Shahla Kazemipour. 2006. "Myths and Realities of the Impact of Islam on Women: Changing Marital Status in Iran." *Critique: Critical Middle Eastern Studies* 15, no. 2: 111–128.

Baker, Nancy V., Peter R. Gregware, and Margery A. Cassidy. 1999. "Family Killing Fields: Honor Rationales in the Murder of Women." *Violence against Women* 5, no. 2: 164–184.

Bakhtiarnejad, Parvin. 2009. "Fajeeye khamush: ghatlhaye namusi" [The silent tragedy: Honour killings]. Unpublished study.

Baroja, Julio Caro. 1966. "Honour and Shame: A Historical Account of Several Conflicts." In *Honour and Shame: The Values of Mediterranean Society*, edited by John G. Peristiany, 79–137. Chicago: University of Chicago Press.

Basu, Nupur. 2013. "Honour Killings: India's Crying Shame." Accessed 18January2018. https://www.aljazeera.com/opinions/2013/11/28/honour-killings-indias-crying-shame.

Begikhani, Nazand, Aisha Gill, and Gill M. Hague. 2010. *Honour-based Violence (HBV) and Honour-based Killings in Iraqi Kurdistan and in the Kurdish Diaspora in the UK*. London: Kurdistan Regional Government.

Begikhani, Nazand. 2005. "Honour-Based Violence among the Kurds: The Case of Iraqi Kurdistan." In *"Honour": Crimes, Paradigms, and Violence against Women*, edited by Lynn Welchman and Sara Hossain, 209–229. London: Zed Books.

Bell, Rudolph M. 1979. *Fate and Honor, Family and Village: Demographic and Cultural Change in Rural Italy since 1800*. Chicago: University of Chicago Press.

Bourdieu, Pierre. 1966. "The Sentiment of Honour in Kabyle Society." In *Honour and Shame: The Values of Mediterranean Society*, edited by John G. Peristiany, 193–241. Chicago: University of Chicago Press.

Bowman, James. 2007. *Honor: A History.* New York: Encounter Books.
Boyer, Richard. 1998. "Honor among Plebeians: *Mala Sangre* and Social Reputation." In *The Faces of Honor: Sex, Shame, and Violence in Colonial Latin America*, edited by Lyman Johnson and Sonya Lipsett-Rivera, 152–178. Albuquerque, NM: University of New Mexico Press.
Brandon, James, and Salam Hafez. 2008. *Crimes of the Community: Honour-based Violence in the UK.* London: Centre for Social Cohesion.
Burkholder, Mark A. 1998. "Honor and Honors in Colonial Spanish America." In *The Faces of Honor: Sex, Shame, and Violence in Colonial Latin America*, edited by Lyman Johnson and Sonya Lipsett-Rivera, 18–44. Albuquerque, NM: University of New Mexico Press.
Campbell, John Kennedy. 1964. *Honour, Family and Patronage: A Study of Institutions and Moral Values in a Greek Mountain Community.* Oxford: Clarendon Press.
Casimir, Michael J. and Susanne Jung. 2009. "'Honor and Dishonor': Connotations of a Socio-symbolic Category in Cross-Cultural Perspective." In *Emotions as Bio-Cultural Processes*, edited by Birgitt Röttger-Rössler and Hans Markowitsch, 229–280. New York: Springer.
Caulfield, Sueann, Sarah C. Chambers, and Lara Putnam, eds. 2005. *Honor, Status, and Law in Modern Latin America.* London: Duke University Press.
Ceasefire. 2019. *Beyond the Veil: Discrimination against Women in Iran.* London: Ceasefire Centre for Civilian Rights.
Chakravarti, Uma. 2005. "From Fathers to Husbands: Of Love, Death and Marriage in North India." In *"Honour": Crimes, Paradigms, and Violence against Women*, edited by Lynn Welchman and Sara Hossain, 308–331. London: Zed Books.
Chamlou, Nadereh. 2016. "Gender Inequality and Income Inequality in Iran." In *Economic Welfare and Inequality in Iran: Developments since the Revolution*, edited by Mohammad Reza Farzanegan and Pooya Alaedini, 129–153. New York: Palgrave Macmillan.
Cialdini, Robert B. 2009. *Influence: The Psychology of Persuasion.* New York: HarperCollins.
Civil Code of the Islamic Republic of Iran. 2015. Retrieved 24 November 2020 from Civil Registration and Vital Statistics Knowledge Base: https://unstats.un.org/unsd/vitalstatkb/KnowledgebaseArticle50545.aspx.
Cohen, Elizabeth S. 1992. "Honor and Gender in the Streets of Early Modern Rome." *Journal of Interdisciplinary History* 22, no. 4: 597–625.
Coulson, Noel J. 1969. *Conflicts and Tensions in Islamic Jurisprudence.* Chicago: University of Chicago Press.
Derayeh, Minoo. 2006. *Gender Equality in Iranian History: From Pre-Islamic Times to the Present.* Lewiston: Edwin Mellen Press.
DeSilva, David A. 2000. *Honor, Patronage, Kinship and Purity: Unlocking New Testament Culture.* Downers Grove, IL: InterVarsity Press.
Dresch, Paul. 1989. *Tribes, Government, and History in Yemen.* Oxford: Clarendon Press.
Ebadi, Shirin. 2002. *Huquq-e Zan Dar Ghavanin-e Jomhoori-e Islami-e Iran* [Women's rights in the laws of the Islamic Republic of Iran]. Tehran: Ganje Danesh Publication.
Elias, Norbert, and John L. Scotson. 2008. *The Established and the Outsiders: A Sociological Enquiry into Community Problems.* Dublin: UCD Press.

Ennaji, Moha, and Fatima Sadiqi, eds. 2011. *Gender and Violence in the Middle East*. Abingdon: Routledge.
Etemaad, Jalil, Bahram Jowkar, Masoud Hoseichari, and Hossein Dabbagh. 2019. "The Effectiveness of Evoking Reminiscence on Nostalgia State and the Role of Nostalgia into Empathy Action: Role of Gender and Personal Justification." *Journal of Applied Psychological Research* 10, no. 2 (Summer): 35–51.
Farahani, Fataneh. 2017. *Gender, Sexuality, and Diaspora*. Abingdon: Routledge.
Feldner, Yotam. 2000. "'Honor' Murders – Why the Perps Get off Easy." *Middle East Quarterly* 7, no. 4 (December): 41–50.
Findlay, Robyn A. 2003. "Interventions to Reduce Social Isolation among Older People: Where Is the Evidence?" *Ageing & Society* 23: 647–658.
Fulu, Emma, and Alice Kerr-Wilson. 2015. *What Works to Prevent Violence against Women and Girls Evidence Reviews Paper 2: Interventions to Prevent Violence against Women and Girls*. UK: What Works to Prevent Violence/United Kingdom Department for International Development. Accessed 30April2018. http://www.whatworks.co.za/documents/publications/35-global-evidence-reviews-paper-2-interventions-to-prevent-violence-against-women-and-girls-sep-2015/file.
Gerrard, Steve. 1994. "Morality and Codes of Honour." *Philosophy* 69, no. 267: 69–84.
Gilsenan, Michael. 1996. *Lords of the Lebanese Marches: Violence and Narrative in an Arab Society*. Berkeley: University of California Press.
Girls Not Brides. 2020. "Child Marriage around the World: Iran." Accessed 24November2020. https://www.girlsnotbrides.org/child-marriage/iran/.
Habibzadeh, M. J., and H. Babi. 1999. "Qatl dar farash" [Honour killing]. *Madares* 4 (Winter): 89–90.
Hagan, John, John Simpson, and A. R. Gillis. 1987. "Class in the Household: A Power-Control Theory of Gender and Delinquency." *American Journal of Sociology* 92, no. 4: 788–816.
Hajnasiri, Hamideh, Reza Ghanei Gheshlagh, Kourosh Sayehmiri, Farnoosh Moafi, and Mohammad Farajzadeh. 2016. "Domestic Violence Among Iranian Women: A Systematic Review and Meta-Analysis." *Iran Red Crescent Medical Journal* 18, no. 6: e34971. 10.5812%2Fircmj.34971.
Haley, Allameh, and Hassan Ibn Yusuf. 1999 (1420 AH). *Tahrir al-Hikam al-Shara'i for the Religion of al-Amamiyya*. Qom, Iran: Imam Sadiq Institute (AS).
Hamzić, Vanja, and Ziba Mir-Hosseini. 2010. *Control and Sexuality: The Revival of Zina Laws in Muslim Contexts*. London: Women Living Under Muslim Laws.
Hardeman, Wendy, Stephen Sutton, Simon Griffin, Marie Johnston, Anthony White, Nicholas J. Wareham, and Ann Louise Kinmonth. 2005. "A Causal Modelling Approach to the Development of Theory-Based Behaviour Change Programmes for Trial Evaluation." *Health Education Research* 20, no. 6 (December): 676–687.
Hasluck, Margaret. 1967. "The Albanian Blood Feud." In *Law and Warfare: Studies in the Anthropology of Conflict*, edited by Paul Bohannan, 381–408. Garden City, NY: The Natural History Press.
Homa, Ava. 2016. "From Self-Rule to Self-Immolation: Kurdish Women's Past and Present." *Iran Human Rights Review: Women and Human Rights*. Accessed 18March2017. https://www.ihrr.org/ihrr_article/women-en_from-self-rule-to-self-immolation-kurdish-womens-past-and-present/.
Home Office. 2019. *Country Policy and Information Note – Iran: Adulterers*. Accessed 18March2017. https://assets.publishing.service.gov.uk/government/uploads/system/

uploads/attachment_data/file/836919/Iran_-_Adulterers_-_CPIN_-_v3.0__October_2019__-_EXT.pdf.
Ibrahim, Faiqa. 2005. "Honour Killings under the Rule of Law in Pakistan." Master's thesis, McGill University.
1991 *Iran: Islamic Penal Code*. 1991. Accessed 26November2020. https://www.refworld.org/docid/518a19404.html.
Jebari, Idriss. 2018. "Therapeutic History and the Enduring Memories of Violence in Algeria and Morocco." *Middle East – Topics & Arguments* 11 (November): 108–119. DOI:10.17192/meta.2018.11.7808.
Kanie, Mariwan. 2015. *Rethinking Roots of Rising Violence against Women in the Kurdistan Region of Iraq*. Hivos, Knowledge Programme Civil Society in West Asia. Special Bulletin (April).
Kar, Mehrangiz. 2008. "Honor Killings." Accessed 20January2017. https://web.archive.org/web/20090304225702/http://www.roozonline.com/english/archives/2008/02/honor_killings.html.
Kazemzadeh, Masoud. 2002. *Islamic Fundamentalism, Feminism, and Gender Inequality in Iran under Khomeini*. Lanham, MD: University Press of America.
Keddie, Nikki R. 1991. "Introduction: Deciphering Middle Eastern Women's History." In *Women in Middle Eastern History: Shifting Boundaries in Sex and Gender*, edited by Nikki R. Keddie and Beth Baron, 1–22. New Haven: Yale University Press.
Koggel, Christine M., ed. 2006.*Moral Issues in Global Perspective - Volume 2: Human Diversity and Equality*. 2nd ed. Peterborough: Broadview Press.
Kressel, Gideon. 1981. "Sororicide/Filiacide: Homicide for Family Honour." *Current Anthropology* 22, no. 2: 141–158.
Kulczycki, Andrzej, and Sarah Windle. 2012. "Honor Killings in the Middle East and North Africa: A Systematic Review of the Literature." *Violence against Women* 17, no. 11: 1442–1464.
Laffin, John. 1975. *Rhetoric and Reality: The Arab Mind Considered*. New York: Taplinger Publishing Company.
Landinfo. 2009. *Honour Killings in Iran*. Accessed 20January2018. https://landinfo.no/asset/960/1/960_1.pdf.
Mahdi, Ali A. 2014. "Perceptions of Gender Roles Among Female Iranian Immigrants in the United States." In *Women, Religion and Culture in Iran*, edited by Sarah Ansari and Vanessa Martin, 189–214. London: Routledge.
Manuello, Tessa. 2014. "Erbil Mission to Boost Canadian Business Opportunities in Kurdistan, Iraq." *Rudaw*. Accessed 20January2018. http://rudaw.net/english/kurdistan/11052014.
Marini, John, and Ken Masugi. 2005. *The Progressive Revolution in Politics and Political Science: Transforming the American Regime*. Lanham, MD: Rowman & Littlefield.
Martin, Vanessa. 2005. *The Qajar Pact: Bargaining, Protest and the State in Nineteenth-Century Persia*. London: I.B. Tauris.
McDonald, Susan. 2001. "Kurdish Women and Self-Determination: A Feminist Approach to International Law." In *Women of a Non-State Nation: The Kurds*, edited by Shahrzad Mojab, 135–157. Costa Mesa, CA: Mazda Publishers.
Mir-Hosseini, Ziba. 2000. *Islam and Gender: The Religious Debate in Contemporary Iran*. London: I. B. Tauris.

Mojab, Shahrzad. 2001. "Women and Nationalism in the Kurdish Republic of 1946." In *Women of a Non-State Nation: The Kurds*, edited by Shahrzad Mojab, 71–93. Costa Mesa, CA: Mazda Publishers.
Mojab, Shahrzad, and Nahla Abdo, eds. 2004. *Violence in the Name of Honour: Theoretical and Political Challenges*. Istanbul: Bilgi University Press.
Mora, Necla. 2009. "Violence as a Communication Action: Customary and Honor Killings." *International Journal of Human Sciences* 6, no. 2: 499–510.
Nanes, Stefanie Eileen. 2003. "Fighting Honor Crimes: Evidence of Civil Society in Jordan." *Middle East Journal* 57, no. 1 (Winter): 112–129.
Napikoski, Linda. 2020. "Patriarchal Society According to Feminism." Accessed 18April2020. https://www.thoughtco.com/patriarchal-society-feminism-definition-3528978.
Nayyeri, Mohammad, and Iran Human Rights Documentation Center (IHRDC). 2013. *Gender Inequality and Discrimination: The Case of Iranian Women*. Accessed 16March2015. https://iranhrdc.org/gender-inequality-and-discrimination-the-case-of-iranian-women/.
Nisbett, Richard E., and Dov Cohen. 1996. *Culture of Honor: The Psychology of Violence in the South*. Boulder: Westview Press.
O'Doherty, Mark. 2017. *Healing Pakistan – Improving Human Rights, Gender Mainstreaming and Religious Education in the Islamic Republic of Pakistan*. N.p.: Lulu.com.
Orywal, Erwin. 1996. "Krieg und Frieden in den Wissenschaften." In *Krieg und Kampf: Die Gewalt in unseren Köpfen*, edited by Erwin Orywal, Aparnar Rao, and Michael Bollig. Berlin: Reimer.
Pervizat, Leyla. 2011. "Lack of Due Diligence: Judgement of Crimes of Honour in Turkey." In *Honour, Violence, Women and Islam*, edited by Mohammad Mazher Idriss and Tahir Abbas, 142–153. Abingdon, Oxon; New York: Routledge.
Pickthall, Muhammad Marmaduke. 2017. *The Holy Qur'an, Arabic Transliteration - English*. India: Adam Publishers.
Pitt-Rivers, J. 1966. "Honour and Social Status." In *Honour and Shame: The Values of Mediterranean Society*, edited by John G. Peristiany, 19–77. Chicago: University of Chicago Press.
Pradel, Jean. 1991. *Histoire des doctrines pénales*. Paris: Presses Universitaires de France.
Rights of the Child in Iran. 2015. Retrieved from UN Treaty Body Database: https://tbinternet.ohchr.org/Treaties/CRC/Shared%20Documents/IRN/INT_CRC_NGO_IRN_19809_E.pdf.
Sadeghi, Mohammad Hadi. 2009. Exclusive Criminal Law; Crimes against Persons, 55–56. Tehran: Mizan, 8th, Spring, ISBN 964-5997-01.
Safilios-Rothschild, Constantina. 1969. "Sociopsychological Factors Affecting Fertility in Urban Greece: A Preliminary Report." *Journal of Marriage and Family* 31, no. 3: 595–606.
Sev'er, Aysan, and Gökçeçiçek Yurdakul. 2001. "Culture of Honor, Culture of Change: A Feminist Analysis of Honor Killings in Rural Turkey." *Violence Against Women* 7, no. 9: 964–998.
Shalinsky, Audrey C. 1986. "Reason, Desire, and Sexuality: The Meaning of Gender in Northern Afghanistan." *Ethos: Journal of the Society for Psychological Anthropology* 14, no. 4 (December): 323–343.

Shojai, Mitra. 2013. "Honor Killing: Black Tradition that Does Not Know the Border." Accessed 20March2018. https://p.dw.com/p/183aR.

Shoro, Shahnaz. 2019. *The Real Stories behind Honour Killing*. Cambridge: Cambridge Scholars Publishing.

Siddiqui, Hannana. 2005. "'There is no "honour" in domestic violence, only shame!' Women's struggles against 'honour' crimes in the UK." In *"Honour": Crimes, Paradigms, and Violence against Women*, edited by Lynn Welchman and Sara Hossain, 263–281. London: Zed Books.

Syngellakis, Anna, and Gabriella Lazaridis. 1995. "Women's Status and Work in Contemporary Greece." *Journal of Area Studies* 3, no. 6: 96–107. DOI:10.1080/02613539508455740.

Taheri, Ahmad Reza. 2012. *The Baloch in Post Islamic Revolution Iran: A Political Study*. Morrisville: Lulu Press.

Tilly, Charles. 2003. *The Politics of Collective Violence*. Cambridge Studies in Contentious Politics. Cambridge: Cambridge University Press.

Tizro, Zahra. 2014. "The Role of Orthodox Jurisprudence in Dealing with Domestic Violence against Women in Iran." *La Camera Blu*, no. 10 (September): 1–27. DOI:10.6092/1827-9198/2794.

Triandis, Harry C. 1989. "The Self and Social Behavior in Differing Cultural Contexts." *Psychological Review* 96, no. 3: 506–520.

Tripathi, Anushree, and Supriya Yadav. 2004. "For the Sake of Honour: But Whose Honour? 'Honour Crimes' Against Women." *Asia-Pacific Journal on Human Rights and the Law* 5, no. 2: 63–78.

Vago, Steven. 2015. *Law and Society*. Abingdon: Routledge.

Van den Haag, Ernest, and John P. Conrad. 1983. *The Death Penalty: A Debate*. New York: Plenum.

Vandello, Joseph A., and Dov Cohen. 2003. "Male Honor and Female Fidelity: Implicit Cultural Scripts that Perpetuate Domestic Violence." *Journal of Personal and Social Psychology* 84, no. 5: 997–1010. DOI:10.1037/0022-3514.84.5.997.

Vandello, Joseph A., and Dov Cohen. 2008. "Culture, Gender, and Men's Intimate Partner Violence." *Social and Personality Psychology Compass*, 2, no. 2: 652–667. DOI:10.1111/j.1751-9004.2008.00080.x.

Vandello, Joseph A., Jennifer K. Bosson, Dov Cohen, Rochelle M. Burnaford, and Jonathan R. Weaver. 2008. "Precarious Manhood." *Journal of Personality and Social Psychology* 95, no. 6: 1325–1339. DOI:10.1037/a0012453.

Vreede-de Stuers, Cora. 1968. *Parda: A Study of Muslim Women's Life in Northern India*. Assen, Netherlands: Van Gorcum.

Warnock, Kitty. 1990. *Land Before Honour: Palestinian Women in the Occupied Territories*. London: Palgrave Macmillan.

Weber, Max, Hans Gerth, and C. Wright Mills. 1946. *From Max Weber: Essays in Sociology*. New York: Oxford University Press.

Wyatt-Brown, Bertram. 1982. *Southern Honor: Ethics and Behavior in the Old South*. New York: Oxford University Press.

Yildiz, Kerim, and Tanyel B. Taysi. 2007. *The Kurds in Iran: The Past, Present and Future*. London: Pluto Press.

3 Child marriage and its consequences: poverty, addiction, and divorce

Introduction

Child marriage, also referred to as early and forced marriage, is a practice that has persisted for centuries. Today, it is defined as a formal or customary union in which one or both parties are under the age of 18 (Vogelstein, 2013: 7). This practice takes place across regions, cultures, and religions, and though it impacts children of both genders, girls are disproportionately affected. The global prevalence of child marriage is on a downward trajectory, particularly among younger girls; however, progress in curbing this tradition has been slow, and in some places, the problem remains intractable. The sheer number of women married as children is staggering: the United Nations estimates that in 2011, one in three women aged 20 to 24 (almost 70 million) had married under the age of 18. Many of these women were far younger than 18 at the time of their marriage; in fact, more than 23 million were married or in a union before the age of 15, which amounts to approximately 13,000 girls under 15 being married every day. Vogelstein (2013: 7) had predicted that by 2020, some 50 million girls would have been married before they reach their 15th birthdays, although, nowadays, these figures may have to be revised given the negative impact that the outbreak of COVD-19 had on girls' schooling and frequency of early marriages. According to UNFPA, COVID-19 has halted the efforts to end child marriage, which could result in 13 million additional child marriages in the next ten years (UNFPA, 2020).

Child marriage is a universal and widespread predicament which impacts "the achievement of more educated, healthier, and stable populations" (Adedokun, Adeyemi, & Dauda, 2016, p. 32). In many cultural settings and traditions, child marriage is synonymous with gender discrimination and a widespread indifference towards issues concerning women. Not only do child marriages directly contribute to the interruption of girls' education, but they are also directly related to other social problems, such as abuse at the hand of husbands, premature child bearing, and poor health. Cultural rationalisation is used as a smokescreen to justify the continuation of this practice and ensure the abuse of young girls and women. Child marriages occur because of a combination of reasons, including environmental conditions, culture and

DOI: 10.4324/9781003208501-3

religion, the number of children in a family, educational level, family problems, poor economic status, and low living standards. It is crucial to bear in mind that they do not only affect the development of individual girls and their offspring by violating basic human rights and contributing to poor health (Bayisenge, 2010), but they also affect the wider health, educational, and social sectors of the society.

In this chapter, I will address the causes and consequences of early marriage, debate the minimum age of marriage in terms of the international standards of human rights, address the differentiating age that is usually proposed as legally permissible for girls and boys to get married, and introduce the rules and standards related to it alongside the Iranian legal system.

Child marriage and the international legal framework

The origins of child marriage are multidimensional and deeply rooted. Historically, early marriage was used as a tool to maximize fertility in the context of high mortality rates. Child marriage was also employed to further economic, political, or social relationships (Vogelstein, 2013: 7). Today, this tradition is partly sustained by widespread poverty and social and cultural norms, and it is perpetuated by the low status of girls and women. Economic considerations are fundamental to the practice of child marriage. In impoverished and rural areas, where this tradition is most prevalent, limited educational and economic opportunities for girls increase their dependency on male breadwinners. This reality is underscored by global data showing that women and girls with greater means marry later (Vogelstein, 2013: 7).

In general, 18 is set as the minimum, permissible age of marriage for both boys and girls and is acknowledged as such by most states and international organisations such as the World Health Organisation (WHO) and UNICEF, since it has been widely recognised that it is not only the physical maturity of the two spouses that matters, but also their mental and social development.

From an international perspective, a forced marriage is a marriage that materialises without the consent of one or both of the parties involved. The United Nations views such a marriage not only as a violation of the principles of freedom and individual autonomy, but also as a human rights violation. As a result, a number of different international human rights treaties and agreements have been enacted that reflect the concern of the international community in this regard. These include the Declaration of Human Rights; the Convention on the Abolition of Slavery (1956); the Convention on the Rights of the Child; the international covenant on Civil and Political Rights; the International Covenant on Economic, Social and Cultural Rights; the Convention on the Elimination of All Forms of Discrimination Against Women; the Codex Convention to Marry Freely and with Full Satisfaction; and even an international treaty approved in

1962 entitled the treaty on Satisfaction with Marriage, Minimum Age Marriage and Marriage Borders. The Supplementary Convention of 1956 on the Abolition of Slavery, in Clause C of Article 1, regards any marriage imposed on a girl or a woman by their families or any other person to be an act of enslavement. Also, forced marriage in some legal and international documents is explicitly recognized as a form of gender-based harassment (Millbank & Dauvergne, 2010: 62–63).

The Universal Declaration of Human Rights, adopted in 1948, stipulates in Article 16 that men and women of "full age" are entitled to marry as equals and start a family, which is the "fundamental group unit of society". Their consent and their enjoyment of full rights is a requirement before, during, and after the dissolution of a marriage. Article 23, second paragraph, of the Covenant on Civil and Political Rights recognises the right to marriage for all men and women of "marriageable age". Similar is the wording used in the European Convention on Human Rights and Fundamental Freedoms, where the phrase "according to the national laws governing the exercise of this right [to marriage and family]" is also added. The UN General Assembly adopted a letter of intent to implement the treaty, with a minimum age limit of 15 years for marriage. According to the Convention on Consent to Marriage, Minimum Age for Marriage and Registration of Marriages, which followed the ratification by the General Assembly of the Resolution 1763 A (XVII) in 1962, state parties are only required to take legislative action in order to establish the minimum legal age of marriage in their respective territories.

With respect to the international legal framework concerning marriage and family, the General Recommendation No. 21, Equality in Marriage and Family Relations, of the Committee on the Elimination of All Forms of Discrimination against Women, paragraph 38, states the following:

Some countries provide for different ages for marriage for men and women. As such provisions assume incorrectly that women have a different rate of intellectual development from men, or that their stage of physical and intellectual development at marriage is immaterial, these provisions should be abolished. In other countries, the betrothal of girls or undertakings by family members on their behalf is permitted. Such measures contravene not only the Convention, but also a woman's right freely to choose her partner.

The General Committee on Economic, Social and Cultural Rights (CESCR) comment No. 11 on Plans of Action for Primary Education, adopted in May 1999, calls upon the states to urgently meet their obligations, which include providing children with free and compulsory education that is considered *inter alia* an economic, social, cultural, civil, and human right. The comment also highlights the aspect of "compulsory" in order to ensure that gender discrimination will not prevent girls from achieving their full potential, as well as the "free of charge" reference so that access to education is ensured for everybody and provided by competent authorities.

Further, Article 16 (2) of the Convention on the Elimination of All Forms of Discrimination against Women, adopted in 1979, stipulates that state parties should eliminate discrimination in all marriage- and family-related matters, with particular emphasis on the free choice to choose a partner. More importantly, it includes the following:

> *The betrothal and the marriage of a child shall have no legal effect, and all necessary action, including legislation, shall be taken to specify a minimum age for marriage and to make the registration of marriages in an official registry compulsory.*

Similarly, the 1993 Vienna Declaration and Programme of Action, adopted by the World Conference on Human Rights in Vienna,[1] aligns itself with all previous international documents and urges their speedy ratification, while at the same time stating that "the human rights of women and of the girl-child are an inalienable, integral and indivisible part of universal human rights".

In September 2013, the United Nations Human Rights Council issued a resolution expressing its concern over the prevalence of forced, early marriage and child marriage around the world, which prevented people from living without violence and posed serious obstacles to their enjoyment of rights such as education. High standards of health, including sexual and reproductive health, call for the prevention and elimination of such marriages that have a disproportionate effect on women's and girls' health.[2] The resolution states that child marriage, in addition to affecting the economic, legal, social, and health rights of women and girls, is an obstacle to the development of society in general, to the empowerment of women and girls, and to their meaningful participation in decisions that affect them. It is also a major obstacle to breaking the cycle of gender inequality, discrimination, violence, and poverty, and it prevents economic growth and the achievement of the Sustainable Development Goals.[3]

Finally, the Committee on the Elimination of Discrimination against Women and the Committee on the Rights of the Child, which are tasked with monitoring the implementation of the Convention on the Elimination of All Forms of Discrimination against Women (CEDAW) and the Convention on the Rights of the Child (CRC), respectively, issued a joint recommendation in 2014 that recognised 18 as the minimum legal age of marriage, while 16 was set at the "absolute minimum" age, allowed only under specific circumstances, which should be strictly defined by law and would require a court order. Children that would enter into this union should do so of their free will, and for this reason, their presence in court is mandatory (Haeri, 2014, p. 19). Marriage registration should be also legally required, while a birth registration system should be also established in order to prevent the abuse of children and their participation in practices such as early marriage. Since 1979, the Islamic Republic of Iran has been a party to the Convention on the Rights of the Child, which recognises that child is a person under the age of 18 (Vogelstein, 2013: 33). In 2010, 342,000 children under the age of 18 were married, and if it was not for the intervention of judicial authorities, this percentage may have been higher (Ahmady, 2021).

It is worth noting that a marriage arranged by the parent may not correspond to forced marriage in its conceptual sense. In this marriage, although parents play a major role in marriage arrangements, the child may not be forced into marriage. However, in international marriage documents, this is considered an example of forced marriage, under the assumption that the child does not have the ability to identify and make a decision about the psychological, emotional, and social obstacles that go along with getting married. The use of the term "compulsory" does not necessarily mean that the child is not consenting to marriage, but even if the child welcomes it and gets satisfaction from the marriage, it is still considered a crime against the child.

In societies where marriage is a requirement for sexual intercourse and is seen as central in maintaining the moral integrity of the youth, the age that a person has the ability to communicate sexually and have meaningful relationships is identified as the minimum age of marriage. But can sexual maturity be the foundation of a common life that has different dimensions and aspects and requires rational understanding and mental maturity?

By the time a child turns 18, they can often act independently and make decisions concerning their life and future choices. Since marriage is an emotional, sexual, economic, and social affair, involving duties and responsibilities in common life, there are a number of essential aspects that one has to take into account: gender, mental maturity and rational understanding of the situation, cultural and social differences, geographical and regional conditions, habits and traditions, personal development, nutrition and education, access to mass media, and communication. Besides reaching puberty, which is closer to adulthood, these indicators may give us a good insight into the personal development and maturity of an individual.

Child marriage and the Iranian legal system

In many societies, the age of maturity coincides with the legally permissible age of marriage. Since these biological and emotional changes occur earlier in girls than boys, it only seems natural that the legally permissible age for marriage is also lower for females than males. If sexual maturity was the only necessary criterion and sufficient condition for marriage, such a difference would be considered objective and rational; however, there are many more biological, psychological, and emotional criteria that could "legally" determine the age that is appropriate to get married. Besides the very different approaches to this topic based on religious, social, and cultural norms, the international legal framework alone should guide national legislature and policy interventions. Reaching maturity is a natural process that can vary from person to person and from region to region, depending on the locally prevailing social and cultural norms. It is often argued that, because of the way children are raised in tropical regions, they reach maturity earlier than those who live in colder regions. Still, even among children that live in tropical regions, maturity varies among different locations. Physical, emotional, and psychological changes take place as the child enters into a new stage of their life.

The institution of marriage is important for most cultures and societies around the world as it plays an important role in people's social identity and feelings. This is especially true for women, whose roles are usually defined as spouses and mothers, not as individuals (Tremayne, 2006: 65). According to contemporary Islam, marriage, or *Nikahh*, is a contract for "possession and use of vagina" (Haeri, 1989: 34). Haeri argues that Hilli's[4] view on marriage is contradictory, since on the one hand he considers it "a form of ownership", while on the other hand he argues that there is a difference between marriage and "ownership", and these two concepts should not be confused. She believes a man can have sex with his slave without marrying her, and should a man decide to marry his slave, he must first release her. Therefore, the "full ownership" of a slave girl, as Haeri (1989, p. 45) argues, is the "owner of a section" of a married woman. Therefore, it is important to note that, in Islamic marriage, only female sex is known as a commodity and not the woman.

In Iran, the tradition of early marriage is very widespread. According to the Iranian Census Office, 5.5% of women are married by the age of 15, and just under 17% of girls marry in Iran before the age of 18. Although the minimum legal age for marriage for girls in Iran is 13, it is widely known that girls as young as nine years old are getting married. In the provinces of Iran where the legal age of marriage is higher, families have found ways to circumvent the law and perpetuate the practice, such as delaying the official registration of the child marriage until the girl grows up or providing fake marriage registration documents. This operation is called "purchase age" in Khuzestan and other provinces of Iran. The latest statistics in Iran show that more than 40,000 children aged ten to 14 are married. Early marriage, which is linked to widespread poverty, does not usually end well, and as of the year 1989, 37,000 children aged between ten and 18 are divorced or widowed in Iran (Ahmady, 2021). Association for the Protection of the Rights of the Child: there are yearly 36,000 "divorced children" in Iran.

Regarding divorce proceedings in the country, the law stipulates that a wife may obtain a divorce if her husband marries without her permission; it also includes a provision that co-wives should be treated equitably before a deliberation at a court. Here, inequality is clear since only a man can have more than one partner. Although a woman can legally file for divorce if the husband marries another woman without her consent, in practice this is not easy. In many cases, the wife is financially dependent on the husband, and due to the laws regarding guardianship of children, in the case of divorce she will most likely lose custody of her children, even if the father is unfit. The fact that Iranian law still permits polygamy not only flies in the face of international standards, it is also clearly disconnected from the social reality and actual practices of Iranian society, which reinforces the notion that the mother is not the guardian of the children, but rather an economic dependent. With the marriage contract, a woman comes under her husband's authority, dominion, and protection, entailing a set of defined rights and obligations for each party; some have a moral sanction and others have legal force. Although the boundaries between the legal and the moral are hazy, those sanctions with legal force revolve around the twin themes of sexual access and compensation, embodied in the concepts of *tamkin* and *Nafaqa*. *Tamkin* implies "submission", defined as sexual accesses as a man's right and thus a woman's duty, whereas *Nafaqa* ("maintenance", defined as shelter, food, and clothing) is a woman's right and a man's duty. A woman becomes entitled to *Nafaqa* only after the consummation of marriage, and she loses her claim if she is in a state of *nushuz* (disobedience), though she has the right to refuse sexual access until she receives *Nafaqa* in full. Nevertheless, and as previously discussed, the minimum age of getting married, both in the city and the countryside, has declined sharply over the years. Many early marriages, and in particular those where there is a big age gap, lead to divorce. It is essential to note that a woman retains full control over the disposal of her property and management of her affairs. The contract establishes neither a shared matrimonial regime nor reciprocal obligations between spouses; the husband is the sole provider and owner of the matrimonial resources and the wife is possessor of her own wealth. The only shared space is that involving the procreation of children, and even here a woman is not expected to breast feed her child unless it is impossible to feed it otherwise (Mir-Hosseini, 1996: 142–169).

In 1935, the minimum legal age of marriage under the Iranian law was 27 years, but now, there is no consensus with regards to the minimum permissible age for marrying in Iran. The minimum legal age was reduced from 15 to 13 years for girls and from 18 to 15 years for boys soon after the Islamic Revolution. The Civil Code nevertheless permits marrying younger children with the guardian's consent and a court's permission. The Islamic law underlying Iran's codified legislation considers a child ready for marriage once they reach puberty; the age of maturity is therefore eight years and nine months (nine lunar years) for girls and 14 years and seven months (15 lunar years) for boys.

In *An Echo of Silence*, Ahmady (2016) uses a mixed method approach to study early child marriage in Iran, conducting a comprehensive field survey of early and child marriage in seven Iranian provinces and in-depth interviews with families and spouses. The main drivers of child marriage in Iran are structural factors, such as deeply entrenched social and cultural norms, as well as the cycle of poverty, which is also socially embedded, since child marriages deprive those affected from completing education and joining the job market, and girls are therefore left with no resources to escape their fate (Ahmady,

2018; Shakib, 2017). Furthermore, Ahmady (2018: 2) argues that "the number of girls married in Iran under the age of 15 increased from 33,383 in 2006 to 43,459 in 2009, a 30% increase in three years". Over ten years, from 2005 to 2014, the rate of registered marriages for girls under 18 in all these seven provinces was approximately 54% (Ahmady, 2018: 4). According to Ahmady's study, at least 48,580 girls between ten and 14 years of age were married in 2011, 48,567 of whom were reported to have had at least one child before they reached 15 years of age. Some 40,635 marriages of girls less than 15 years of age were also registered between March 2012 and March 2013, of which more than 8,000 involved men who were at least ten years older. Furthermore, at least 1,537 marriages of girls less than ten years of age were registered in 2012 (Ahmady, 2018: 2). A recent study in a village outside of Tabriz found poverty, traditional culture, and lack of awareness of the risks involved contribute to early marriages of girls (Azizi Zeinalhajlou et al. 2017). Large numbers of households headed by underage girls in Iran result in divorce, widowhood, or abandonment of young brides, especially those married to men quite a lot older than themselves. Such families are usually, of course, challenged by poverty (Ahmady 2018: 131–132).

In the Iranian legal system, according to Article 1070 of the Civil Code, the satisfaction of couples is a condition for the permissiveness of the marriage, and it is not possible to decide on the marriage against the consent of the parties involved (Mehrpour, 1993: 55). Still, it is worth wondering how it is possible to obtain the consent of a child under 18 years old, when, by law, they cannot intervene. How can this type of marriage be considered valid? The question of whether someone under 18 years old is mentally mature enough is the reason for the significant relationship between age and marital satisfaction (Probiter quoted in Smith & Anker, 2005: 245). Under Article 1041 of the Civil Code, the legal permissible minimum age for marriage is 15 years for boys and 13 for girls. In this case, what the law considers important is the age reached, not the restrictive boundaries set concerning what is internationally regarded as child marriage. Nowadays, even in many Islamic countries, marriage before reaching puberty is prohibited, since getting married at an age when the children do not have the mental maturity to make decisions and choose a suitable spouse can be severely harmful (Mehrpour, 1993 53). Article 3 of the Amendment to the Law on Marriage adopted in 1938 also states that

> *If a man, contrary to the provisions of Article 1041 of the Constitution, is found with someone who has not yet reached the age of marriage, he is sentenced to six months to two years' imprisonment. If the girl has not reached the age of 13, she will be sentenced to at least two to three years' imprisonment, and in each case, in addition to the sentence of imprisonment, he can be fined two thousand rials up to 20,000 rials, if any. If the effect of marriage, contrary to the above rules, results in an outbreak of a woman organ or a permanent illness of a woman, the punishment of a*

couple of 5 to 10 years imprisonment is intense, and if he leads to the death of a woman, the punishment of the couple is permanent imprisonment. The accused and suitor and other persons who participated in the crime are also sentenced to the same punishment imposed on the deputy of the offense.

Under the marriage regulation, it is only possible for parties to declare their intention to marry to a competent state official, and this statement must be in the welfare state and free from coercion, fraud, and fear. This regulation is complemented by the second paragraph of Article 23, which recognizes the right of marriage only to those who have reached the legally permissible age. According to this regulation, the member states are required to prohibit the marriage of persons who do not have the status of a person and those who, at the time of marriage, are mentally ill, under the influence of alcohol, or under the influence of psychotropic substances. It is clear that such a regulation is not only necessary for the support of the individual, but also for their partner.

Forty years later, under Article 23 of the Family Protection Act 1353 (1974), the legal ages of marriage for boys and girls were increased to 18 and 20 years respectively, and with court authorisation, it could be reduced to 15 years for girls if it was considered urgent for them to get married. The article further foresaw punishment for those who violated the law. The amendment to Article 1041 of the Criminal Code was submitted to the parliament in 2002. Finally, on 1 July 2002, this article was changed in accordance with the resolution of the Expediency Council.

In detail, according to the resolution of the Expediency Council[5] on 1 July 2002, the article reads as follows: "Marriage before the age of 13 is subject to permission, but subject to the expediency of a competent court". Marriage was allowed before puberty, but it was prohibited without permission as envisaged in Article 3 of the Revised Law on Marriage, which was also approved in 1937. In the event of law violation, the perpetrator would be sentenced from six months to two years' imprisonment. If the girl had not reached the age of 13, she would be sentenced to two to three years of correctional imprisonment. If a marriage contravened the aforementioned rules and led to a member's defect or permanent illness, the couple's sentence could be five to ten years in prison; nevertheless, according to the jurisprudential views of some clerics, 13 is a permissible age for girls to get married. In fact, even before that age, a marriage can take place, provided the court determines that it is in the best interest of the girl to get married and her father allows it. Before the revolution, the girl could not get married before she turned 18, but after the revolution, the age of marriage was determined on the basis of religious maturity. Regarding the registration of civilians in Tehran of the marriage of 75 children under ten in the year 2012, Ahmed Tuisarkani, head of the State Organisation of Property and Immigration, said: "Registration of marriage below the legal age for girls and boys, without a court ruling is prohibited and if it is witnessed it has be reported".[6]

A functional marriage should centre on a meaningful relationship between two consenting adults leading to full satisfaction. Lowering the minimum age for marriage below the age of physical maturity conflicts with the objective of marriage within the meaning of the Convention and the requirements for the full and free consent of Article 23 (3). It should be noted that the determination of a minimum age of more than the age of maturity or legal maturity may also conflict with the right of men and women to marry, as well as the fact that in some countries, the marriage age, especially for boys, is 21.

Child and forced marriages: in women's own words

The practice of child marriage is a violation of human rights. Every day, girls around the world are forced to leave their families, marry against their will, endure sexual and physical abuse, and bear children while still in childhood themselves. This practice is driven by poverty, deeply embedded cultural traditions, and pervasive discrimination against girls. According to some human rights experts, it is tantamount to sexual slavery, yet, in many parts of the world, this ancient practice still flourishes; estimates show that nearly five million girls are married under the age of 15 every year, and some are as young as eight or nine years old (UNFPA United Nations Population Fund, 2012).

According to the Covenant on Civil and Political Rights and the Covenant on Economic, Social and Cultural Rights, which came into force as early as 1976, member states are required to determine the minimum age for marriage. This age should be determined in such a way that the consent of the person to marriage can be considered valid. Of course, determining the age without addressing the root causes of early and forced marriages does not solve the problem, since it undermines other rights of the individual. Although it has considerably changed over the centuries, the institution of marriage is one of the oldest institutions in existence. As previously discussed, today, in order to protect vulnerable groups of people, governments impose certain conditions that qualify a marriage as legally permissible. When it comes to the international human rights framework, in Article 16 of the Universal Declaration of Human Rights, the family is considered to be a natural and essential part of the community, which has the right to benefit from state support (paragraph 3). Article 23 of the Covenant recognizes the rights of adult women, as well as men and women who have reached the age of sexual consent, to marry and to form a family. Article 10 of the Economic and Social Covenant also calls for the provision of assistance for the establishment of the family by referencing paragraph 3 of the Universal Declaration of Human Rights and paragraph 1 of the Covenant on Civil and Political Rights, without reference to the concept of the family. Further, Article 16 of the Covenant on the Elimination of all Forms of Discrimination against Women only refers to the commitment of states to eliminate discrimination against women in all matters relating to family marriage. One of my informants from Sannandaj narrates:

> *I had not completed the third grade of primary school; I was only 14 years old when my father told me to marry my aunt's grandson. The only criterion and reason was the wealth of Ahmed's father. My two other sisters married the same way. We did not disagree with our father, or maybe we were afraid of him. Ahmed was already married, but I was indifferent towards his wife. There was not much connection between us. The first days after the wedding, I felt that his behaviour was abnormal. A few months later I was sure there was a problem. After a while, when he got worse, his family was forced to take him to a doctor and it was only there that I realized that Ahmed had a problem with his nerves and he was taking medication, but he had stopped responding to this medication. His family said that it was not important. My parents also told me to stay by him, so, although it was difficult, I had to put up with all of his problems for many years. No one was helping out. I was forced to live under the influence of the elders; their only goal was for Ahmed to get better! I was only 20 years old when my daughter was born, but Ahmed got worse. My life was hell. Every day he was taking a handful of pills and was sleeping for hours. When he was up he would always talk to himself and his friends. Then he would slap me and talk to me. I knew what he was saying was from his illness, so I did not cry and answered to him. I've lost my nerves. His father, despite his great wealth, only spent money on his son's medicines, and if my husband could not cover our monthly expenses, we could not live. How could someone hide his son's illness from a 14-year-old girl, especially when he is in no position to work? I know Ahmed is no longer well. My parents told me before that I should have left my husband. These days they say if you want to get separated, you have to leave your daughter behind! With a four-year-old girl, you cannot re-marry and nobody would want to marry you. How can I leave my daughter with this father? His doctor says that he has not long to live.*

According to the Statistical Office of Iran, between 2011 and 2012, 761,903 girls were married under the age of 19, and 588,128 boys were married under the age of 20.[7] During nine months of the year 2017 (1396), 7,328 marriages had been registered in the province of Northern Khorasan, with more than 900 cases involving girls under the age of 15.[8] A study in Tehran showed that literacy and military service were key factors in determining the timing of marriage (Maroufi, 1968). Yet, in many communities, girls were assigned a groom by their parents at birth or even earlier. Sometimes this was a sign of friendship between the two families, or one family was given a gift or service for many years so that the daughter's family can live up to their commitment. Girls enter the husband's family as auxiliary staff and, despite their youth, they have to quickly produce offspring in order to please the elders of the family before they die. Sometimes the girl's family tries to prevent sexual intercourse within this marriage.

One of my informants from Kermanshah told me the following: "Forced marriages happen because of the poverty and the uncertainty that reigns among families who try to dominate their girls". My informant's eyes were red, sometimes she stuttered, her lips were constantly bloated and her head shook too much. The inability to follow up with her education had severely affected her mentally and disrupted her personal development. She had firstly attempted to commit suicide in order to put pressure on her parents; after a while she developed a nervous tick due to her failure to carry through the attempt. In details, she said:

> *I'll be 35 years old tonight. We were three sisters and two brothers, and I was the first child of my family. My father was insignificant and irrelevant, and he always lived off my mother's work. Our financial situation was awful. I was going with my mom to work in the fields. I was 18 when I fell in love with a 40-year-old man who had a wife and three children. The following year I went to college. We did not have a lot of money; I paid for the first semester with great difficulty, but we could not do anything for the next semester. I threatened the family with suicide if I could not continue with my education. My mother could not do anything. I went to a doctor's office and said that I had left my medicine for my nerves. I copied the doctor's prescription and I took a lot of tablets, but I only fell asleep and woke up, dizzy and sleepy, the following morning, so, I went to the pharmacy again. Again, I pretended that my medication was lost. I took the tablets and fell asleep again. I do not know how many days I was sleeping, maybe three days. During this time my family thought I was dying because I was upset and depressed. When I opened my eyes, I saw my sister sitting and worried next to me. I saw a shadow. I said to my sister, "I am devastated; we have no money to study…". On the other hand, my sister, who thought that I had committed suicide because of a man, rushed to her office on the very first day and told my family that I did not want to live without him! To summarize, this neurological disease and drug use lasted two years to compensate for the failure of suicide. I could not go to the university and I was lying depressed all day at home, where, contrary to the doctor's advice, I stopped all medication. I went to work with my mother and sisters and my brother again. Once, the driver of the agency insisted that I should talk to him, and so I did. He said to my mother that he lost his parents and wants to marry me. My mother allowed him to show me a ring and as soon as my father died, she let everyone know. Everybody was wondering who he was. All this was accompanied by crying and crying. After six months I got tired of my life. Because he could not marry me officially, I gave him back the ring and told him, "I have nothing for you".*

One of my informants from Kangavar told me the following:

> *My dad was addicted to drugs. We lived in a half-cement, semi-circular room. When I was sixteen years old he forced me to marry because we were too poor. My husband was a handsome man who was working at the factory. After my marriage, we lived in a place like my father's house, and I became pregnant. Little by little I also became an addict; I wanted to leave him but I could not afford it. When my child was four years old I divorced him. I went to my father's house; my younger sister was also divorced. I was forced to re-marry and my second son is now two years old. My husband is a good man. The husband of my little sister, Maryam, who was 14 when she married, beat her and brutally raped her. Maryam knows that her husband had already killed his first wife. Finally, they separated.*

Forcing women to marry due to social pressures or enacting laws whereby marriage to a woman is violated by the relaxation or denial of punishment for the husband, especially when she is a victim of child abuse, a factor in the reduction of the age of marriage, are other factors that exaggerate the satisfaction of marriage. Inter-marital problems relate to disordered developmental processes, but the emphasis is on emotional security; it affects the way individuals feel secure. Other detected problems can be behavioural or physiological in nature, for example, sleep disruption, which leads to problematic environmental adjustment and poor academic performance.

As mentioned in previous discussions, free and full marriage is one of the most important provisions of the Covenant on Civil and Political Rights (art. 23), which is intended to prevent underage marriages that are prevalent in certain societies in accordance with their local culture. In some societies, such as Iran, the free and complete consent to marriage is provided exclusively by the adult males and the girl's family, both in childhood and in gestation, so that even when men are old, they can still get married to a child. Of course, as previously mentioned, child marriage is inconsistent with the provisions of the covenant and other international instruments. There are two forms of discrimination here: one is that permission is only required for the daughter of the family and not for the son; and, secondly, only the father's or even the grandfather's permission is necessary, while the mother has no say in the matter. It is worth wondering at this point whether, in the event that a girl or a boy does not have a father or a grandfather, could the mother's permission be considered acceptable and binding?

Similarly, while further analysing Article 1041 of the Civil Code, it becomes obvious that the marriage of a girl requires only the permission of the father or ancestor: in the event of "the marriage of a virgin daughter who has reached the age of maturity, the permission is granted to the father or ancestor of the father". Therefore, a boy after the age of 15 does not require permission, but the girl requires it at any age. Of course, again, regardless of the limitations of child welfare, the minimum aspect of support for boys aged 15 to 18 was deemed discriminatory compared to girls. According to Katouzian, this distinction is as follows: "In general ethics, the importance of son's marriage and the daughter's marriage is not equal and tolerable. The girl's failure at this stage of life seems to be more difficult. For this reason, the legislator has not equated the two and granted the permission of the daughter of a girl to marry after adulthood" (Katouzian, 2003: 72).

Negin is one of those women who was forced to marry. Of course, she was not that young, but in her own words, she was foolish and uninterested in studying. Negin says:

> *There was a kid who would sometimes beat me, for example, he pulled my hair! I was 17 years old when he said that a suitor came to you. It's better to accept a good guy. I was a horrified and timid girl. I was afraid of it. I remember a night when we were wandering around and started talking. I was so embarrassed and afraid, but eventually we got married. Reza was 13 years older than me. I was frustrated. He kept telling me about sexual intercourse and I was more worried. The wedding night came and I cried and pushed Reza away from me. Finally, eight days later, he came to me and beat me. I'm tired; I do not like him. A few months ago I applied for divorce.*

All in all, it seems that, in situations where getting married before reaching 18 in certain countries is not forbidden, parents would still be required to have the child's consent before a court. The consideration of child protection could be seen as guaranteeing the court's permission, especially in the case of parents who want to see their children married because they are poor or addicts. A common attitude in traditional Kurdish families is that girls are not worth educating as their destiny is marriage and motherhood. The continuation of cultural practices such as forced marriage often results in a fierce opposition, mainly on the part of fathers, to furthering the education of girls.

In the south-east, extreme poverty caused by forced migration, loss of assets, and unemployment makes families dependent upon child labour. Such extreme poverty and high rates of unemployment cause many Kurdish children, particularly girls, to drop out of school. In addition, the practical expenses of sending children to school (e.g., clothes, shoes, stationery, and transport) are often too high for families to afford. Although allowances are paid by the state to the very poorest of families—namely those without any family member in employment—in order to enable them to send their children to school, this does not suffice to cover all necessary expenses. An additional obstacle cited is the language barrier; while private language schools can teach Kurdish, the only language of instruction in mainstream schools is Persian.

Early marriages, especially when the parties involved do not yet have the required mental and sexual maturity, can cause serious harm to the individual and the community. Tradition, habit, and local customs to preserve family dignity and religious fanaticism can all be viewed as cultural causes of early marriages. Other causes include the conviction that girls are inferior to boys, poverty, lack of education, lifestyle choice, illiteracy, mental disorders of the parents, etc. Limited education, lack of maturity, exposure to domestic violence, exploitation, and early pregnancy are some of the main consequences of such a union. Furthermore, it endangers the health of the mother and the child, and children grow with inadequate paternal or maternal support, since their parents are themselves very young. Additionally, the foundations of the family are weak and can easily lead to divorce, the development of suicidal behaviour, depression, running away, prostitution, addiction, and deprivation. Certain aspects of the socio-economic consequences that stand out are the ramifications that a divorce in this particular setting can have on women and children, for example, it can intensify women's poverty, social displacement, helplessness, and frustration (Jain & Kurz, 2007; Pinheiro et al., 2006). In fact, all cognitive, biological, and social processes are affected; but again, more importantly, the emotional security of young mothers who have to raise young children by themselves is an area of grave concern. Because of this, we end up with a vicious circle where everybody's developmental process has been affected, with severe ramifications for the cohesion and social fabric of the community and the society in general (Cummings & Miller-Graff, 2015).

My study reveals that, although a number of the participants intended to postpone their marriage, certain factors, such as family structure, lack of self-decision-making, and social pressure fuelled by social, emotional, and sexual needs, forced them to marry. My research highlighted underlying factors at various levels associated with the marriage-related decision-making process among teenage girls. These findings have implications for policymakers, planners, and health practitioners developing culturally sensitive programs and interventions tailored to the needs of teenage girls. These programs should focus on empowering girls to make proper decisions and preparing them for marriage at the appropriate time and in the appropriate manner. Given that early marriage is a multidimensional and intersectional issue, effective and comprehensive programs aimed at raising awareness among families and communities regarding the negative consequences of early marriage are of the utmost importance. In addition, in order to understand the issues related to early marriage, much more qualitative research is needed to address young people's perceptions in different cultural contexts (Montazeri et al., 2016).

My informant Marzieh from Ilam was a victim of poverty and child marriage. Marzieh did not have a normal family. Her brothers were married to girls who were poorer than their family, and they all lived in their father's house. She was 15 years old when she married a poor man and went to a small, remote village. But, apart from poverty, many families believe that if girls marry at a young age they will not be "corrupted", meaning that they will not be enticed to have premarital sex. This logic is no different to the generalised tendency to control women's sexual and reproductive rights, which directly contributes to an increase in child marriages. These girls are not given the choice and have no access to the appropriate educational and health care services in order to make an informed decision about how their sexual lives will unfold. Of course, this mentality should be gauged against Islam, where premarital (as well as outside the marriage) sex is considered a grave sin and should be punished.

Another informant, a young man from Ilam, was 31 years old. He said that he was 18 years old when he finished military service. His family arranged an engagement with a nine-year-old girl. They married a few years later when she turned 15 years old. She was very nervous. She became pregnant and had a lot of gynaecological problems. The doctor said her veins became inflamed. The young man said that all the girls in the village had similar experiences because, once girls completed the fifth grade, they left school, which is why the primary school had plenty of girls enrolled and the secondary school had only boys. Many of these marriages end up in divorce; for example, one of the causes of divorce was the position of the girl at her husband's house: "They say that the girl wakes up in the morning looking for her toy doll. That's why he divorced her—she is still a child".

Moreover, economic transactions related to marriage often place a lot of pressure on youth, which drives poor families to marry off their daughters to increase their own economic stability. Traditions such as dowry, in which the bride's family provides money, goods, or property to the groom, can be less expensive when paid on behalf of young brides, creating an economic incentive for early marriage. Practices such as bride price or bride wealth—in which the groom's family gives money or property to the bride's family—also encourage early marriage, since it is believed that younger brides have a higher value because they can contribute more over time to the groom and his family (Nasimiyu, 1997). Ending abusive marriages can be especially difficult if a bride's family is not able to repay money or goods received at the time of marriage, which can leave girls trapped and exposed to violence.

A lawyer from Ilam told me the following:

> *For some time, killing by guns had become very common in one of the surrounding neighbourhoods in Iranian Kurdistan, and the last killing we witnessed was one or two months ago. A young man killed his wife and his daughters. Nobody knows why. Most likely, this is not because of poor financial conditions. The man was operating as a drug dealer. When the police tried to arrest him, he threw the drugs at his wife. His wife, who was pregnant, was imprisoned and gave birth to a child. After she was released from prison they divorced. The baby the woman was impregnated with at the time of her imprisonment is now a woman and they lived together with her sisters at their grandfather's house. A while after, the older girl wanted to marry. Her father came a few days before the wedding and told her: "I want us to go outside together". Then he shot her and then killed her sisters and mother. The man is in prison today and there is no verdict yet.*

> *His ex-wife used to cry and complain: It's been a while that my husband was complaining to my daughter that she was spending a lot. "I do not know what you are doing, and how should I stop you doing that. In the end, I'll do everything to get rid of this and I will kill you".*

Regional or national instability, including conflict, displacement, and natural disaster, are also associated with the practice of child marriage. Recent research suggests that families in crisis situations are more likely to marry their daughters early in order to either preserve resources by offloading economic responsibility for their children or in an attempt to ensure their daughters' safety from conflict-related sexual violence (World Vision, 2013). Of course, as previously mentioned, there are many parents who support early marriage in order to avoid premarital intimacy and pregnancy, loss of virginity, or out-of-wedlock births, which would bring shame and dishonour to the family. Some communities subscribe to cultural beliefs that marrying young girls will protect or bring blessings to their families.

The poor status of girls and women is at the root of child marriage. The low value ascribed to girls renders them particularly susceptible to economic and cultural pressures. Endemic son preference and restrictive notions about the appropriate role for women limit investments in female education, skills, and economic potential, which further reinforce perceptions of girls as drains on family resources. Child brides sometimes request to visit their father's house every day, something that could lead to a family dispute and even divorce. Girls are chosen and engaged from the age of seven to 11 years, and they are married three or four years later. And if a girl is not married before the age of 14 or 15, then everyone says that she is defective and life is going to be very hard for her.

Early marriage and childbearing are connected with poor maternal health. Child brides are frequently unable to negotiate sexual relationships with their husbands and lack access to contraception, which leads to early childbearing; of the 16 million adolescent girls who give birth every year, approximately 90% are married. Forty percent of pregnancies in adolescence truncate physical growth and increase the risk of death. A large number of marriages occurring at an early age are not recorded in any way, and therefore, the children from these marriages lack identity cards and are not registered as Iranian citizens. Early marriages are also associated with the growing number of injection drug users (IDUs) in marginal areas, deprivation of education, and the increase in the number of widowed children. The connection between early marriages and drug abuse is one that requires additional explanation, namely in the sense that in a troublesome marriage relationship, the desperate spouse may resort to drug abuse. It has also been often the case that if their partner is already a drug addict, girls follow their husbands' example and begin to use illegal substances as well. In most cases, it also seems that girls are not at first aware of their husbands' disastrous habits, but soon thereafter they follow anyway. At the same time, it is truly remarkable that although a high percentage of Kurdish youth use drugs, the Iranian regime has not come up with a cogent policy for tackling the drug problem in this region (Saleh, 2013). Furthermore, the jobless in Tehran often turn to begging, prostitution, or drug dealing. (Drugs are a booming business, despite the threat of death if caught and convicted of using or selling.) It is roughly estimated that 100 people start using drugs every day, and 70% of them become addicted, according to an official government report. Three million of the country's nearly 80 million people are estimated to suffer from drug addiction. Nine percent of those are women (Von Hein, 2016).

In my research in Ilam, I came across a mother who said her son was an addict, unemployed, and had morally inappropriate behaviour. For some time she insisted that her son should get married. He was not the first addict among her relatives. He eventually committed suicide. One of his wives was 14 years old and the second 30 years old. The girl could not even speak out of fear. The mother was addicted and was psychologically unbalanced.

Another example is Nashmil from Kermanshah, who was married to her cousin on her sixth birthday. From the age of five, she separated from her mother and moved to her cousin's home. She was 11 when they officially married, and she went to her husband's house two years later. At the age of 15, she was a mother of a one-year-old child; later on she divorced. Her son was taken from her and she moved to her father's house and lived in difficult conditions. Because she was beautiful and stout, she always had a suitor. Her father forced her to marry a rich man, who already had a wife and two children, since it was not considered acceptable for a young divorced woman to be on her own.

All in all, as already discussed, the implications of child marriages are diverse and far-reaching, ranging from political ramifications, such as lack of identity cards and registration, to social ramifications, such as the emergence of widowed children, domestic violence, and spousal abuse, to further socioeconomic and long-term consequences, like the unpredicted growth of illegal population in marginal areas, homelessness, self-immolation, and suicide. Society is also deprived of a qualified work force, unemployment rises, and the societal fabric lacks cohesion because of poor parenting skills, poverty, and child labour. To this long list, one has to add the biological and physiological consequences, such as abortions, premature baby deliveries, increased numbers of low-birthweight babies, HIV-related diseases, increased vulnerability to social isolation, early puberty, malnutrition, severe bleeding, lack of awareness of reproductive health and family planning, etc. Finally, getting married at a young age and being exposed to less than ideal marital and family situations, including violence and coercion, also has a number of psychological complications: disorders such as depression, anxiety, obsessive-compulsive disorder, panic disorder, lack of personal autonomy and intellectual maturity, separation from family and friends, loss of support, loss of freedom to engage with peers in social activities, limited opportunities for growth and development, and the imperfect phase-out of psychosocial development.

Zahra Sajjadi, Secretary of the Association of Educated Women of the Islamic Revolution, stated that 17% of girls' marriages in Iran were before the age of 18, and, according to the latest data registered with the country's Civil Registration Organisation, during the first nine months of the 2016, more than 5% of women married were under 15 years old. In other words, 28,242 women were married before the age of 15, and more than 204,000 girls were married between the ages of five and 19.[9]

Fatima, a 17-year-old girl from Sanandaj, was about to divorce. Her father forced her to marry when she was 13 years old. She said:

> *My dad sold me. My father has been in prison for many years. When our neighbour asked me to marry him, my father and my grandmother did not object, and my grandmother actually told me that this was a very good opportunity for me. By getting married I would take money from my husband to release my dad from prison. I got engaged and later, I realized that my husband was older than admitted; around 10 years older than me. His behaviour was unnatural. He was a liar and an addict. When I protested, I was beaten.*

Early marriages contribute to increased gender-based violence and have additionally negative effects on women's self-worth and their ability to meaningfully support the advancement of society (Amoakohene, 2004: 2375). Moreover, early marriage leads to dysfunctional marital relationships that expose a child to psychological, sexual, financial, and emotional pressure (Bayisenge, 2010). Since marriage is associated with childbearing and most girls are not physically and sexually mature enough, there are certain complications during pregnancy and childbirth. Unfortunately, pregnant women in Iran are also subject to domestic violence. In addition to the trauma of being pregnant and giving birth at such a young age, these girls also have to worry about protecting themselves and their babies from abusive husbands. In a study of 600 Iranian women who had to give birth in a hospital, 338 of them reported domestic violence during their pregnancies, Early marriages also result in higher maternal mortality rates as a result of limited access to health care in many rural societies (Bayisenge, 2010). Due to the age of the brides, they are also often subject to marital rape, which gives girls long-term psychological trauma (Somerset, 2000); the exposure of girls to domestic violence such as sexual and emotional abuse does not receive public and societal acknowledgement. Early marriage is mostly practiced in rural communities where sexual violence and rape are not uncommon and are traditionally accepted, hence, these issues receive no further publicity and attention (Jain & Kurz, 2007; Otoo-Oyortey & Pobi, 2003).

The following interview was given to me by two sisters from an extremely poor family in Sanandaj whose father was a drug addict. Both girls married early; one at the age of 16 to an impotent boy who later became an addict, and the other one at the age of 14 to a 40-year-old man because she wanted to escape the extreme poverty. Besides failed marriages and cohabiting with addicts, they also had to work in order to keep their families afloat. Sahar was a young woman who suffered from premature aging. Her body was thin and her face flat and lean. She loved to study and was a gifted student, but she was not allowed to study.

> *I was just 14 years old. I had just received my school books when my father said it is enough. A girl only needs to read and write. I begged my mother to mediate, but she also said: "Do you want to end up old and without a husband?" I went to my husband's house crying. My husband was evil and uncontrollable. If something went wrong, he would scream at me and hit me. I have been working with him for four years now. I even worked for him throughout most of my pregnancy and, when I delivered, I only stayed at home for a couple of months. I went to the doctor because of the hair loss and weight loss I experienced and he said that it was due to extreme stress and tiredness.*

Forced marriages take place not just among the poor and more conservative segments of the population in the countryside, but also, especially with the increasing urbanization and migration of younger people to big urban cities, among urban families and different social classes. The victims of forced marriages have no legal rights or social protection. The authorities force girls who have run away from home to return to their parents instead of giving them a place in a shelter. Schools, teachers, and others who work with children cannot intervene in forced marriages. Married girls are also not allowed to attend the same schools as unmarried girls and instead have to take evening classes with adults if they wish to continue their education. In this way, child marriages invariably lead to the interruption of the young bride's schooling.

Girls who enter into a marriage are also expected to perform their marital sexual duties. Intercourse is forbidden until a girl reaches the Islamic age of maturity of nine lunar years, but underage wives can still be sexually abused in other ways under Ayatollah Khomeini's well-known Fatwa. For example, and as stated: "It is not illegal for an adult male to 'thigh' or enjoy a young girl who is still in the age of weaning; meaning to place his penis between her thighs, and to kiss her" (Khumaini, 2014: 241).

Early marriage exposes girls to various harmful events such as domestic violence and sexual abuse. The age difference between young brides and their husbands limits their participation in decision-making concerning the growth and structure of the family (Jain & Kurz, 2007). Girls who are married early are unlikely to be educated and could become school dropouts. Consequently, they may not be aware of the use of contraception or family planning. Often, young brides refuse to speak out for fear of being beaten. Girls usually see their older husbands as their fathers and live with perpetual fear under their strict control. In addition, young girls believe that once a bride price was paid on their head, they are bought and owned by their husbands (Adongo et al., 1997), which is the general perception of many traditional men. Often, the lower status of girls leaves them with less ability to voice their opinions on issues, such as sex in their marriage. In addition, girls also have less ability to demand husbands' fidelity (Bruce & Clark, 2003; Somerset, 2000).

Chiman from Ilam has a different story to tell: she was six months old when the elders promised her to her cousin. Five years later, her uncle said that Chiman should live in her husband's household. It was also a tradition that the girl and her husband grew up together so that they could get to know each other and grow to become compatible. When she was seven years old, her uncle told her that she should discontinue her schooling and forbade her from attending it. However, the school director provided her with literacy classes for reading and writing. When she got married, one day, her husband did not come home. She thought that he was in prison for stealing. Her family warned him that if he repeats it, Chiman would divorce him. However, he stole again and the police arrested him. Chiman divorced him and stayed in her father's home. After the divorce, many men offered to marry her, however they were all already married with children. As she said: "they came because I was beautiful, I did not want to be second wife of someone, but my father forced me, at the age of 16, to marry a man with a wife and two children".

Conclusion

All in all, child marriage becomes a confinement to a helpless lifetime of domestic and sexual subservience for girls, and they are robbed of their access to education that would have benefitted them (Adedokun, Adeyemi, & Dauda, 2016 5). Loss of self-esteem, social withdrawal, and depression have been observed as consequences of early and forced sexual activities that married young girls experience (Somerset, 2000). Household duties, repeated pregnancies, and early motherhood take their toll on young girls who are exhausted and look older than expected. They are forced to mature before they are physically or psychologically ready (Adedokun, Adeyemi, & Dauda, 2016). It is important when trying to fix these deeply rooted issues to consider that changing everything drastically may not be the safest option. These practices are so far embedded in Iranian culture that ripping them out entirely could cause more issues for the girls trapped in these situations. Therefore, a careful approach is needed when working to free these girls from their abusers and the dark parts of their cultures.

Restricting women's rights to education also results in limited access to information about their rights, especially their right to choose how they live, their right to be free from violence, and their access to justice. Depriving girls of education constitutes a form of economic discrimination, since they are less likely to fulfil their employment potential and engage within the political sphere. For example, in a country like Turkey, more than 640,000 girls do not receive compulsory education, although women have the right to equal education by law. Low levels of enrolment, lack of interest in receiving education, and the inability of students to use the Kurdish language within schools are mainly responsible for preventing Kurdish women and girls in particular from improving their status within the community. Due to a generally perceived hopelessness that breeds from this situation, disadvantaged Kurdish women and girls are most at risk of attempting or committing suicide. According to the head of the organisation's literacy movement, almost three and a half million people aged between ten and 49 years old were illiterate as of the census of 2010. In the past five years, illiteracy rates in the country decreased to under 1.2 million. Based on statistics from the 1990s, illiteracy is worse in the provinces of Sistan and Baluchestan, West Azerbaijan-Kurdistan, part of Kerman province, Lorestan, and North Khorasan. The rate of literacy increases in the western provinces. Girls account for 77% of all enrolments to the Literacy Movement; the head of the Literacy Movement said that in Iran, the rate of illiteracy is higher in girls than boys, mainly because of prevailing cultural norms and early marriages. Is it estimated that 77% of illiterate people are women and girls. It comes as no surprise that terms such as the "feminisation of poverty" found a particular relevance in such a harsh environment.

In this chapter, I sought to exemplify how early marriage is one of the leading harmful practices against women, since it has severe biological and physiological implications for their personal health, inhibits personal growth, strains family and community relations, and impedes social, political, and economic development of a region and a country. It is because of the very complex, diverse, and far-reaching consequences of child marriages that women are driven to desperation, depression, and suicide. Child marriage is not simply a human rights violation. It is also a threat to the prosperity and stability of the countries in which it is prevalent; it undermines development and societal cohesion. Child marriage perpetuates poverty over generations and is linked to poor health, curtailed education, violence, instability, and disregard for the rule of law. Its effects are harmful not only to girls, but also to families, communities, and economies.

Notes

1 Vienna Declaration and Programme of Action: https://www.ohchr.org/en/professionalinterest/pages/vienna.aspx.
2 UN Human Rights Council, *Promotion and Protection of All Human Rights, Civil, Political, Economic, Social and Cultural Rights, Including the Right to Development: Note/By the United Nations High Commissioner for Human Rights*, 17 November 2008, A/HRC/10/24.
3 The Sustainable Development Goals, or the 2030 Agenda, were set in 2015 by the United Nations General Assembly to achieve a better and sustainable future by that year and include targets and indicators in different areas, such as no poverty,

zero hunger, quality education, decent work and economic growth, climate action, peace, justice and strong institutions, partnerships for the goals, etc.
4 The renowned Shia jurist from the 13th century Muhaqqiq al-Hilli had defined a marriage as a contract which "ensures domination over the vagina, *buz* without ownership, *milkyyat*, as in the case of a slave girl" (Haeri, 1989: 33).
5 The Expediency Discernment Council is an administrative body tasked to advise the Supreme Leader. It was established in 1988 following the revision of the Constitution of the Islamic Republic of Iran.
6 http://www.tabnak.ir/fa/news/294842. 31 December 2012, accessed February 24, 2020.
7 News online: https://www.khabaronline.ir/detail/232286/society/social-damage. Wednesday, 11 August 2012, accessed March 3, 2018.
8 http://www.khabaronline.ir/detail/741900/provinces/Khorasan-shomali.
9 https://www.isna.ir/news/95092112286/%D8%AC%D8%AF%DB%8C%D8%AA%D8%B1%DB%8C%D9%86-%D8%A2%D9%85%D8%A7%D8%B1-%D8%A7%D8%B2-%D8%A7%D8%B2%D8%AF%D9%88%D8%A7%D8%AC-%DA%A9%D9%88%D8%AF%DA%A9%D8%A7%D9%86-%D8%AF%D8%B1-%D8%A7%DB%8C%D8%B1%D8%A7%D9%86. 11 December 2016, accessed March 15, 2018.

References

Adedokun, Olaide, Oluwagbemiga Adeyemi, and Cholli Dauda. 2016. "Child Marriage and Maternal Health Risks among Young Mothers in Gombi, Adamawa State, Nigeria: Implications for Mortality, Entitlements and Freedoms." *African Health Sciences* 16, no. 4: 986–999. DOI:10.4314/ahs.v16i4.15.

Adongo, Philip B., James F. Phillips, Beverly Kajihara, Cornelius Debpuur, and Fred N. Binka. 1997. "Cultural Factors Constraining the Introduction of Family Planning among the Kassena-Nankana of Northern Ghana." *Social Science and Medicine* 45, no. 12: 1789–1804. DOI: PII: S0277-9536(97)00110-X.

Ahmady, Kameel. 2016. *An Echo of Silence: A Comprehensive Research Study on Early Child Marriage (ECM) in Iran*. http://kameelahmady.com/wp-content/uploads/2016/10/English-final-web.pdf.

Ahmady, Kameel. 2018. "Feminization of Poverty – The Causes and Consequences of Early Childhood Marriages in Iran." *Swift Journal of Social Sciences and Humanities* 4, no. 1: 1–10.

Ahmady, Kameel. 2021. "The Role of Temporary Marriage (TM) in Promoting Early Child Marriage (ECM) in Iran." In *Temporary and Child Marriages in Iran and Afghanistan: Historical Perspectives and Contemporary Issues*, edited by S. Behnaz Hosseini, 47–66. UK: Springer.

Amoakohene, Margaret I. 2004. "Violence against Women in Ghana: A Look at Women's Perceptions and Review of Policy and Social Responses." *Social Science and Medicine* 59, no. 11: 2373–2385. Accessed 15May2017. https://pubmed.ncbi.nlm.nih.gov/15450710/. DOI: 10.1016/j.socscimed.2004.04.001.

Bayisenge, Jeannette. 2010. "Early Marriage as a Barrier to Girl's Education: A Developmental Challenge in Africa." In *Girl-Child Education in Africa*, edited by C. Ikekeonwu, 43–66. Nigeria: CIDJAP Press.

Bruce, Judith, and Shelley Clark. 2003. "Including Married Adolescents in Adolescent Reproductive Health and HIV/AIDS Policy." Paper presented for Technical Consultation on Married Adolescents, World Health Organization, Geneva.

Cummings, E. Mark, and Laura E. Miller-Graff. 2015. "Emotional Security Theory: An Emerging Theoretical Model for Youths' Psychological and Physiological Responses Across Multiple Developmental Contexts." *Current Directions in Psychological Science* 24, no. 3 (June): 208–213. DOI: 10.1177/0963721414561510.

Haeri, Shahla. 1989. *Law of Desire: Temporary Marriage in Shi'i Iran*. New York: Syracuse University Press.

Haeri, Shahla. 2014. *Law of Desire: Temporary Marriage in Shi'i Iran*. Rev. ed. New York: Syracuse University Press.

Jain, Saranga, and Kathleen Kurz. 2007. *New Insights on Preventing Child Marriage: A Global Analysis of Factors and Programs*. ICRW, International Center for Research on Women.

Katouzian, Nasser. 2003. *Family Law*, Civil Rights Foundation.

Khumaini, Ayatu Allah Al. 2014. *Tahrir Al-Wasila*. no. 2. CreateSpace Independent Publishing Platform.

Maroufi, Nasser. 1968. "The Effect of Literacy and Employment on Age at First Marriage of Women in Various Parts of Tehran City." In *Tenth International Seminar on Family Research, Institute for Social Studies and Research*. Tehran: University of Tehran.

Mehrpour, Hossein, ed. 1993. *Majmu'eh-ye nazariyāt-e shurā-ye negahbān* [Collected opinions of the Guardian Council, vol. 1]. Tehran: Center for the Islamic Revolution Documents.

Millbank, Jenni, and Catherine Dauvergne. 2010. "Forced Marriage and the Exoticization of Gendered Harms in United States Asylum Law." *Columbia Journal of Gender and Law* 19, no. 4. Accessed 20February2020. DOI: 10.7916/cjgl.v19i4.2612.

Mir-Hosseini, Ziba. 1996. "Women and Politics in Post-Khomeini Iran: Divorce, Veiling and Emerging Feminist Voices." In *Women and Politics in the Third World*, edited by Haleh Afshar, 145–173. London and New York: Routledge.

Montazeri, Simin, Maryam Gharacheh, Nooredin Mohammadi, Javad Alaghband Rad, and Hassan Eftekhar Ardabili. 2016. "Determinants of Early Marriage from Married Girls' Perspectives in Iranian Setting: A Qualitative Study." *Journal of Environmental and Public Health* 2016, article ID 8615929. DOI: 10.1155/2016/8615929.

Nasimiyu, R. 1997. "Changing Women's Rights Over Property in Western Kenya." In *African Families and the Crisis of Social Change*, edited by Thomas, C. B., S. Weisner, and P. L. Kilbride (in collaboration with A. B. C. Ocholla-Ayayo, Joshua Akong'a and Simiyu Wandibba). Westport, Connecticut: Bergin and Garvey.

Otoo-Oyortey, Naana, and Sonita Pobi. 2003. "Early Marriage and Poverty: Exploring Links and Key Policy Issues." *Gender and Development* 11, no. 2: 42–51.

Pinheiro, R. T., P. V. S., Magalhaes, B. L., Horta, K. A. T., Pinheiro, R. A., de Silva, and R. H., Pinto. 2006. "Is Paternal Postpartum Depression Associated with Maternal Postpartum Depression? Population-Based Study in Brazil. *Acta Psychiatrica Schandinavica* 113: 230–232.

Saleh, Alam. 2013. *Ethnic Identity and the State in Iran*. New York: Palgrave Macmillan.

Shakib, Shirin. 2017. "Child Marriage in Iran Forces Girls into a Life of Oppression." *Deutsche Welle*. Accessed 18March2020. https://tinyurl.com/yy35etl7.

Smith, Rhona K. M., and Christien van den Anker. 2005. *The Essentials of Human Rights*. London: Hodder Arnold.

Somerset, Carron. 2000. *Early Marriage: Whose Right to Choose?* London: Forum on Marriage and the Rights of Women and Girls.

Tremayne, Soraya. 2006. "Modernity and Early Marriage in Iran: A View from Within." *Journal of Middle East Women's Studies* 2, no. 1: 65–94.

UNFPA (United Nations Population Fund). 2012. *Marrying Too Young: End Child Marriage.* New York: UNFPA. Accessed 14March2017. https://www.unfpa.org/sites/default/files/pub-pdf/MarryingTooYoung.pdf.

UNFPA (United Nations Population Fund). 2020. *Adapting to COVID-19: Pivoting the UNFPA–UNICEF Global Programme to End Child Marriage to Respond to the Pandemic.* New York: UNFPA. Accessed 17December2020. https://www.unfpa.org/sites/default/files/resource-pdf/Responding_to_COVID-19_Pivoting_the_GPECM_to_the_pandemic.pdf.

Vogelstein, Rachel B. 2013. *Ending Child Marriage: How Elevating the Status of Girls Advances U.S. Foreign Policy Objectives.* USA: Council on Foreign Relations.

Von Hein, Shabnam. 2016. "Child Trafficking a Growing Problem in Iran." *Deutsche Welle.* https://p.dw.com/p/2T8uo.

World Vision. 2013. *Untying the Knot: Exploring Early Marriage in Fragile States.* UK: World Vision.

Zeinalhajlou, Azizi, Hossein Matlabi Akbar, Mohammad Hasan Sahebihagh, Sarvin Sanaie, Manouchehr Seyedi Vafaee, and Fathollah Pourali. 2017. "Nutritional Status of the Community-Dwelling Elderly in Tabriz, Iran." *Elderly Health Journal* 3, no. 2: 80–86. Accessed 24March2017 http://ehj.ssu.ac.ir/article-1-100-en.html.

4 Marriage and life after divorce: caught between tradition, poverty, and suicide

Introduction

According to international statistics, nearly one million people in the world commit suicide every year. The global suicide rate is 16 per 100,000 people and, on average, a person takes their own life every 40 seconds.[1] Suicide is an act of self-harm that leads to death (Tartaro & Lester, 2010: 5). In English, the word suicide was used for the first time in 1642 based on the Latin words SUI and CARDER, which mean "self-destructive" and "inventive killing", respectively (Curra, 2013: 7). According to the theory of Edwin Shneidman, there is a correlation with unmet or failed needs, the feeling of helplessness and frustration, the duality of conflict, and tolerance of the intolerable stress of escape (Lester, 2001: 134). A suicide attempt is one that is said to be incomplete and which has not resulted in death. In fact, suicide attempts can be considered complex psychological phenomena that are subjected to mutual interactions between personal and environmental factors and among the individual factors of age, gender, and marital status. These can be distinguished among environmental factors, time, and place or the availability of a suicide device that plays a decisive role in a person's decision to commit the act. Mental disorders, especially depression, and drug abuse are among the most common causes of suicide attempts. Suicide occurs in cases of inter-family disputes, death of a loved one, or chronic medical conditions and has a higher incidence in highly stressful circumstances, such as in cases of sexual abuse and emotional failure, or when individuals feel particularly frail (Takahashi, 2001).

Naturally, when it comes to divorce, women are abandoned and exposed. The most common reason stated for filing for divorce is the husband's aggressiveness; divorce is seen as the last resort if no other legal means can put an end to the violence. Another reason for filing for divorce is infertility, as procreation is one of the main goals of marriage. The outcomes vary considerably, especially in those cases that are dependent on an individual judge's take on the circumstances (Mir-Hosseini, 2001: 254).

Suicide is the 15th leading cause of death with over 800,000 victims worldwide; 75% of suicides occur in low-income and middle-income countries.

DOI: 10.4324/9781003208501-4

Throughout my fieldwork, I conducted interviews in order to better understand the association between suicidal ideation and behaviours and economic poverty in low-income and middle-income countries. My findings show a consistent trend at the individual level indicating that poverty, particularly in the form of worsening economic status, diminished wealth, and unemployment, are associated with suicidal ideations and behaviours (Iemmi et al., 2016).

This chapter explores the correlation between an increased suicide rate among women in the Kurdish regions of Iran and the prevailing poverty, unequal access to the job market, and social norms, such as marriage and life after divorce. It identifies continued societal, political, and economic inequalities as key factors that leave women vulnerable, both in the public and the private spheres. It also identifies the root causes that drive women to suicide.

Women in Iran confront an array of legal and social barriers, restricting not only their lives but also their livelihoods and contributing to starkly unequal economic relations. Although women make up over 50% of university graduates, their participation in the labour force is only 17%. The 2015 Global Gender Gap report, produced by the World Economic Forum, ranked Iran among the last five countries (141 out of 145) for gender equality, including equality in economic participation. Moreover, these disparities exist in every layer of the economic hierarchy; women are severely underrepresented in senior public positions and as private sector managers. This significant participation gap in the Iranian labour market has occurred in a context in which Iranian authorities have extensively violated women's economic and social rights. Specifically, the government has created and enforced numerous discriminatory laws and regulations limiting women's participation in the job market while also failing to stop, and sometimes actively participating in, widespread discriminatory employment practices against women in the private and public sectors.

Tradition and family

In general, Islam promotes early marriage and the importance of preserving family institutions. As previously discussed, prior to the creation of the Iranian Civil Code in 1935, Iran did not have any restrictions on the age of marriage. Following the Islamic Revolution, the civil law set the minimum marriage age for women at 15, and, provided there was a court order and the parents' permission, girls could marry as early as 13 (Haeri, 2020). Unemployment also contributed to the frequency of early marriages along with limited education. As Afshar (1998) points out, marriage in Islam can be regarded as a "commercial transaction" in which women sell sex services to their husbands. Mir-Hosseini (1993: 36) argues that each aspect (all rights and duties) of Islamic marriage follows logically from the central concepts of exchange: the exchange of sexual services for financial security (the price of a bride, maintenance, household expenses). Sheikh Khalil, a prominent lawyer of Maliki, sees the relationship in marriage as follows: when a woman marries, a part of her person is sold. In the market, man buys one of the products, paying homage to the genital mutilation in his marriage (Mir-Hosseini, 1993: 32).

One of the most important components of Islamic marriage is obedience (*Tamkin*), which explicitly recognises dominance as a right of the man, and therefore a woman is subjected to his authority, including in the most diminutive aspects of her relationships. According to Article 1105 of the Iranian Civil Code, the husband is the only and undisputable "head of the family", while in accordance with Articles 1106 and 1107[2], he is obliged to provide his wife with accommodation, clothing, furniture, and food. The legal term for a spouse's refusal is *ushūz* ("rebellion" or "disobedience"), a husband's refusal to provide maintenance costs is punishable under the law (he may be fined or imprisoned) (Haeri, 2020).

Another clause that exemplifies the relation between the two spouses and is inspired by the Islamic Sharia and Islamic Republic laws is from verse 34 of the Nisa chapter of the Qur'an, which discusses the husband's role and how he should deal with the disloyalty of his wife. Besides looking after his wife, as demonstrated in the civil code articles mentioned above, he is also the protector, and he should enjoy her obedience. Those who are not obedient should be punished. This is interpreted by many as encouraging domestic violence. Undoubtedly, this is more relevant for women who are completely dependent upon their husbands and, as a result, lack necessary survival skills. Kar (2015) argues that, because the legislature offers men power as the absolute leader of the household, this can easily spread to other spheres of marital life, such as sexual relations and, as a result, sexual violence. Others dispute this reasoning by arguing that being in charge of a household is more of a managerial task and that a man is expected to act wisely and fairly (Mohammadi, 2004). Economic dependence on men, in the view of judges, automatically makes men more powerful in their role as husbands (Tizro, 2014). The director general of the Social Affairs Bureau of Kermanshah Governorate said in 2018 that 14% of marriages in Kermanshah end in divorce.[3]

There have been cases where women were left with no other option but to learn how to survive: for example, in many families that were persecuted or where men were executed, their widows decided to become politically active and joined Kurdish political parties. Many of them tried to make ends meet by knitting socks; they also worked as midwives, cleaners, and carers for children. Certain women were also put under political pressure because of their politically active spouses. Yet, their status in society never corresponded to their productivity. In cities, unemployment, poverty, and lack of opportunities for women to work have worsened their position.

Discrimination in the job market and the feminisation of poverty

Discrimination against women in the Iranian labour market is shaped in part by the political ideology that has dominated Iran since the Islamic revolution, which pushed women to adopt perceived "ideal roles" as mothers and wives and sought to marginalise them from public life. Yet, what often goes unmentioned in narratives on women's role in Iranian society is that discriminatory laws towards women in the economic realm long predate this period. Many discriminatory laws can be found in Iran's 1936 civil code. After the Islamic Revolution in 1979, the authorities rolled back the progress made by legislation enacted in 1976 promoting gender equality, particularly in family law, and returned to these earlier legal provisions while also enforcing a dress code as a prerequisite for appearing in public life.

In the past three decades, authorities have punished and often imprisoned women's rights activists for their efforts to promote gender equality in law and practice. The government's prosecution of prominent members of the "One Million Signatures" campaign[4] to change these discriminatory laws also illustrates that the battle for women's social and economic freedoms cannot be disentangled from the broader struggle for political and civic rights in Iran. Iranian law is likely a culprit in creating this unequal economic reality. Domestic laws directly discriminate against women's equal access to employment, including restricting the number of professions women can enter and denying equal benefits to women in the workforce. The government also fails to enforce laws designed to stop widespread discrimination by employers against women, and Iranian law contains inadequate legal protections against sexual harassment in the workplace. Moreover, while Iranian law prohibits discrimination against women in the workplace, its application is not extended to the hiring process, where it is critically needed. Although the legal, minimum working age is 15, the government has taken no measures whatsoever to prevent children in rural areas who start working from the age of ten (Haeri, 2014: 56).

Although women make up about 50% of Iran's population,[5] only 30% of them are actively participating in the workforce. According to the Centre for Strategic Statistics and Information in Iran, the number of actively working women in Iranian Kurdistan is only between 16.2% and 19.7%.[6] In the more backward areas of the country, women depend entirely on men. The tribal economy is not in good shape, there are limited jobs, and women are mostly involved in producing artefacts. Poverty is widespread, and it has often led to public unrest. Due to the prevailing patriarchy, women are not encouraged to work, making their financial dependence on the men complete (Fallah Safavi, 2019). In cities where the number of educated women is higher, job prospects remain very poor.

Prostitution is considered a way to overcome economic problems for many following a divorce, and it is caused by generalized poverty, destruction of the economy and the society, high unemployment, drug consumption, major demographic shifts, lack of education, etc. Although prostitution is strictly illegal, in 2004 there was a 635% increase in the number of teenage girls engaged in prostitution in Iran. In Tehran alone, there were an estimated 84,000 women and girls working as prostitutes.

Unemployment of roughly 28% among youths aged between 15 and 29 and 43% unemployment among women aged between 15 and 20 have created a particularly economically vulnerable population. The rising number of drug addicts, street children, and young female runaways contributed further to create a highly marginalised population (Hughes & Sepehrrad, 2004).

Publicly available data shows that government and private sector employers routinely prefer to hire men over women, in particular for technical and managerial positions. Employers in both the public and the private sectors regularly specify gender preferences when advertising vacancies and do so based on arbitrary and discriminatory criteria. As a result, some parts of the country have seen unemployment rise among women, as high as 70%. In 2015 Iran's vice president for Women's Affairs openly criticised the unequal employment opportunities for women and men. Shahindokht Molavardi referred to the government's recruitment practices as fuelling gender discrimination and running contrary to the pledges of Hassan Rouhani. In a country where half the graduates are women, out of the approximately 2,800 jobs advertised for positions in governmental posts, 2,300 jobs were allocated for men, 500 were for men and women, and only 16 jobs were targeted specifically at women. There have also been rumours that in exchange for a position, sex was required. The structure of the labour market and widespread discrimination mean that more and more women will have to stay home (Molaverdi, 2015).

The lack of economic growth and underdevelopment in the Kurdish provinces is so obvious that as soon as entering the region, one easily witnesses the stark difference between them and the rest of the country: there is a complete lack of highways, industrial estates, large investments, and development projects. Economic underdevelopment and the disregard for people's livelihoods are tantamount to economic sanctions, are the main causes for rising unemployment, and precipitate the need for the male population to resort to jobs such as Kulbari. People often face the dilemma to either seek employment in big cities or become a Kulbar (Border der Couriers, "Return Delivery"),[7] couriers who are often murdered. Further, a report published by the Human Rights Association in Iranian Kurdistan-Geneva (KMMK-G) refers to high unemployment and environmental pollution as a result of the landmines and the unexploded ordnances, remnants from the Iran–Iraq war. People in cities, but also farmers, nomads, shepherds, and traders, have a very challenging life. Kurdish youth and farmers in the provinces of Kurdistan, Kermanshah, Ilam, and Wermê (West Azerbaijan) are involved in smuggling goods such as tea, tobacco, and fuel (Human Rights Association in Kurdistan of Iran-Geneva).[8]

Pursuant to paragraphs 8 to 15 of Principles 3 and Principles 29, 43, 44, 45, 48, 49, 101, and 104 of the constitution, provinces are obliged to administer national and public resources, revenues, and wealth fairly and without discrimination to all regions for the purpose of progress and development. Central authorities should prioritise and redistribute wealth so that each region has the necessary capital and facilities at its disposal according to its needs and growth potential. Yet, the Kurdish territories are completely neglected, and there is not even the slightest indication that some sort of economic revival with the active participation of the local population is taking place. In the Kurdish areas, local investors are not allowed to open factories. Obtaining a license for any large investment that promotes economic prosperity and job creation requires the permission of the Revolutionary Guards, and privileges and facilities are granted to a limited number of individuals and families loyal to the system. Preventing the promotion of economic expansion from a certain level in this direction and forced migration is the result.

The head of the Imam Khomeini Relief Committee (in Persian *Komitteh Emdad Imam Khomeini*) has argued that the Iranian government is forbidden to inform the general population about the precise unemployment rate because of the political implications that such a statement would have, since although more than 30 million people are hungry and do not have food security, the government has the capacity to provide—potentially—jobs for only half of them. Unfortunately, not only does the Iranian government decide the system of welfare and state support for low-income people, but it also shapes the overall structure of the economy such that it limits people's creativity, while highly educated students end up with no jobs and the average income decreases.[9] Yet, poverty should be understood as more than a shortage of income. It is the denial of opportunities and choices most basic to human development.[10] According to a statement issued by the chairman of the relief committee on 17 February 2016, the number of poor people in the country is increasing.

The term "culture of poverty" was coined by the anthropologist Oscar Lewis (1975) and is defined as a set of ideas and values transferred from one generation to the next among poor families (Bradshaw, 2007). According to this theory, the culture of poverty gradually dominates in a poor society and continues to transmit from one generation to the next. According to Lewis (1975), the culture of poverty seems to be an interrelated and complementary set of family- and attitude-related behavioural and personality properties, which poor people have gotten used to and adjusted to under dire financial circumstances. It requires a setting of cash economy, high rate of unemployment and underemployment, low wages, and low-skilled workers. In the absence of voluntary or state support and a stable family, the low-income population tends to develop a culture of poverty against the dominant ideology of wealth accumulation of the middle class. The poor realise that they have a marginal position within a highly stratified and individualistic capitalistic society that does not offer them any prospect for upward mobility. This results in cultural values that are transferred from one generation to the next. This process is mostly witnessed in societies that are transformed rapidly. Due to the rapid and often unpredictable transformations that a society experiences, people with low skills and income remain in low positions; they detach themselves from society and become isolated while they gradually create a new culture which is different from the public, prevailing culture. In this way, poverty itself does create a special culture, and this culture itself will reproduce poverty (Abouchedid & Nasser, 2002; Faver, Cavazos, & Trachte, 2005). This kind of culture indicates that the poor themselves contribute to producing, reproducing, and maintaining poverty; it also indicates that a care-centred and protective watch mechanism has actually made the poor dependent on government support, while at the same time the same governmental mechanisms possess no genuine willingness or intention to address their root causes of poverty and change their situation. These care-centred approach has taken the agency, change, and rehabilitation power from the poor so they accept the formal aid and do not feel any need for rehabilitation. Unemployment, lack of safe shelter for women, and other factors have involved a major stratum of people, with economic, social, and mental consequences (Gorski, 2008; Ludwig & Mayer 2006; Small, Luis, & Lamont 2010). However, this point does not abate the intense need for the study of the ruling culture of the families under support; it even helps them manage the people under support better.

Of the world's poor, 60–70% are women (Allen & Thomas, 1992), and the fact that they are particularly prone to poverty is one of the major concerns of policymakers in developing countries. There are many factors that place women in a disadvantaged position, such as wage inequality, lack of civil rights, unequal opportunities to access the job market, and the uneven consequences of structural readjustment policies. The feminisation of the informal economy and the deprivation of formal employment benefits, migrations and wars, shrinking families, and formal support networks have contributed to what is widely known as the "feminisation of poverty" and have created a special class of women known as caretaker women, which is "the poorest" group.

Social development, as one of the main aspects of the development process, determines social justice, quality of life, and the promotion of human empowerment. By properly engineering social development, it is expected that all people, especially women, would have a better life. The association between women and poverty is a particularly damaging one and has to be urgently addressed. Policies and resources have to be directed in such a way as to financially empower women. Gender inclusive indicators have to be identified and used, given the fact that women's rights are also human rights. Fallah Safavi (2019) conducted an urban ethnographic fieldwork on the culture of poverty in the Hadyabad District of Ghazvin Township. Using participant observation and in-depth interviews, he concluded that the physical features of a district and lack of urban possibilities and social opportunities have created a context for maintaining poverty and a rising culture of poverty among residents. Ahmadi & Iman (2005) in their research on marginalisation and delinquency among youths in the Dehpiale district of Shiraz found that the culture of poverty produces and reproduces delinquency among youths.

They also demonstrated that there exists a significant relationship between urban marginalisation and a rising culture of poverty in the region.

The way that poverty is reproduced and internalised—especially by women—is a feature of many societies across the world. Shin (2006), who studied Korean immigrant women, determined that women shared a common subculture of working ethos that included low aspirations and relying on God for the future. Behind a common subculture that these women shared lay their fear of appearing as tough wives to the outside world, their passive participation in the family migration decision, and their constrained mobility as a result of their gender roles and their economic status. While their culture of reproducing poverty served a positive function, their subculture, as a consequence, constrained these women's agency and freedom. Claypool (2009) examined antipoverty programs in Chicago's Near North Side neighbourhood. According to his findings, like the nationwide war on poverty, Chicago's effort did little to end poor people's economic disadvantage through direct job creation or increased welfare payments. Instead, reformers attempted to modify poor people's values and behaviours to prepare them to enter the existing social structure and labour market. Often, reformers' narrowly constructed definitions of work, family, and gender roles, along with their faith in the capitalist economy and the American ideal of self-reliance, shaped their initiatives.

As previously discussed, poverty creates its own culture and establishes a certain life-pattern that is conveyed from generation to generation; poverty is the cause of borrowing from formal and informal sources, using second-hand clothes and home appliances, and living in overcrowded houses, and it contributes to a lack of welfare and privacy (Mohammadpur, Karimi, & Alizadeh, 2014). Caretaker women and their children are members of vulnerable groups exposed to abuses such as sexual exploitation by opportunists. Perhaps moral and sexual vulnerability embody the furthermost painful and delicate features of caretaker women's culture of poverty; since these poor women are abused by opportunists, they have developed certain additional psychological problems, affecting their life and their children's lives (Mohammadpur, Karimi, & Alizadeh, 2014). In other words, poverty exacerbates women's exposure to sexual vulnerability, including child marriage, forced remarriage, and prostitution. This is why studying women's culture of poverty is considered vital in comprehending their situation and identifying policies that will contravene the current effect of applied measures that contribute to reproducing the status quo. Otherwise, in the future, we will probably witness an increase in the number of women under the care of caretaker organisations as well as the reinforcement and expansion of the culture of poverty among them and their children.

Following their husbands' death or divorce, these caretaker women tend to resort to remarriage due to financial considerations, psychological problems, peer pressure, and other factors. They usually have limited choices. In most cases, it is a marriage of convenience, a shotgun marriage, or an escape from their present situation. These new marriages are strongly influenced by the women's previous life condition. In a way, a new marriages feel more like providing a shelter for women. The unnerving experiences of the current study's caretaker mothers have made them pessimistic about the patriarchal society they live in; they generally allow their daughters to participate in the community, but with many precautions. Not only does fanaticism against girls' unimpeded participation in society limit their educational opportunities, but it also undermines their chances to find employment. The researchers have observed that especially girls in rural areas who were forbidden to have a full-time job or to work alongside male co-workers were encouraged and given priority for positions at the nearest possible distance in order to appease the concerned families (Mohammadpur, Karimi, & Alizadeh, 2014).

Finally, another point to consider is that nowadays, the women's development indices are considered among the main human development indices (HDI), which consist of three indices: literacy, gross national income, and life expectancy. In other words, the women's situation and life quality are directly linked to the society's development level, hence the central role that women play or are expected to play in development and modernisation programs in the contemporary world. At the same time, the level of gender equality and female empowerment that a country has achieved is assessed through three main factors: (1) the number of women among parliamentarians; (2) the number of women participating in legislative, managerial, professional, and technical positions; and (3) women's financial strength, which indicates their level of achievement. In view of this, the gender empowerment index in Iran is underperforming when compared with the human development index, and women's capacity and abilities have not yet reached their full potential. This is set against the fact that sustainable development is only possible with the participation of all segments of society. Similarly to many other countries, women in Iran are considered a vulnerable group that has limited access to resources and opportunities. This issue is especially more acute among caretaker women because they lack support and have the additional responsibility of caring for a family.

A brief socio-psychological approach to the question of suicide

"Life" and "death" are two simple, ordinary, everyday words, but since the beginning of civilisation, man has sought to look for their deeper philosophical meaning and connection. We are accustomed to the concept of "life", but we are still wary against the unfamiliar and mysterious concept of "death". Throughout the centuries, philosophers, anthropologists, sociologists, and scientists have sought to understand and decipher what "death" really is.

Suicide is, in fact, a voluntary act of death. At first, humans sacrificed themselves for the sake of the gods and tradition, and even in recent centuries, philosophers, scientists, and writers considered suicide a meaningful and philosophical action. On the other hand, suicide was sometimes the only viable option for ordinary people who were overwhelmed with personal, psychological, economic, and social challenges. Many of them saw death as a wish and an escape from their problems. Suicide could be also seen as a symbol or protest against the family as well as society and its institutions and structures. Unfortunately, in the society in question, Kurdistan, this is seen as a reaction to social, economic, and political problems. It has become a sort of civic protest and a declaration of the death of society, its structures, and its institutions.[11]

Suicide should not be solely approached from a personal and psychological angle. On the contrary, it should also be seen as a social problem, which is frequently met at the interplay between social, economic, and political circumstances. Why does a bride, under the age of 25 and living in a village in Sardasht, commit suicide? The obvious answer is that because she lives in a closed and rigid system of patriarchy, and cannot speak up and demand her rights. According to one suicide witness, a young girl in Sardasht had this exchange with her mother: Girl: "I'm going to kill myself, I'm setting myself on fire". Her mother replied: "Go to hell", adding after the fact: "And that's true, and that's the suicide and the death of my daughter. That easy!" This is an heartbreaking response of the community to the demands and protest of the people! The problem is that the people cannot be empowered by uncritically following centuries of old tribal and Islamic traditions. By doing so, we automatically exclude from our community and the society anyone who is different and criticises or wishes to change things.

Suicide doesn't just happen because of a one-off, singular issue or event. In our case, it tends to be the result of a prolonged period of violence and oppression and years of harassment and psychological damage that have taken their toll on women's physical and mental health. Psychological violence depends on factors that encourage suicide and their power to influence the individual, control and oppress women, and deny them individual agency and freedom in a way that makes life unbearable (Breault & Barkey, 1982). Durkheim draws on the idea that suicide is a social phenomenon and that it is the social and psychological atmosphere in a society that determines the extent of suicidal tendencies. In any society, there are collective forces that have a certain power and lead the individual to suicide.

At the individual level, it is well established that suicidal behaviour is associated with mental illness and individual personality factors (Fliege et al., 2009: p. 47; Hawton et al., 2013: 17). Nonetheless, the relationship between suicide and mental ill-health is complex. At the macro level, sociocultural, economic, and contextual factors also play a significant role in the aetiology of a suicide (Colucci & Lester, 2012; Vijayakumar et al., 2005:19), such as a positive association between unemployment and a successful suicide (Nordt et al., 2015: 11) and between economic crises and suicide. I focused on economic indicators at the individual level, including poverty, economic status, wealth, unemployment, economic or financial problems, debt, and welfare support at the national level. Pathological-psychological causes include physical illness and mental illness such as depression. Economic causes include unemployment, economic problems, dismissal from work, bankruptcy, and the loss of social bases. Emotional causes include loss of love, loss of a person's interest, death or serious illness of a loved one, conflicts, and family disputes.

Khalid Tavakoli, a sociologist in the field of social harms, said that the number of suicides in the western provinces of Iran has increased over the past 20 years due to conflicts caused by traditional and patriarchal culture. Tavakoli told the Persian news agency IRNA: "Women in the western regions of the country have a long history of suicide; yet, we have studied suicide rates for the past 20 years, and it has to be noted that the suicide rate nowadays is the highest and in provinces of Ilam, Kermanshah and Kurdistan is at the top of the country". "The existence of society" and "the rule of patriarchal values" are among the reasons for this. "It leads to problems with emotional, mental, and fragile attachments". The sociologist described the suicide attempt as a "protest" against the status quo. Tavakoli also cited the Coronavirus crisis, poverty, and unemployment as contributing factors to the escalation of domestic violence, adding that another worrying trend nowadays is the decreasing age of those committing suicide.

Suicide is the second and fifth leading causes of death in young adults aged 15–29 and 30–49 years, respectively, and it surpasses maternal mortality as the leading cause of death among girls aged 15–19 globally (Petroni, Patel, & Patton, 2015: 2031–32). Economic and epidemiological theories of suicide have been built on these ideas (Hamermesh & Soss, 1974). In the six months prior to October 2018, a human rights group reported that more than 100 Kurds had lost their lives, accounting for 40% of suicides, due to unemployment and extreme poverty (Nawzad, 2018). Official statistics show a 66% increase in women's suicide over the past five years. Eighty-two percent of suicide attempts occur among women under the age of 34. Through my fieldwork, my goal has been to analyse the high rate of suicides in Sardasht and other Kurdish cities, where the beginning of spring usually coincides with a new wave of suicides. This time we see a "third wave of suicides". In the "first wave" of suicides, which occurred a few years ago and were only a few cases, they were seen as a "social problem". They were not adequately researched, because the number of cases was considered minimal. During the "second wave" of suicides, the number of cases slightly rose, and we can now remember men and women in their early or mid-thirties having committed suicide a few years back. On account of the unusually high number of suicides due to self-immolation registered among women in the province, the UN Special Rapporteur on Violence against Women visited Ilam in 2005.[12] The report published after the visit cited social pressure, the lack of legal protection for women who are victims of violence, the lack of shelters, family legislation that favours men in divorce and child custody cases, and widespread discrimination against women as the main reasons for the high rate in suicides. Some of the suicides appeared to be honour-related. Yet, it is the third wave of suicides in Sardasht, Piranshahr, and Marivan that has been marked both by an increase in the total number of cases such that it now resembles more of an epidemic, as well as by a decrease in the average age of the victims—the majority of whom are between 20 and 25 years old. If the root causes behind this third wave of suicides remain unaddressed and are not promptly accompanied by structural, cultural, and social changes, we will soon see an even more spectacular rise in the overall number of female suicides (Alizadeh et al., 2010).

Female suicide in Iranian Kurdistan: tragic stories through personal narratives

According to the latest World Health Organization (WHO) report, about 800,000 people a year commit suicide. From this figure, 4,069 are Iranians. This places Iran at number 120th in the world with about 11 people dying each day in the country.[13] What does the third wave of suicides mean in Sardasht and the cities of Kurdistan? What is the rate of suicide in Kurdistan and Kurdish cities? Why are there no available statistics on suicide in Kurdish cities? Is the concealment of a problem a way to solve it? Why are suicide rates rising in Kurdish cities? Why is the average age of the victims in Sardasht, Marivan, and Piranshahr between 20 and 25 years old? What causes suicide in Sardasht and other Kurdish cities? Which provinces have the highest rates of suicide? Who is truly responsible for such a deplorable situation?

Kermanshah's suicide rate is between those of Ilam and Lorestan. Seyyed Kazem Malekuti, head of the Iranian Scientific Society for the Prevention of Suicide, said that Ilam, Lorestan, West Azerbaijan, and Kurdistan are the provinces with the highest rates of suicides in the country. The suicide rate in the western part of the country is higher than the global rate. Suicide is also higher among female students, married women, and unemployed and low-income people.[14] Despair is the main cause of suicide in Iran. Yet, there are no accurate and reliable statistics regarding suicides in the country. Instead of looking for the root causes behind this disaster at the urban, rural, and regional levels, authorities behave as if these cases are not actually occurring. They treat them indifferently, consider them unimportant, and turn a blind eye to the suffering they entail. In fact, when incidents of domestic violence and suicide are reported in Kurdistan, the Iranian government uses them to further persecute the Kurds, rather than seeking a solution (Fallah Safavi, 2019).

The increasing suicide rate among women in the Ilam province can be attributed to slander and defamation; forced marriages and honour; deeply embedded patriarchal structures, especially in rural areas; conflicts and family disputes; marriages where the age gap is significant; and other factors. This results in a lack of genuine relationship between children and parents and an abundance of unemployed, unqualified, and socially deprived young girls.

Against this background, where women are seen as assets, they are also exposed to sexual harassment; polygamy; poverty, both material and cultural; and large, financially unsustainable families. A survey of suicides among Kurdish women shows that women are being subjected to violence by their brothers, fathers, and sometimes mothers. As they always view themselves in a subordinate position with no substantial rights and little value, sometimes suicide is seen as the only way out of a life with very few prospects.

Some Iraqi Kurdish women living in a conservative and patriarchal society believe that the only way to solve their problem is having it recognised through a dramatic gesture. They resort to setting themselves on fire with kerosene heaters, conveniently found at home (Romm, Combs, & Klein, 2008). Self-destructive behaviours, such as self-immolation, are seen among young, uneducated women who are exposed to domestic violence or arranged marriages and live in absolute frustration and helplessness. Since no institutional body is available to support these women, they have no choice but to destroy themselves (Fallah Safavi, 2019).

In Kuhasht region, I interviewed a friend of Zahra, who committed suicide:

> *"Bahman and Zahra were in love and they looked good together. They would never disagree with each other. But even after the marriage, their families did not leave them in peace. Zahra's father had problems with the father of Bahman. He wanted his daughter to divorce and marry the person he wanted to. Finally, Bahman and Zahra took their decision; the only way to escape the family pressure was death. Both of them took poison. In the end Bahman survived and Zahra died".*

Below follows a narrative by one of my informants in Kangavar city, whose girlfriend committed suicide after he told her that he was interested in marrying another girl:

> *"She was 16 and I wanted her for friendship, but not marriage. However, we became much closer and we had a relationship. After a while, she became dependent on me. We were very close and we had a close relationship, but then I decided to get married to another girl. I spoke to her, but she could not accept it. She constantly contacted me and cried that she could not forget me and live without me. Our relation was a secret and our families knew nothing about it. I threatened her that I would let her family know about us, but I did not really mean it. I did not think she was going to hurt herself, but after some days she committed suicide. Now, a few months after this, I can still not forgive myself. From time to time I fall asleep and cry in my sleep. It still hurts a lot".*

The head of the Social Emergency Department in Iran said that 95% of people who commit suicide have psychological disorders, and the main cause of this is depression and "disappointment".[15] What makes suicide among the Kurdish people different from other societies is the rate among women. Research on suicide epidemiology has shown that when attempting suicide, women nowadays use mild procedures such as taking pills or poison, while research conducted in Ilam, Kermanshah, and Kurdistan has shown the old habit of Kurdish women resorting to self-immolation has decreased in prevalence, as they also now prefer taking poison or pills.[16] The common characteristic among those who commit suicide is believing that suicide is the only way to overcome the unpleasantness of their daily life. Committing suicide ultimately ends these intolerable emotions associated with oppression and hopelessness.

Kurdish women are severely controlled and subjected to gender discrimination and psychological pressures in a male-dominated society. In a tribal community, an unwritten punishment exists for women who protest against forced marriage or have outspoken views about sexual and romantic relationships. Under the pretence of honour, women are simply forced to die. Self-immolation among Kurdish women has come to symbolise a sort of opposition and rebellion. Those who commit self-immolation also try to make the people around them and the community aware of their suffering. In this case, this action is a cry for help. In the Kurdish regions, especially in the provinces of Kermanshah and Ilam, many women and girls commit self-immolation to free themselves from gender, social, and tribal norms and expectations. The rural areas of Kurdistan and Ilam are plagued by ancient traditions and cultural norms that do not allow women to develop independent decision-making skills and make informed decisions.

My informant in Kermanshah, Venus, is about 50 years old and suffers from muscular dystrophy syndrome:

> *"I have no trouble going out of the house, but he will not allow me attending a class. I have been controlled by him for so many years that I cannot any more postpone my decision to get a divorce. I opened a bank account last year. A few months ago, I realised that my husband was asking the head of the bank who is his friend to activate my own bank account number. Since I opened this account, I'm more likely to save some money. But this is very difficult because I had to use my own money to even pay for my son's school registration and the purchase of his books".*

According to the law, if a man dies, the custody of the children goes to his parents even if their mother is competent to look after them. The mother can have her children with the consent of her husband's parents and uncles. If a woman wants a divorce, she will lose her children, unless she can prove that her husband is addicted to drugs or has cheated on her, for example. The latter is almost impossible to prove because she must have witnesses; that is, two men or the woman with whom her husband cheated. It is worth highlighting at this point that a man's testimony at the court of law equals that of two women.

My informant Hana, who is 34 years old, from Ilam, was a victim of forced marriage. Not only did she share with me her story, but she also gave me a very acute insight into the desperate situation of the region:

> *"I was 20 years old when my husband collapsed at the age of 28 and died. We were all mourning for a long time. A few months later, his parents said that since there were unmarried men at home, I could not live with them. As a result, I had to leave home and leave my child with them or I should marry the brother of my dead husband. I was desperate. They finally said that if you want to stay in this house, you have to marry your brother-in-law. Mostafa was just a year older than me and still had no diploma. I got stuck. There was a difference between the families and my parents divorced. Women have to work so that they are not forced into a similar situation. There are many such women around us. Some heads of households are very young and are often not well educated. Some can't even read and write, which makes their life even more difficult. I often asked when I was smaller why families who are affluent often have one or two kids, while the poor have several children whom they cannot afford. For quite some time now we have come to an answer: poverty. When you are poor, you are not just starving; you are born poor, you do not need to study, you cannot think about it, you just do not want to. In the third world, the poor have no access to education. A woman is born in poverty because her mother could not prevent her pregnancy. Every birth multiplies poverty!"*

All of us experience loneliness, depression, disappointment, and despair throughout life. The death of a family member and failure to communicate are just two of the things that affect our confidence, creating a sense of unworthiness in us. Financial bankruptcies are also major issues that some of us face in life. Since each person's emotional structure is unique, each one of us reacts differently to different situations. In determining whether a person really wants to commit suicide, it is necessary to assess the situation/ circumstances from the person's own point of view.[17] Based on the results of various studies, men over 45 with a history of alcoholism, violence, and irritability; a loss of physical health; depression; and previous hospitalisation in a mental hospital are at high risk for suicide (Ryazi & Najafianpour, 2016). Studies also show that more than two-thirds of those who commit suicide had shared their intention with others and threatened to follow through. Therefore, a successful way of preventing suicide is to identify any intent in the thoughts or speech of an affected person and to direct that person to a psychologist or psychiatrist (Sue et al., 2012: 252).

As already discussed, financial issues have always been one of the driving forces behind forced marriages. Many families may not approve of or easily resort to violence, but they hardly tolerate their daughters voicing their own opinions about their future. That future usually involves the choice of a perspective spouse, whom they often reject in advance. What really matters to them is to find someone who is in a good financial standing. For example, in one of the cases I examined, a girl refused to marry someone when she realised he was a drug dealer (it was considered common to buy drugs in Kurdish areas). Despite her opposition, within a week's time their wedding was arranged. The girl begged her mother that she did not want to marry him, but she wasn't taken seriously. The wedding preparations went ahead, and the young girl set herself alight before the ceremony.

The advancement of new communication tools, such as the internet and mobile phones, have expanded our horizons of interpersonal relations and acquaintances. Yet lack of economic incentives and the prevailing cultural norms have limited women's ability to experience the possibilities that these new communication tools have to offer. Tradition and culture make up the group identity, which is usually practiced through the elders of the family and the community. However, in the last decade, people, particularly women, have experienced a shift in the sources that traditionally provided their identity. Of course, changing the traditional roles of women means that the society will also gradually change. In this regard, the influence of traditional power-holders, such as the family and the community, will gradually decline, and religious and ethnic values will also lose their grip on people. In fact, in today's Kurdistan, there are a lot of people who base their lifestyle and parenting choices on information they receive through media, universities, and trans-regional interactions.

Mina is 30 years old and from Ilam. She is one woman who experienced a bitter marriage. She says:

> *"I was sixteen years old when I fell in love. The love of those days was honest. We talked twice a week by phone, although his mother was opposed to our relation. Because in the village the name of the girl is destroyed when everybody knows about her relationship, in the end, no one asked me to marriage. My boyfriend married another girl the same year. I was depressed and stayed indoors. The next year, when I had a suitor, it did not matter to me whether I loved him or not; I just wanted to get married and go. Even when my dad disagreed, I insisted to marry him. We married the same week. A few months later he finished the military service. Soon, I figured out how my husband was lazy and irresponsible. Finally, after a year, he went to work. I also went with him. He worked at a greenhouse outside the city. At night, we went home to two dirty rooms. In the meantime, Said became addicted to drugs. After my childbirth, he did not stay there either. He went to Tehran and disappeared, and I travelled for six months with my state subsidy for myself and my twins. Ten years passed. In all these years, we have even cultivated crops. Now I'm a saleswoman and he is unemployed. His addiction has got worse. My father says to get divorced. But I cannot. The government is taking my children*

and giving them to my husband. I waited so long so that the kids grow up and come with me".

Another informant, a mother, who had come to pay back a loan to a well-to-do individual in Kangwar, told me:

"My girl was 16 years old when she married. I've been working with my husband and I've got three more daughters. One day my daughter told me that a lawyer asked her to marry. Despite our objections, she eventually got married, but their life together lasted three months and my daughter returned home. They were very different. The groom was a traditional man and the girl was still a teenager. My daughter said they were not like a husband and wife. My daughter was full of energy and her husband expected an obedient housewife".

Another case from Kangavar involves a woman named Masoume, who committed suicide when she was only 24 years old. She was forced to marry when she was 14 without knowing anything about married life. Following a lot of fighting and two years of common life, she became a depressed, divorced widow at the age of 18. Three years later, she was forced to marry a 40-year-old man, who already had a six-year-old daughter; he was a man who was just looking for a mother for his daughter. Three years later, when she was 24, she had a baby, and when he turned ten months, she committed suicide by taking tablets.

Another informant is a young woman, Samaneh, from Kangavar. She is 17 years old and married to an older man. She consented to that marriage in order to satisfy her parents. Shortly after the marriage, she realised that her husband was involved with other women. At first, she doubted his betrayal, but then she found a certificate of temporary marriage among her husband's clothes. She had a good relationship with her husband's family, and she felt embarrassed to proceed with a separation, so she endured her husband's infidelity for a long time hoping for a better life until her family became aware of the issue and she divorced. She still decided to remarry. This time she chose someone who soon proved to be a drug addict. When I asked her about her choice of husbands, she replied: *"I was not comfortable living in my father's house. Everything I wanted was provided. Every morning I woke up, my father would give me money, I was embarrassed. Being married and at my age having to go back to my father's house for money and help is truly an embarrassing experience. It was difficult for me not to feel guilty".* Samaneh chose not to separate, and despite her husband's addiction, she lives with him. She borrowed money and she launched a small shop.

Since Kurdistan is not considered an industrial region, according to Mr. Shakir Ebrahimi, head of the Islamic Council of the Kurdistan Provincial Council of the Islamic Republic of Iran, the implementation of projects such as the Kurdistan Arrangement Project will result in a drop of living standards by leaving workers below the poverty line since they will receive only one-third of the benefits they are entitled to. Those types of polices only make people poorer. Instead of introducing an apprenticeship plan, the government should allow young people who have shops and those who work in Kulbari to freely trade and export Iranian products. Meanwhile, a representative from the Ilam Province at the Supreme Council of the Provinces said that Ilam is the suicide capital of the country. The same official mentioned that Ilam is situated on the poverty line because of the very high unemployment rate (IRNA news). Based on the reports, the parliamentary research centre announced the poverty line of 2019 was equal to 1.8 million tomans or around 200 USD.[18]

Kurdistan is one of the least developed provinces, which in the last few decades has not been able to keep up with the development of other provinces of the country. More than 70% of industries have closed down, and the unemployment rate has reached 30%. However, the province is considered one of the safer areas in the country, and the reopening of the border crossings, which are used by Kolbars to smuggle prohibited goods, can have an impact on sustainable security development in the area. Still, this deprives the state's treasury of additional income and affects other government agencies and organisations such as the border regiment.

Abdolreza Masri, a representative of Kermanshah, said that Kermanshah has no proper social or unemployment benefits. Unemployment is a factor in suicide and social harm, including addiction and theft. Social damage is like an iceberg, where only a little shows and the rest, the real and serious problems that any society faces, remain hidden.[19] In the first six months of year 2017, 1,187 people committed suicide. To get a better picture of this unique pattern, a comprehensive registry was established in the Ilam province from 1995 through 2002. In this registry, the information about all suicide and DSH (deliberate self-harm) cases that occurred within Ilam were recorded based on multiple sources, including the records of the Ilam Bureau of Statistics, emergency medical services, hospitals, police, and forensic medical examiners. According to this registry, during the period of investigation, 611 cases of suicide (438 females vs. 172 males) and 1807 cases of DSH (1074 females vs. 728 males) were registered in Ilam (Rezaeinasab, Sheikhi, & Shahri, 2018).

It should be noted that the genders of one suicide victim and five DSH cases were missing. The fatality rates were 25.3% for both genders and 29% and 19.1% for females and males, respectively (Rezaeian & Sharifirad, 2012). Between 1998 and 2003, 98 cases of attempted suicides by self-immolation were identified and ascertained in Sina University Hospital of Tabriz University of Medical Sciences, Tabriz, Iran (Dastgiri, Kalankesh, & Pourafkary, 2005). The age range for self-immolation victims in Iran is between 18 and 27 years old (Groohi, Alaghehbandan, & Lari, 2002: 569–74). Several studies have identified disputes between married couples, (95% of suicide attempts are due to some type of mood disorder and depression,

September 2017, Reporter: Azam Shami, Publisher: Roya Rafiei) bigamy, poverty, frustration in education, and physical and mental illnesses including addiction and alcoholism as the main reasons for committing suicide. Both successful and unsuccessful suicide attempts have mostly occurred among housewives who had no independent incomes (Askari, 1998: 37–42).[20]

According to a report published by Human Rights Watch, 20% of all suicide victims from the major Kurdish towns are children and adolescents. In more detail, there are 225 people, 103 women and 122 men, who committed suicide in the four provinces of Ilam, Kurdistan, Kermanshah, and West Azerbaijan in the period December 1998 to December 1999. Twenty percent of them were teenagers under the age of 18, including 26 girls and 18 boys. Suicides of school children as young as 11 have also been reported.[21] Poverty and problems associated with poverty are listed as the main reason behind this very high number of suicides. For example, according to the Riga Kurdistan, a young man called Soltanpour ended his life mainly due to extreme poverty. He was married and had a child and attempted suicide by taking tablets. Eventually, he died from poisoning.

Some previous studies have shown that incidences of self-immolation have risen by 30–40% in the Kermanshah and Elam provinces over the past few years.[22] Further, the occurrence of self-immolation among females is much higher than males. This difference between females and males is similar to the research data reported from the provinces of Mazandaran, Ahvaz, and Kurdistan (Dastgiri, Kalankesh, & Pourafkary, 2005: 14–19). In western Iran, where 80% of self-immolation cases were committed by young women; the most common reasons were identified as excessive depression, family honour, and poverty (Suhrabi, Delpisheh, & Taghinejad, 2012).

My 35-year-old informant from Kohdasht in Lurestan said:

> *"Over the past ten years, suicide among women has declined, and the rate of male suicides has risen mainly due to the use of aluminium phosphide or as it is commonly known, rice pill. Here the suicides among women predominantly resulted from self-immolation. Perhaps the main reason is the closed community. An emotional woman who has been widowed and socially under pressure by men (father and brother), usually resorts to suicide".*

An interview in Eyvan with a 22-year-old boy follows:

> *"Eyvan city is one of the main centres of Kalhor tribe. It has a good weather but it is a deprived area. It is less developed than elsewhere. There are almost no facilities. Do not come here. It is as if Eyvan has vanished from the map. Even the pilgrims' paths do not meet so that they do not pass through this place. In this situation, the only thing that comes to the minds of many is suicide. At times, young people gather together when they say goodbye. Well, I'm going to throw myself off a cliff one says.*

These jokes about suicide are very common. My childhood friend killed himself a few years ago. Right on the day of his marriage. The best day for a human. His fiancée said that I'm not going to live in your father's house. He did not have the money to buy a home for his wife, so he killed himself. If the young people have jobs, if they have money, they will marry a woman and have hope for life".

Gender inequality refers to unequal treatment or perceptions of individuals based on their gender. Men are the ones who usually hold all the powerful positions in the workplace. Men in a position of power will typically promote or hire other men, resulting in discrimination against women, whose income, even when they are employed, will be less than that of their male colleagues. There are still many who believe that a woman's place is at home. Functionalists in sociology claim that gender inequality is necessary for achieving balance in society, employment, politics, education, family, and reality. Human sexual dimorphism theory says that physical differences define the line between male and female (Ferris & Stein, 2008). Although the lack of adequate representation of Kurdish women in political life has not been cited directly as a possible cause of suicides or attempted suicides, it is clear that fair representation of women in political life is essential in order to ensure that at last female-focused issues, such as limited access to the job market, poverty, unfair treatment after a divorce, and high suicide rates, receive the attention they deserve.

One of my friends living in Bāneh has this to say about the city's atmosphere:

"For many years, people's behaviour was based on backward tradition. Most of the population and households lived in a relatively normal way, while the old patriarchal system is gradually losing more and more of its grip on the society. Admittedly there is still a long way to go. Still nowadays, there are marriages under the age of 20, but there is no more a lot of violence, at least, not as much as before. And there are less and less families who forbid their girls from continuing with their education; there are not that many parents who choose to hide their teenage girls because they are afraid of their behaviour. Yet, the old-fashioned view that an educated girl may become too modern still persists and poses an obstacle to the pursuit of further education for girls. But at the same time, the idea of committing suicide is gradually, also, losing ground, and if a married woman finds herself in difficult circumstances and divorces, the parents may even offer some support. Most women's problems here are rooted in the lack of awareness of marital relationships. Males compensate for their marital relationship by starting a parallel relationship, and eventually a divorce is inevitable. Or vice versa, women who are not satisfied with their spouse, they may also end up having relationships with other men. Alongside this new reality, suicide and self-immolation still happen.

Unfortunately, families do not have the right information or they are not happy when someone asks too many questions".

There is a correlation between several factors that prepare the ground for a young girl's suicide: patriarchal society and family pressure, including forced marriage, honour killings, and polygamy; domestic violence; lack of education; language barriers; lack of access to political processes; lack of access to health care and psychological care; and economic problems. Equally common are cases where a young woman burns herself alive because of a dispute with her husband's family. Lack of communication and proper advice are also partly to blame. In January 2017, a 13-year-old girl, who was dissatisfied with the separation of her parents and her father's marriage with a young woman, self-immolated. The reason why this teenage girl did not explore any other avenues to vent her frustration is not clear. Research in this field has been very challenging, and I have, personally, found it extremely difficult to uncover the real reasons behind each suicide. Parents were, understandably, not always forthcoming to share information. Similarly, neighbours were unwilling to help and they often provided inaccurate information. The point is that such a disaster—a 13-year-old committing suicide—should have been prevented at all costs.

Under regular circumstances, the available healing methods for those contemplating suicide include: individual counselling, guidance, and support; education and the development of problem-solving skills; individual psychotherapy sessions; family interventions; and therapy groups. Considering that we will have to adjust these suicide prevention strategies to the reality of Ilam Province, we can determine that treatment should focus on the following: firstly, training through the organisation of urban workshops and public media on anger and excitement control skills should be provided. Secondly, theatre playing or drama therapy should be utilised since they have been proven to assist people, making them aware of all the negative emotions they have. This type of therapy includes techniques such as role-playing, story-telling, miming, improvising, and using puppets. Another measure would be to undertake information campaigns aiming at breaking the taboo of divorce among people by providing them with information about the positive and negative consequences of divorce and its impact on the life of divorcees and children. Other techniques involve the identification of suicidal subjects using a screening plan and the creation of job opportunities and tailor-made trainings suitable for the conditions of those contemplating suicide to help them achieve job satisfaction. It is also of key importance to teach people verbal and non-verbal skills in marital life in order to use negotiation and compromise when approaching their partner instead of constant argumentation and altercations that lead to bitter divorce proceedings. Further, people should learn activities and exercises that promote emotional stability, such as physical exercise, expressing feelings with words, active listening skills, exhibiting pride for accomplishments, checking expectations, and devising an adjustable action plan, among many others. Finally, NGOs should be promoted and used as centers of dialogue for people in need of empath; they should additionally provide opportunities for counselling and publicize their work through media so that people become aware of the possibilities available.

The training and deployment of additional social workers, psychologists, and psychiatrists and the provision of more shelters for women fleeing domestic violence, while essential, will take many years to realise. Furthermore, in the climate of conflict, danger, and poverty, it is questionable as to how effective these initiatives may be, since the crucial issues of prevailing culture, patriarchy, conservatism, and language may represent insurmountable obstacles. As for family therapy, efforts to penetrate the family circle and reach out to the men and the older women who often accept the oppression of women are frequently rebuffed. It is exceptional for a family to come together to be counselled following a suicide attempt. The lack of education among Kurdish women has been cited by a number of interviewees as one of the main causes of suicides and attempted suicides. As a result, it is of utmost significance to promote and enforce women's education. After all, women's education is integral to their mental health, as well as to the overall health of men and children. It has been established that educated women are less likely to tolerate domestic violence and abuse and more likely to find employment and engage in public health programs (Desjarlais et al., 1995).

Conclusion

Women in the Kurdish regions resort to suicide in order to gain some control over their lives and escape repressive values imposed upon them by close family and society, as well as to avoid gender-based violence and state neglect. The scourge of honour killings only highlights the pressures that women in Iran—in particular Kurdish women—endure in order to conform to societal and family expectations. Despite the absence of concrete and reliable government statistics concerning suicide rates in the Kurdish regions, a small number of women's NGOs and regional human rights organisations possess a limited amount of data, which was presented in detail above. However, the ability of these NGOs to provide reliable statistical information is severely hampered by the pervading political, social, and economic situation in the region and the unwillingness of families, clans, neighbours, and the larger Kurdish community to report or discuss the issue of suicide. Although it is difficult to provide a conclusive answer as to whether or not there has been an increase in female suicides and attempted suicides in the Kurdish regions in Iran due to the dearth of reliable and independent statistical data, it is clear that Kurdish women and girls in Iran experience multiple disadvantages, over and above those experienced by women in Iran generally. These additional disadvantages are specific to their position within a well-established patriarchal society. In such circumstances, women and girls are especially prone to depression and desperation, which inevitably lead to a great number of attempted and often successful suicides.

Harassment, negative attitudes towards women from both men and women in the community, and discrimination against girls in a family setting are all part of the reality of being a woman in Iran, which, in other words, means accepting coming second in the family and society. A disadvantaged starting position in the job market, discriminatory inheritance laws,[23] and prevailing cultural norms cause women to feel immense pressure, and they face outright discrimination and violence. What they in fact experience is a well-embedded patriarchal culture where their rights are violated, and an endless list of limitations curtail their potential. Despite some modest changes, their overall status has been hardly improved over the past decades.

It is well known that the education system provides individuals with a realistic opportunity to break away from poverty by enabling them to find employment; overcome mental distress, disability, and despair; and have access to health care and benefits and, in this way, feel less vulnerable and more in control. Still, various forms of racial and gender discrimination can lead to salary inequalities and poverty. Even when all members of a workforce are equally productive, men are paid more than women. (While racial and gender discrimination still exist, economists do generally agree that discrimination at work is decreasing.)

Further, let us not forget that education is a basic human right and an essential tool for achieving the goals of equality, development, and peace. It is crucial that Kurdish girls and young women are educated in order to reverse the desperate situation in which so many of them find themselves later on in life that is responsible for the number of suicides and attempted suicides witnessed in the region. It is therefore imperative that the Ministry of Education, in co-operation with the State Ministry responsible for Women's Affairs, Family and Child Protection, work with the NGO community in order to realise these objectives. There is a dire need for workshops and economic opportunities in the area in order to provide employment for the increased numbers of women who live in the cities. The majority of the women who commit suicide are women who are abandoned and neglected, face severe financial problems and have zero prospects for the future, or suffer under the socio-cultural norms and expectations that the traditional patriarchal society has placed upon them.

It is hoped that the international community will eventually pay attention to the plea of the thousands of women in the region and will work together with the Iranian government in order to reach a viable solution. In doing so, they would need to closely consult and collaborate with locally inspired civil society organisations and especially women's NGOs. At a political level, the creation of a democratic platform for dialogue regarding the ongoing conflict, and the amendment of the Iranian Constitution to recognise the rights of the Kurdish minority, will definitely contribute towards improving the situation of Kurdish women in Iran.

Unfortunately, the COVID-19 pandemic has had disastrous consequences for women in Iran, where honour killings are not condemned. Due to the new restrictions being placed all over the world, such as lockdowns, closing businesses, and not being able to leave the home, women are in a more vulnerable place than ever. "Financial insecurity, increased stress, restricted access to personal space in the home, isolation, and poor economic conditions lead to damage to mental health and poor socioeconomic status" (Pirnia, Pirnia, & Pirnia, 2020). All of these conditions also create even more tension in the home, leading to a higher likelihood of violence against women. With the desperation associated with forced isolation (due to lockdown restrictions), it is possible that more women may even try to run away from their situations, leading to their families' honour being compromised and perhaps resulting in honour killings.

Notes

1 https://www.who.int/news/item/09-09-2019-suicide-one-person-dies-every-40-seconds. 19 September 2019. Accessed 18 October 2019.
2 Article 1106 - The cost of maintenance of the wife is at the charge of the husband in permanent marriages. Article 1107 - Cost of maintenance includes dwelling, clothing, food, furniture in proportion to the situation of the wife, on a reasonable basis, and provision of a servant if the wife is accustomed to having servants or if she needs one because of illness or defects of limbs.
3 https://www.isna.ir/news/kermanshah-77987/%D8%AE%D8%AA%D9%85-14-%D8%AF%D8%B1%D8%B5%D8%AF-%D8%A7%D8%B2-%D8%AF%D9%88%D8%A7%D8%AC-%D9%87%D8%A7%DB%8C-%DA%A9%D8%B1%D9%85%D8%A7%D9%86%D8%B4%D8%A7%D9%87-%D8%A8%D9%87-%D8%B7%D9%84%D8%A7%D9%82-%D8%AF%D8%B1-5-%D8%B3%D8%A7%D9%84-%D8%A7%D9%88%D9%84-%D8%B2%D9%86%D8%AF%DA%AF%DB%8C. Accessed 1 July 2019.
4 The "One Million Signatures" campaign was initiated by women in Iran to repel discriminatory laws against women in the country. The campaign has received worldwide attention, while some of the activists involved have been incarcerated by the Iranian regime.
5 "Iran Population Female Percent of Total," https://tradingeconomics.com/iran/population-female-percent-of-total-wb-data.html.
6 Center for Strategic Stats and Information. "What proportion of women make up the country's labor supply?" 2018.
7 Called Qachax ("border trafficking") by IRS.
8 "The Association for Human Rights in Kurdistan of Iran-Geneva (KMMK-G)," last modified 5 September 2017. http://www.kmmk-ge.org/2017/09.
9 "Wave: The Unemployed Homeowners Are on Their Way." 2016. http://rigakurdistan.ir/postID=2046/%D8%B3%D9%88%D9%86%D8%A7%D9%85%DB%8C-%D8%AE%D8%A7%D9%86%D9%87%E2%80%8C%D9%86%D8%B4%DB%8C%D9%86%D8%A7%D9%86-%D8%A8%DB%8C%DA%A9%D8%A7%D8%B1-%D8%AF%D8%B1-%D8%B1%D8%A7%D9%87-%D8%A7%D8%B3%D8%AA. Accessed 2 August 2016.

10 M. Z., "Chairman of the Relief Committee: The number of poor people in the country is increasing," 17 February 2016. https://p.dw.com/p/1HwuV. Accessed 20 March 2017.
11 According to the latest statistics published by the World Health Organization (WHO), every 40 seconds someone commits suicide. An analysis of suicide in Sardasht and other Kurdish cities, release date: 5 June 2017.
12 https://www.radiofarda.com/a/295830.html. 2 March 2005. Accessed 25 October 2017.
13 https://www.asriran.com/fa/news/688253/%D9%87%D8%AB%D8%A7%D9%86%DB%8C%D9%87-%DB%8C%DA%A9-%D9%86%D9%81%D8%B1-%D8%AF%D8%B1-%D8%AC%D9%87%D8%A7%D9%86-%D8%A8%D8%B1-%D8%A7%D8%AB%D8%B1-%D8%AE%D9%88%D8%AF%DA%A9%D8%B4%DB%8C-%D9%85%DB%8C%E2%80%8C%D9%85%DB%8C%D8%B1%D8%AF
14 Usman Mahmoudi, social researcher, "An Analysis of Suicide in Sardasht and Other Kurdish Cities," 5 June 1395. http://rigakurdistan.ir/postID=754/%D8%AA%D8%AD%D9%84%DB%8C%D9%84%DB%8C-%D8%A8%D8%B1-%D9%85%D8%B3%D8%A7%D9%84%D9%87-%D8%AE%D9%88%D8%AF%DA%A9%D8%B4%DB%8C-%D8%B3%D8%B1%D8%AF%D8%B4%D8%AA-%D8%B4. Accessed 2 March 2018.
15 95% of suicide attempts are due to a type of mood disorder and depression. https://www.irna.ir/news/82660073/95-%D8%AF%D8%B1%D8%B5%D8%AF-%D8%A7%D9%82%D8%AF%D8%A7%D9%85-%D8%A8%D9%87-%D8%AE%D9%88%D8%AF%D9%83%D8%B4%D9%8A-%D9%87%D8%A7-%D9%86%D8%A7%D8%B4%D9%8A-%D8%A7%D8%B2-%D9%8A%D9%83-%D9%86%D9%88%D8%B9-%D8%A7%D8%AE%D8%AA%D9%84%D8%A7%D9%84-%D8%AE%D9%84%D9%82%D9%8A-%D9%88-%D8%A7%D9%81%D8%B3%D8%B1%D8%AF%DA%AF%D9%8A. Accessed 11 November 2019.
16 Suicide with pills and poison replaced female self-immolation in Ilam, 7 November 2019. https://www.radiozamaneh.com/473085. Accessed 10 November 2019.
17 Statistically speaking, Iran ranks 58th in the world, with 6 suicides per 100,000 population. The breakdown is 42.5% by hanging, 30% by self-immolation, and 13.5% with pills and poison. The Elam province tops the list with 26 suicides per 100,000 people, and Kermanshah province is second with 23 per 100,000 people.
18 "Tehran's poverty line has almost doubled in two years," emphasis nor government propaganda has affected the youth, 5 September 2020. https://www.dw.com/fa-ir/%D8%AF%D9%88%DB%8C%DA%86%D9%87-%D9%88%D9%84%D9%87-%D9%81%D8%A7%D8%B1%D8%B3%DB%8C/s-9993
19 https://www.saat24.news/news/260854/عبدالرضا-مصری-عضو-شورای-رقابت-شد (Translation: Abdolreza Mesri become member of competition council). 10 May 2017. Accessed August 2017.
20 The average age (standard deviation) of cases was 27 (12) years (range: 11–68 years). The female/male ratio was 3.3. In the majority of the cases, victims were married (55%). Kerosene was the most common ingredient (85%) used to commit suicide by self-immolation. The average burn size was 63% of the total body surface. The case fatality rate was 76%. Of these cases, 28% and 15% had a history of family conflicts and mental disorders, respectively. The lowest and highest incidence rates (per 100,000 population) of self-immolation occurred in Tabriz (2, CI 95%: 1.2–2.8) and Mianeh (209, CI 95%: 72.5–346), respectively. There was a significant increasing trend in the incidence rate (per 100,000 population) of self-immolation from 1998 (1.48, CI 95%: 0.2–2.8) to 2003 (7.7, CI 95%: 4.8–10.5). The majority of suicides by self-immolation occurred in March every year. Two- and five-week survival rates for suicide by self-immolation were

25% (CI 95%: 16–34) and 15% (CI 95%: 6–24), respectively. The median survival time was 4.3 days (CI 95%: 3.9–4.5) (Dastgiri, Kalankesh & Pourafkary, 2005: 14–19).
21 https://iranintl.com/%D8%A7%D9%8A%D8%B1%D8%A7%D9%86/%D8%A8%DB%8C%D8%B3%D8%AA-%D8%AF%D8%B1%D8%B5%D8%AF-%D8%A7%D8%B2-%D9%82%D8%B1%D8%A8%D8%A7%D9%86%DB%8C%D8%A7%D9%86-%D8%AE%D9%88%D8%AF%DA%A9%D8%B4%DB%8C-%D8%AF%D8%B1-%D8%B4%D9%87%D8%B1%D9%87%D8%A7%DB%8C-%DA%A9%D9%8F%D8%B1%D8%AF%D9%86%D8%B4%DB%8C%D9%86-%D8%A7%DB%8C%D8%B1%D8%A7%D9%86-%D8%B7%DB%8C-%DB%8C%DA%A9-%D8%B3%D8%A7%D9%84-%DA%AF%D8%B0%D8%B4%D8%AA%D9%87%D8%8C-%DA%A9%D9%88%D8%AF%DA%A9-%D9%88-%D9%86%D9%88%D8%AC%D9%88%D8%A7%D9%86-%D8%A8%D9%88%D8%AF%D9%87%E2%80%8C%D8%A7%D9%86%D8%AF.
22 Iran Newspaper. Available at: www.Iran-newspaper.com. Accessed 10 August 2004.
23 One of the issues that has become an excuse for attacking Islam in the nature of the early sects of Islam and the proponents of the full equality of women and men in the present age is the issue of women's inheritance. The problem is that Islam has ignored the human value of women in terms of inheritance by approving that women are entitled to less than men.

References

Abouchedid, Kamal, and Ramzi Nasser. 2002. "Attributions of Responsibility for Poverty among Lebanese and Portuguese University Students: A Cross-cultural Comparison." *Social Behavior and Personality: An International Journal* 30, no. 1: 25–36.
Afshar, Haleh. 1998. *Islam and Feminisms: An Iranian Case-Study*. London: Macmillian Press.
Ahmadi, Habib, and Mohammadtaghi Iman. 2005. "Culture of Poverty and Attitude toward Delinquency among Youth of Dehpileh District of Shiraz." *Journal of Isfahan University medical science* 19, no. 2: 99–118.
Alizadeh, Narges, Abdolrahim Afkhamzadeh, B. Mohsenpour, and B. Salehian. 2010. "Suicide Attempt and Related Factors in Kurdistan Province." *Scientific Journal of Kurdistan University of Medical Sciences* 15: 79–86. Accessed 10December2019. http://sjku.muk.ac.ir/article-1-321-fa.pdf.
Allen, Tim, and Alan Thomas, eds. 1992. *Poverty and Development in the 1990s*. Oxford: Oxford University Press.
Askari, S. 1998. "Special Report on Women." *Farhang-e-Tose's J* 1998: 34–42.
Bradshaw, Ted. 2007. "Theories of Poverty and Anti-Poverty Programs in Community Development." *Community Development* 38, no. 1: 7–25. 10.1080/15575330709490182.
Breault, K. D., and Karen Barkey. 1982. "A Comparative Analysis of Durkheim's Theory of Egoistic Suicide." *Sociological Quarterly* 23, no. 3: 321–331. DOI: 10.1111/j.1533-8525.1982.tb01015.x.
Claypool, W. A. 2009. "Fighting the Culture of Poverty: Values and Opportunities on Chicago's Near North Side." MA thesis, Roosevelt University.
Colucci, Erminia, and David Lester, eds. 2012. *Suicide and Culture: Understanding the Context*. Göttingen: Hogrefe Publishing.
Curra, John. 2013. *The Relativity of Deviance*. Thousand Oaks, CA: SAGE Publications.
Dastgiri, S., L. R. Kalankesh, and N. Pourafkary. 2005. "Epidemiology of

Self-Immolation in the North-West of Iran." *European Journal of General Medicine* 2, no. 1: 14–19. 10.29333/ejgm/82260.

Desjarlais, Robert, Leon Eisenberg, Byron Good, and Arthur Kleinman. 1995. *World Mental Health Problems and Priorities in Low-Income Countries*. New York: Oxford University Press.

Fallah Safavi, M. 2019. "Urban Ethnography with Emphasis on Culture of Poverty: A Case Study of Hadi Abad District of Ghazvim." MA thesis, Tehran University.

Faver, Catherine A., Alonzo M. Cavazos, and Brian L. Trachte. 2005. "Social Work Students at the Border: Religion, Culture, and Beliefs about Poverty." *Journal of Baccalaureate Social Work* 11, no. 1: 1–15.

Ferris, Kerry, and Jill Stein. 2008. *The Real World: An Introduction to Sociology*. New York: W.W. Norton.

Fliege, Herbert, Jeong-Ran Lee, Anne Grimm, and Burghard F. Klapp. 2009. "Risk Factors and Correlates of Deliberate Self-Harm Behavior: A Systematic Review." *Journal of Psychosomatic Research* 66, no. 6 (June): 477–493.

Gorski, Paul. 2008. "Beyond the 'Culture of Poverty': Resources on Economic Justice." *Multicultural Perspectives* 10, no. 1: 27–29.

Groohi, Bahram, Reza Alaghehbandan, and Abdolaziz Rastegar Lari. 2002. "Analysis of 1089 Burn Patients in Province of Kurdistan, Iran." *Burns* 28, no. 6 (September): 569–574.

Haeri, Shahla. 2014. *Law of Desire: Temporary Marriage in Shi'i Iran*. Rev. ed. New York: Syracuse University Press.

Haeri, Shahla. 2020. *The Unforgettable Queens of Islam: Succession, Authority and Gender*. Cambridge: Cambridge University Press.

Hamermesh, Daniel, and Neal M. Soss. 1974. "An Economic Theory of Suicide." *Journal of Political Economy* 82, no. 1: 83–98.

Hawton, Keith, Carolina Casañas I. Comabella, Camilla Haw, and Kate Saunders. 2013. "Risk Factors for Suicide in Individuals with Depression: A Systematic Review." *Journal of Affective Disorders* 147, no. 1–3 (May): 17–28. DOI: 10.1016/j.jad.2013.01.004.

Hughes, Donna M., and Ramesh Sepehrrad. 2004. "Sex Slavery New Face of Oppression of Women in Iran." Accessed 21March2019. https://womensenews.org/2004/02/sex-slavery-new-face-oppression-women-iran/.

Iemmi, Valentina, Jason Bantjes, Ernestina Coast, Kerrie Channer, Tiziana Leone, David McDaid, Alexis Palfreyman, Crick Lund, and Bevan Stephens. 2016. "Suicide and Poverty in Low-Income and Middle-Income Countries: A Systematic Review." *Lancet Psychiatry* 3, no. 8: 774–783. 10.1016/S2215-0366(16)30066-9.

Kar, M. 2015. "Rape of Young Girl in Iran Met with Muted Responses." 10 April. http://www.mehrangizkar.net/english/.

Lester, David, ed. 2001. *Suicide Prevention: Resources for the Millennium*. Series in Death, Dying, and Bereavement. UK: Routledge.

Lewis, Oscar. 1975. *Five Families: Mexican Case Studies in the Culture of Poverty*. New York: Basic Books.

Ludwig, Jens, and Susan Mayer. 2006. "'Culture' and the Intergenerational Transmission of Poverty: The Prevention Paradox." *The Future of Children* 16, no. 2: 175–196.

Petroni, Suzanne, Vikram Patel, and George Patton. 2015. "Why Is Suicide the Leading Killer of Older Adolescent Girls?" *Lancet* 386, no. 10008: 2031–2032.

Mir-Hosseini, Ziba. 1993. *Marriage on Trial: A Study of Islamic Family Law: Iran and Morocco Compared*. London: I.B. Tauris.
Mir-Hosseini, Ziba. 2001. *Marriage on Trial: A Study of Islamic Family Law: Iran and Morocco Compared*. Rev. ed. London: I.B. Tauris.
Mohammadi, M. 2004. "Tamkin; Ghodrat-e Zanan ya Khooshunat-e Mardan" [Obedience; women's power or men's violence]. *Ketab Zanan in Women's Socio-Cultural Council Quarterly* 23: 12–20.
Mohammadpur, Ahmad, Jalil Karimi, and Mehdi Alizadeh. 2014. "Women and Culture of Poverty (A Qualitative Study of the Culture of Poverty among the Iranian Caretaker Women)." *Quality & Quantity: International Journal of Methodology* 48, no. 1 (January): 1–14.
Molaverdi, Shahindokht. 2015. "Female Unemployment; This Is Not a Priority for the Government." *Deutsche Welle*. Accessed 15November2020. https://www.dw.com/fa-ir/بیکاری-زنان-معضلی-که-اولویت-اصلی-دولت-نیست/a-18507670.
Nawzad, Kosar. 2018. "Over 100 Kurds in Iran Commit Suicide in 6 Months, Many over Poverty." Kurdistan24. Accessed 1November2020. https://www.kurdistan24.net/en/news/078ad429-62bb-4ab7-b6d1-fcc0e53e4bab.
Nordt, Carlos, Ingeborg Warnke, Erich Seifritz, and Wolfram Kawohl. 2015. "Modelling Suicide and Unemployment: A Longitudinal Analysis Covering 63 Countries, 2000–11." *Lancet Psychiatry* 2, no. 3: 239–245.
Pirnia, Bijan, Fariborz Pirnia, and Kambiz Pirnia. 2020. "Honour Killings and Violence against Women in Iran during the COVID-19 Pandemic." *Lancet Psychiatry* 7, no. 10: e60.
Rezaeian, Mohsen, and Gholamreza Sharifirad. 2012. "Case Fatality Rates of Different Suicide Methods within Ilam Province of Iran." *Journal of Education and Health Promotion* 1: 15–17.
Rezaeinasab, Zahra, Mohammad Taghi Sheikhi, and Fatemeh Jamilei Kohaneh Shahri. 2018. "Self-immolation of Women in Ilam City, Iran: A Descriptive Study." *Journal of School of Public Health and Institute of Public Health Research* 15, no. 4: 365–376. https://sjsph.tums.ac.ir/files/site1/user_files_edcd0e/admin-A-10-1-53-531e029.pdf.
Romm, Sharon, Heidi Combs, and Matthew B. Klein. 2008. "Self-Immolation: Cause and Culture." *Journal of Burn Care & Research* 29, no. 6 (November–December): 988–993.
Ryazi, S. Abolhassan, and Banoudokht Najafianpour. 2016. "Comparison of Effective Socio-cultural and Psychological Factors in Women Suicide in Iran and Tajikistan." *Iranian Journal of Cultural Research* 8, no. 4: 143–167. Accessed 14October2019. https://www.sid.ir/en/Journal/ViewPaper.aspx?ID=508304.
Shin, Gi-Wook. 2006. *Ethnic Nationalism in Korea: Genealogy, Politics, and Legacy*. Stanford, CA: Stanford University Press.
Small, Mario, David J. Harding Luis, and Michèle Lamont. 2010. "Reconsidering Culture and Poverty." *The ANNALS of the American Academy of Political and Social Science* 629, no. 1 (May): 6–27.
Sue, David, Derald Wing Sue, Stanley Sue, and Diane Sue. 2012. *Understanding Abnormal Behavior*. US: Cengage Learning.
Suhrabi, Zainab, Ali Delpisheh, and Hamid Taghinejad. 2012. "Tragedy of Women's Self-Immolation in Iran and Developing Communities: A Review." *International Journal of Burns and Trauma* 2: 93–104.

Takahashi, Yoshitomo. 2001. "Depression and Suicide." *Japan Medical Association Journal* 44, no. 8: 359–363.

Tartaro, Christine, and David Lester. 2010. *Suicide and Self-Harm in Prisons and Jails*. Lanham, MD: Lexington Books.

Tizro, Zahra. 2014. "The Role of Orthodox Jurisprudence in Dealing with Domestic Violence against Women in Iran." *La Camera Blu*, (September). Accessed 18March2017. DOI:10.6092/1827-9198/2794.

Vijayakumar, Lakshmi, Sujit John, Jane Pirkis, and Harvey Whiteford. 2005. "Suicide in Developing Countries (2): Risk Factors." *Crisis* 26, no. 3: 112–119.

References

Abdi, Kamyar. 2003. "The Early Development of Pastoralism in the Central Zagros Mountains." *Journal of World Prehistory* 17, no. 4 (December): 395–448.

Abouchedid, Kamal, and Ramzi Nasser. 2002. "Attributions of Responsibility for Poverty among Lebanese and Portuguese University Students: A Cross-cultural Comparison." *Social Behavior and Personality: An International Journal* 30, no. 1: 25–36.

Abu Zayd, Nasr. 1988. "The Perfect Man in the Qur'ân: Textual Analysis." *Journal of Osaka University of Foreign Studies* 73: 111–133.

Abu-Odeh, Lama. 1996. "Crimes of Honor and the Construction of Gender in Arab Societies." In *Feminism and Islam: Legal and Literary Perspectives*, edited by Mai Yamani and Andrew Allen, 141–193. New York: NYU Press.

Adedokun, Olaide, Oluwagbemiga Adeyemi, and Cholli Dauda. 2016. "Child Marriage and Maternal Health Risks among Young Mothers in Gombi, Adamawa State, Nigeria: Implications for Mortality, Entitlements and Freedoms." *African Health Sciences* 16, no. 4: 986–999. DOI: 10.4314/ahs.v16i4.15.

Adongo, Philip B., James F. Phillips, Beverly Kajihara, Cornelius Debpuur, and Fred N. Binka. 1997. "Cultural Factors Constraining the Introduction of Family Planning among the Kassena-Nankana of Northern Ghana." *Social Science and Medicine* 45, no. 12: 1789–1804. DOI: PII: S0277-9536(97)00110-X.

Afary, Janet. 2009. *Sexual Politics in Modern Iran*. New York: Cambridge University Press.

Afshar, Haleh. 1998. *Islam and Feminisms: An Iranian Case-Study*. London: Macmillian Press.

Ahmadi, H., and M. T. Iman. 2005. "Culture of Poverty and Attitude toward Delinquency among Youth of Dehpileh District of Shiraz." *Journal of Isfahan University Medical Science* 19, no. 2: 99–118.

Ahmady, Kameel. 2016. *An Echo of Silence: A Comprehensive Research Study on Early Child Marriage (ECM) in Iran*. http://kameelahmady.com/wp-content/uploads/2016/10/English-final-web.pdf.

Ahmady, Kameel. 2018. "Feminization of Poverty – The Causes and Consequences of Early Childhood Marriages in Iran." *Swift Journal of Social Sciences and Humanities* 4, no. 1: 1–10.

Ahmady, Kameel. 2021. "The Role of Temporary Marriage (TM) in Promoting Early Child Marriage (ECM) in Iran." In *Temporary and Child Marriages in Iran* and Afghanistan: Historical Perspectives and Contemporary Issues, edited by S. Behnaz Hosseini, 47–66. UK: Springer.

Ajzen, Icek. 1991. "The Theory of Planned Behavior." *Organizational Behavior and Human Decision Processes* 50, no. 2: 179–211.

Ajzen, Icek. 2001. "Nature and Operation of Attitudes." *Annual Review of Psychology* 52, no. 1: 27–58.

Ajzen, Icek. 2011. "The Theory of Planned Behaviour: Reaction and Reflection." *Psychology and Health* 26, no. 9: 1113–1127.

Akbari, Daniel, and Paul Tetreault. 2014. *Honor Killing: A Professional's Guide to Sexual Relations and Ghayra Violence from the Islamic Sources*. USA: AuthorHouse.

Ali, Kecia. 2002. "Rethinking Women's Issues in Muslim Communities." In *Taking Back Islam: American Muslims Reclaim Their Faith*, edited by Michael Wolfe and Beliefnet. Emmaus, PA: Rodale Press.

Alinia, Minoo. 2013. *Honor and Violence against Women in Iraqi Kurdistan*. New York: Palgrave Macmillan.

Alizadeh, Narges, Abdolrahim Afkhamzadeh, Bezad Mohsenpour, and Bayan Salehian. 2010. "Suicide Attempt and Related Factors in Kurdistan Province." *Scientific Journal of Kurdistan University of Medical Sciences* 15: 79–86. Accessed 10 December 2019. http://sjku.muk.ac.ir/article-1-321-fa.pdf.

Al-Khayyat, Sana. 1990. *Honour and Shame: Women in Modern Iraq*. London: Saqi Books.

Allen, Tim, and Alan Thomas, eds. 1992. *Poverty and Development in the 1990s*. Oxford: Oxford University Press.

Amin, A. 2000. "Violence against Women. Sanandaj, Islamic Republic of Iran." *Women's Participation Research Center of Kurdistan Province* 9: 180–197.

Amnesty International. 2019. "Iran: Thousands Arbitrarily Detained and at Risk of Torture in Chilling Post-protest Crackdown." Accessed 17 April 2020. https://www.amnesty.org/en/latest/news/2019/12/iran-thousands-arbitrarily-detained-and-at-risk-of-torture-in-chilling-post-protest-crackdown/.

Amoakohene, Margaret I. 2004. "Violence against Women in Ghana: A Look at Women's Perceptions and Review of Policy and Social Responses." *Social Science and Medicine* 59, no. 11: 2373–2385. Accessed 15 May 2017. https://pubmed.ncbi.nlm.nih.gov/15450710/. DOI: 10.1016/j.socscimed.2004.04.001.

Ansari, Ali. 2003. *Modern Iran since 1921: The Pahlavis and After*. London: Longman (Pearson education series).

Antoun, Richard T. 1976. "Anthropology." In *The Study of the Middle East: Research and Scholarship in the Humanities and Social Sciences*, edited by Leonard Binder, 137–228. New York: John Wiley & Sons.

Araji, Sharon K. 2000. "Crimes of Honor and Shame: Violence against Women in Non-Western and Western Societies." *The Red Feather Journal of Postmodern Criminology* 8: 1–12.

Aranchi, Mahboub J., and Latif Ebadpour. 2017. "Madhur-Al-Dam (A Person Whose Blood is Void) in Iran's Criminal Law with Emphasis on the Issued Verdicts by Judiciary Courts." *Quid*, Special Issue no. 1: 2126–2133.

Asano-Tamanoi, Mariko. 1987. "Shame, Family, and State in Catalonia and Japan." In *Honor and Shame and the Unity of the Mediterranean*, edited by David Gilmore, 104–120. Washington, DC: American Anthropological Association Special Publication, no. 22.

References

Associated Press. 28 May 2020. "Romina Ashrafi: Outcry in Iran over So-Called 'Honour Killing' of 14-Year-Old Girl." Accessed 24 November 2020. https://www.theguardian.com/world/2020/may/28/romina-ashrafi-outcry-in-iran-over-so-called-honour-killing-of-14-year-old-girl.

Awde, Nicholas, ed. 2000. *Women in Islam: An Anthology from the Qur'an and Hadith*. Translated by Nicholas Awde. New York: St. Martin's Press.

Azadi, Pooya. 2020. "The Structure of Corruption in Iran." Stanford Iran 2040 Project. Accessed 21 April 2020. https://iranian-studies.stanford.edu/sites/g/files/sbiybj6191/f/publications/the_structure_of_corruption_in_iran.pdf.

Azizi Zeinalhajlou, Akbar, Hossein Matlabi, Mohammad Hasan Sahebihagh, Sarvin Sanaie, Manouchehr Seyedi Vafaee, and Fathollah Pourali. 2017. "Nutritional Status of the Community-Dwelling Elderly in Tabriz, Iran." *Elderly Health Journal* 3, no. 2: 80–86. Accessed 24 March 2017 http://ehj.ssu.ac.ir/article-1-100-en.html.

Bahramitash, Roksana, and Shahla Kazemipour. 2006. "Myths and Realities of the Impact of Islam on Women: Changing Marital Status in Iran." *Critique: Critical Middle Eastern Studies* 15, no. 2: 111–128.

Baker, Nancy V., Peter R. Gregware, and Margery A. Cassidy. 1999. "Family Killing Fields: Honor Rationales in the Murder of Women." *Violence against Women* 5, no. 2: 164–184.

Bakhtiarnejad, Parvin. 2009. "Fajeeye khamush: ghatlhaye namusi" [The silent tragedy: Honour killings]. Unpublished study.

Baroja, Julio Caro. 1966. "Honour and Shame: A Historical Account of Several Conflicts." In *Honour and Shame: The Values of Mediterranean Society*, edited by John G. Peristiany, 79–137. Chicago: University of Chicago Press.

Barth, Fredrik. 1969a. "Introduction." In *Ethnic Groups and Boundaries: The Social Organization of Culture Difference*, edited by Fredrik Barth, 9–38. London: Allen & Unwin.

Barth, Fredrik. 1969b. "Pathan Identity and Its Maintenance." In *Ethnic Groups and Boundaries: The Social Organization of Culture Difference*, edited by Fredrik Barth, 117–134. London: Allen & Unwin.

Basu, Nupur. 2013. "Honour Killings: India's Crying Shame." Accessed 18 January 2018. https://www.aljazeera.com/opinions/2013/11/28/honour-killings-indias-crying-shame.

Bayisenge, Jeannette. 2010. "Early Marriage as a Barrier to Girl's Education: A Developmental Challenge in Africa." In *Girl-Child Education in Africa*, edited by C. Ikekeonwu, 43–66. Nigeria: CIDJAP Press.

Begikhani, Nazand, Aisha Gill, and Gill M. Hague. 2010. *Honour-based Violence (HBV) and Honour-based Killings in Iraqi Kurdistan and in the Kurdish Diaspora in the UK*. London: Kurdistan Regional Government.

Begikhani, Nazand. 2005. "Honour-Based Violence among the Kurds: The Case of Iraqi Kurdistan." In *"Honour": Crimes, Paradigms, and Violence against Women*, edited by Lynn Welchman and Sara Hossain, 209–229. London: Zed Books.

Bell, Rudolph M. 1979. *Fate and Honor, Family and Village: Demographic and Cultural Change in Rural Italy since 1800*. Chicago: University of Chicago Press.

Beoku-Betts, Josephine. 1994. "When Black Is Not Enough: Doing Field Research among Gullah Women." *NWSA Journal* 6, no. 3: 413–433. Accessed 12 June 2020. www.jstor.org/stable/4316353.

References

Bourdieu, Pierre. 1966. "The Sentiment of Honour in Kabyle Society." In *Honour and Shame: The Values of Mediterranean Society*, edited by John G. Peristiany, 193–241. Chicago: University of Chicago Press.

Bowman, James. 2007. *Honor: A History*. New York: Encounter Books.

Boyer, Richard. 1998. "Honor among Plebeians: *Mala Sangre* and Social Reputation." In *The Faces of Honor: Sex, Shame, and Violence in Colonial Latin America*, edited by Lyman Johnson and Sonya Lipsett-Rivera, 152–178. Albuquerque, NM: University of New Mexico Press.

Bradshaw, Ted. 2007. "Theories of Poverty and Anti-Poverty Programs in Community Development." *Community Development* 38, no. 1: 7–25. 10.1080/15575330709490182.

Brandon, James, and Salam Hafez. 2008. *Crimes of the Community: Honour-based Violence in the UK*. London: Centre for Social Cohesion.

Brannick, Teresa, and David Coghlan. 2007. "In Defense of Being 'Native': The Case of Insider Academic Research." *Organizational Research Methods* 10, no. 1 (January): 59–74.

Breault, K. D., and Karen Barkey. 1982. "A Comparative Analysis of Durkheim's Theory of Egoistic Suicide." *Sociological Quarterly* 23, no. 3: 321–331. DOI: 10.1111/j.1533-8525.1982.tb01015.x.

Bruce, Judith, and Shelley Clark. 2003. "Including Married Adolescents in Adolescent Reproductive Health and HIV/AIDS Policy." Paper presented for Technical Consultation on Married Adolescents, World Health Organization, Geneva.

Bucerius, Sandra Meike. 2013. "Becoming a 'Trusted Outsider': Gender, Ethnicity, and Inequality in Ethnographic Research." *Journal of Contemporary Ethnography* 42, no. 6 (December): 690–721. DOI: 10.1177/0891241613497747.

Burkholder, Mark A. 1998. "Honor and Honors in Colonial Spanish America." In *The Faces of Honor: Sex, Shame, and Violence in Colonial Latin America*, edited by Lyman Johnson and Sonya Lipsett-Rivera, 18–44. Albuquerque, NM: University of New Mexico Press.

Campbell, Jacquelyn. 1992. "Wife-Battering: Cultural Contexts Versus Western Social Sciences." In *Sanctions and Sanctuary: Cultural Perspectives on the Beating of Wives*, edited by Dorothy Counts, Judith K. Brown, and Jacquelyn C. Campbell, 229–249. Boulder, CO: Westview Press.

Campbell, John Kennedy. 1964. *Honour, Family and Patronage: A Study of Institutions and Moral Values in a Greek Mountain Community*. Oxford: Clarendon Press.

Casimir, Michael J. and Susanne Jung. 2009. "'Honor and Dishonor': Connotations of a Socio-symbolic Category in Cross-Cultural Perspective." In *Emotions as Bio-Cultural Processes*, edited by Birgitt Röttger-Rössler and Hans Markowitsch, 229–280. New York: Springer.

Caulfield, Sueann, Sarah C. Chambers, and Lara Putnam, eds. 2005. *Honor, Status, and Law in Modern Latin America*. London: Duke University Press.

Ceasefire. 2019. *Beyond the Veil: Discrimination against Women in Iran*. London: Ceasefire Centre for Civilian Rights.

Chakravarti, Uma. 2005. "From Fathers to Husbands: Of Love, Death and Marriage in North India." In *"Honour": Crimes, Paradigms, and Violence against Women*, edited by Lynn Welchman and Sara Hossain, 308–331. London: Zed Books.

Chamlou, Nadereh. 2016. "Gender Inequality and Income Inequality in Iran." In *Economic Welfare and Inequality in Iran: Developments since the Revolution*, edited by Mohammad Reza Farzanegan and Pooya Alaedini, 129–153. New York: Palgrave Macmillan.

Charmaz, Kathy. 2006. *Constructing Grounded Theory: A Practical Guide Through Qualitative Analysis*. London: SAGE Publications.

Cialdini, Robert B. 2009. *Influence: The Psychology of Persuasion*. New York: HarperCollins.

Civil Code of the Islamic Republic of Iran. 2015. Retrieved 24 November 2020 from Civil Registration and Vital Statistics Knowledge Base: https://unstats.un.org/unsd/vitalstatkb/KnowledgebaseArticle50545.aspx.

Claypool, W. A. 2009. "Fighting the Culture of Poverty: Values and Opportunities on Chicago's Near North Side." MA thesis, Roosevelt University.

Cohen, Elizabeth S. 1992. "Honor and Gender in the Streets of Early Modern Rome." *Journal of Interdisciplinary History* 22, no. 4: 597–625.

Colucci, Erminia, and David Lester, eds. 2012. *Suicide and Culture: Understanding the Context*. Göttingen: Hogrefe Publishing.

Conrad, Clifton, A. Neumann, Jennifer Grant Haworth, and P. Scott. 1993. *Qualitative Research in Higher Education: Experiencing Alternative Perspectives and Approaches*. Needham Heights, MA: Ginn Press.

Coulson, Noel J. 1969. *Conflicts and Tensions in Islamic Jurisprudence*. Chicago: University of Chicago Press.

Cummings, E. Mark, and Laura E. Miller-Graff. 2015. "Emotional Security Theory: An Emerging Theoretical Model for Youths' Psychological and Physiological Responses Across Multiple Developmental Contexts." *Current Directions in Psychological Science* 24, no. 3 (June): 208–213. DOI: 10.1177/0963721414561510.

Curra, John. 2013. *The Relativity of Deviance*. Thousand Oaks, CA: SAGE Publications.

Danish Immigration Service. 2020. *Iranian Kurds: Consequences of Political Activities in Iran and KRI*. Accessed 16 April 2020. https://www.ecoi.net/en/file/local/2024578/Report+on+Iranian+Kurds+Feb+2020.pdf.

Dastgiri, S., L. R. Kalankesh, and N. Pourafkary. 2005. "Epidemiology of Self-Immolation in the North-West of Iran." *European Journal of General Medicine* 2, no. 1: 14–19. 10.29333/ejgm/82260.

Derayeh, Minoo. 2006. *Gender Equality in Iranian History: From Pre-Islamic Times to the Present*. Lewiston: Edwin Mellen Press.

DeSilva, David A. 2000. *Honor, Patronage, Kinship and Purity: Unlocking New Testament Culture*. Downers Grove, IL: InterVarsity Press.

Desjarlais, Robert, Leon Eisenberg, Byron Good, and Arthur Kleinman. 1995. *World Mental Health Problems and Priorities in Low-Income Countries*. New York: Oxford University Press.

Dobash, Russell, Rebecca Emerson Dobash, Margo Wilson, and Martin Daly. 2005. "The Myth of Sexual Symmetry in Marital Violence." In *Violence against Women*, edited by Raquel Kennedy Bergen and Claire M. Renzetti, 31–54. UK: Rowman & Littlefield.

Dresch, Paul. 1989. *Tribes, Government, and History in Yemen*. Oxford: Clarendon Press.

Eagleton, William Jr. 1963. *The Kurdish Republic of 1946*. London: Oxford University Press.
Ebadi, Shirin. 2002. *Huquq-e Zan Dar Ghavanin-e Jomhoori-e Islami-e Iran [Women's rights in the laws of the Islamic Republic of Iran]*. Tehran: Ganje Danesh Publication.
Edwards, Rosalind. 1990. "Connecting Method and Epistemology: A White Woman Interviewing Black Women." *Women's Studies International Forum* 13, no. 5: 477–490.
Eickelman, Dale F. 1998. *The Middle East and Central Asia: An Anthropological Approach*. Upper Saddle River, NJ: Prentice Hall.
Elias, Norbert, and John L. Scotson. 2008. *The Established and the Outsiders: A Sociological Enquiry into Community Problems*. Dublin: UCD Press.
Ennaji, Moha, and Fatima Sadiqi, eds. 2011. *Gender and Violence in the Middle East*. Abingdon: Routledge.
Esfandiari, Golnaz. 2020. "Iran Passes Child-Protection Law Following Gruesome Killing of Teenager." Radio Free Europe / Radio Liberty. Accessed 18 November 2020. https://www.rferl.org/a/iran-passes-child-protection-law-gruesome-killing-teenager-father/30660956.html.
Etemaad, Jalil, Bahram Jowkar, Masoud Hoseichari, and Hossein Dabbagh. 2019. "The Effectiveness of Evoking Reminiscence on Nostalgia State and the Role of Nostalgia into Empathy Action: Role of Gender and Personal Justification." *Journal of Applied Psychological Research* 10, no. 2 (Summer): 35–51.
Fallah Safavi, M. 2019. "Urban Ethnography with Emphasis on Culture of Poverty: A Case Study of Hadi Abad District of Ghazvim." MA thesis, Tehran University.
Farahani, Fataneh. 2017. *Gender, Sexuality, and Diaspora*. Abingdon: Routledge.
Faver, Catherine A., Alonzo M. Cavazos, and Brian L. Trachte. 2005. "Social Work Students at the Border: Religion, Culture, and Beliefs about Poverty." *Journal of Baccalaureate Social Work* 11, no. 1: 1–15.
Feldner, Yotam. 2000. "'Honor' Murders – Why the Perps Get off Easy." *Middle East Quarterly* 7, no. 4 (December): 41–50.
Ferris, Kerry, and Jill Stein. 2008. *The Real World: An Introduction to Sociology*. New York: W.W. Norton.
Findlay, Robyn A. 2003. "Interventions to Reduce Social Isolation among Older People: Where Is the Evidence?" *Ageing & Society* 23: 647–658.
Fliege, Herbert, Jeong-Ran Lee, Anne Grimm, and Burghard F. Klapp. 2009. "Risk Factors and Correlates of Deliberate Self-Harm Behavior: A Systematic Review." *Journal of Psychosomatic Research* 66, no. 6 (June): 477–493.
Fulu, Emma, and Alice Kerr-Wilson. 2015. *What Works to Prevent Violence against Women and Girls Evidence Reviews Paper 2: Interventions to Prevent Violence against Women and Girls*. UK: What Works to Prevent Violence/United Kingdom Department for International Development. Accessed 30 April 2018. http://www.whatworks.co.za/documents/publications/35-global-evidence-reviews-paper-2-interventions-to-prevent-violence-against-women-and-girls-sep-2015/file.
Gerrard, Steve. 1994. "Morality and Codes of Honour." *Philosophy* 69, no. 267: 69–84.
Ghanea-Hercock, Nazila. 2003. "Ethnic and Religious Groups in the Islamic Republic of Iran: Policy Suggestions for the Integration of Minorities through Participation in Public Life." Paper presented at the United Nations Commission on Human Rights, Sub-commission on the Promotion and Protection of Human Rights, Working

Group on Minorities. 9th session. Accessed 17 April 2018. https://ap.ohchr.org/documents/E/SUBCOM/other/E-CN_4-SUB_2-AC_5-2003-WG_8.pdf.

Gilsenan, Michael. 1996. *Lords of the Lebanese Marches: Violence and Narrative in an Arab Society*. Berkeley: University of California Press.

Girls Not Brides. 2020. "Child Marriage around the World: Iran." Accessed 24 November 2020. https://www.girlsnotbrides.org/child-marriage/iran/.

Gorski, Paul. 2008. "Beyond the 'Culture of Poverty': Resources on Economic Justice." *Multicultural Perspectives* 10, no. 1: 27–29.

Griffiths, Paul. 2002. "Juvenile Delinquency in Time." In *Becoming Delinquent: British and European Youth, 1650-1950*, edited by Pamela Cox and Heather Shore, 23–40. Dartmouth: Ashgate.

Groohi, Bahram, Reza Alaghehbandan, and Abdolaziz Rastegar Lari. 2002. "Analysis of 1089 Burn Patients in Province of Kurdistan, Iran." *Burns* 28, no. 6 (September): 569–574.

Gunter, Michael M. 2020. "Iran's Forgotten Kurds." *Journal of South Asian and Middle Eastern Studies* 43, no. 2: 54–67.

Habibzadeh, M. J., and H. Babi. 1999. "Qatl dar farash" [Honour killing]. *Madares* 4 (Winter): 89–90.

Haeri, Shahla. 1989. *Law of Desire: Temporary Marriage in Shi'i Iran*. New York: Syracuse University Press.

Haeri, Shahla. 2014. *Law of Desire: Temporary Marriage in Shi'i Iran*. Rev. ed. New York: Syracuse University Press.

Haeri, Shahla. 2020. *The Unforgettable Queens of Islam: Succession, Authority and Gender*. Cambridge: Cambridge University Press.

Hagan, John, John Simpson, and A. R. Gillis. 1987. "Class in the Household: A Power-Control Theory of Gender and Delinquency." *American Journal of Sociology* 92, no. 4: 788–816.

Hajnasiri, Hamideh, Reza Ghanei Gheshlagh, Kourosh Sayehmiri, Farnoosh Moafi, and Mohammad Farajzadeh. 2016. "Domestic Violence Among Iranian Women: A Systematic Review and Meta-Analysis." *Iran Red Crescent Medical Journal* 18, no. 6: e34971. 10.5812%2Fircmj.34971.

Haley, Allameh, and Hassan Ibn Yusuf. 1999 (1420 AH). *Tahrir al-Hikam al-Shara'i for the Religion of al-Amamiyya*. Qom, Iran: Imam Sadiq Institute (AS).

Hamermesh, Daniel, and Neal M. Soss. 1974. "An Economic Theory of Suicide." *Journal of Political Economy* 82, no. 1: 83–98.

Hamzić, Vanja, and Ziba Mir-Hosseini. 2010. *Control and Sexuality: The Revival of Zina Laws in Muslim Contexts*. London: Women Living Under Muslim Laws.

Hardeman, Wendy, Stephen Sutton, Simon Griffin, Marie Johnston, Anthony White, Nicholas J. Wareham, and Ann Louise Kinmonth. 2005. "A Causal Modelling Approach to the Development of Theory-Based Behaviour Change Programmes for Trial Evaluation." *Health Education Research* 20, no. 6 (December): 676–687.

Hasluck, Margaret. 1967. "The Albanian Blood Feud." In *Law and Warfare: Studies in the Anthropology of Conflict*, edited by Paul Bohannan, 381–408. Garden City, NY: The Natural History Press.

Hawton, Keith, Carolina Casañas I. Comabella, Camilla Haw, and Kate Saunders. 2013. "Risk Factors for Suicide in Individuals with Depression: A Systematic Review." *Journal of Affective Disorders* 147, no. 1–3 (May): 17–28. DOI: 10.1016/j.jad.2013.01.004.

Hesse-Biber, Sharlene Nagy. 2007. "The Practice of Feminist In-Depth Interviewing." In *Feminist Research Practice*, edited by Sharlene Nagy Hesse-Biber and Patricia L. Leavy, 110–148. Thousand Oaks, CA: SAGE Publications, Inc. 10.4135/9781412984270.n5.

Hiro, Dilip. 2013. *Iran under the Ayatollahs*. London: Routledge.

Homa, Ava. 2016. "From Self-Rule to Self-Immolation: Kurdish Women's Past and Present." *Iran Human Rights Review: Women and Human Rights*. Accessed 18 March 2017. https://www.ihrr.org/ihrr_article/women-en_from-self-rule-to-self-immolation-kurdish-womens-past-and-present/.

Home Office. 2017. *Country Policy and Information Note – Iran: Honour Crimes against Women*. Accessed 17 April 2018. https://assets.publishing.service.gov.uk/government/uploads/system/uploads/attachment_data/file/653537/CPIN_-_Iran_-_Honour_crimes_October_2017_ex.pdf.

Home Office. 2019. *Country Policy and Information Note – Iran: Adulterers*. Accessed 18 March 2017. https://assets.publishing.service.gov.uk/government/uploads/system/uploads/attachment_data/file/836919/Iran_-_Adulterers_-_CPIN_-_v3.0__October_2019__-_EXT.pdf.

Hughes, Donna M., and Ramesh Sepehrrad. 2004. "Sex Slavery New Face of Oppression of Women in Iran." Accessed 21 March 2019. https://womensenews.org/2004/02/sex-slavery-new-face-oppression-women-iran/.

Human Rights Watch. 2019. "Iran: Events of 2018." *World Report 2019*. Accessed 21 March 2020. https://www.hrw.org/world-report/2019/country-chapters/iran#.

Human Rights Watch. 2020. "Iran: Events of 2019." *World Report 2020*. Accessed 17 April 2020. https://www.hrw.org/world-report/2020/country-chapters/iran#be6679.

Ibrahim, Faiqa. 2005. "Honour Killings under the Rule of Law in Pakistan." Master's thesis, McGill University.

Idriss, Mohammad Mazher. 2011. "Honour, Violence, Women and Islam—An Introduction." In *Honour, Violence, Women and Islam*, edited by Mohammad Mazher Idriss and Tahir Abbas, 1–15. Abingdon, Oxon; New York: Routledge.

Iemmi, Valentina, Jason Bantjes, Ernestina Coast, Kerrie Channer, Tiziana Leone, David McDaid, Alexis Palfreyman, Crick Lund, and Bevan Stephens. 2016. "Suicide and Poverty in Low-Income and Middle-Income Countries: A Systematic Review." *Lancet Psychiatry* 3, no. 8: 774–783. DOI: 10.1016/S2215-0366(16)30066-9.

Iran: Islamic Penal Code. 1991. Accessed 26 November 2020. https://www.refworld.org/docid/518a19404.html.

Jain, Saranga, and Kathleen Kurz. 2007. *New Insights on Preventing Child Marriage: A Global Analysis of Factors and Programs*. ICRW, International Center for Research on Women.

Jebari, Idriss. 2018. "Therapeutic History and the Enduring Memories of Violence in Algeria and Morocco." *Middle East – Topics & Arguments* 11 (November): 108–119. DOI:10.17192/meta.2018.11.7808.

Julios, Christina. 2016. *Forced Marriage and "Honour" Killings in Britain: Private Lives, Community Crimes and Public Policy Perspectives*. UK: Routledge.

Kanie, Mariwan. 2015. *Rethinking Roots of Rising Violence against Women in the Kurdistan Region of Iraq*. Hivos, Knowledge Programme Civil Society in West Asia. Special Bulletin (April).

Kar, Mehrangiz. 2008. "Honor Killings." Accessed 20 January 2017. https://web.archive.org/web/20090304225702/http://www.roozonline.com/english/archives/2008/02/honor_killings.html.

Katouzian, Nasser. 2003. *Family Law*. Civil Rights Foundation.
Kaviani Rad, Morad. 2007. "Political Regionalism in Iran: The Case of Iranian Baluchestan." *Strategic Studies Quarterly* 10, no. 35: 89–101.
Kazemzadeh, Masoud. 2002. *Islamic Fundamentalism, Feminism, and Gender Inequality in Iran under Khomeini*. Lanham, MD: University Press of America.
Keddie, Nikki R. 1991. "Introduction: Deciphering Middle Eastern Women's History." In *Women in Middle Eastern History: Shifting Boundaries in Sex and Gender*, edited by Nikki R. Keddie and Beth Baron, 1–22. New Haven: Yale University Press.
Khayati, Khalid. 2008. *From Victim Diaspora to Transborder Citizenship? Diaspora Formation and Transnational Relations among Kurds in France and Sweden*. Linköping, Sweden: Linköping University.
Khumaini, Ayatu Allah Al. 2010. *Tahrir Al-Wasila*. no. 12.
Koggel, Christine M., ed. 2006. *Moral Issues in Global Perspective - Volume 2: Human Diversity and Equality*. 2nd ed. Peterborough: Broadview Press.
Koohi-Kamali, Farideh. 2003. *The Political Development of the Kurds in Iran: Pastoral Nationalism*. New York: Palgrave-Macmillan.
Kressel, Gideon. 1981. "Sororicide/Filiacide: Homicide for Family Honour." *Current Anthropology* 22, no. 2: 141–158.
Kulczycki, Andrzej, and Sarah Windle. 2012. "Honor Killings in the Middle East and North Africa: A Systematic Review of the Literature." *Violence against Women* 17, no. 11: 1442–1464.
Kurdistan Human Rights Network. 2020. "Two Kurdish Porters Wounded in the Border Areas of Baneh and Sardasht." Accessed 17 April 2020. http://kurdistanhumanrights.net/en/two-kurdish-porters-wounded-in-the-border-areas-of-baneh-and-sardasht/.
Laffin, John. 1975. *Rhetoric and Reality: The Arab Mind Considered*. New York: Taplinger Publishing Company.
Landinfo. 2009. *Honour Killings in Iran*. Accessed 20 January 2018. https://landinfo.no/asset/960/1/960_1.pdf.
Lester, David, ed. 2001. *Suicide Prevention: Resources for the Millennium*. Series in Death, Dying, and Bereavement. UK: Routledge.
Lewis, Oscar. 1975. *Five Families: Mexican Case Studies in the Culture of Poverty*. New York: Basic Books.
Ludwig, Jens, and Susan Mayer. 2006. "'Culture' and the Intergenerational Transmission of Poverty: The Prevention Paradox." *The Future of Children* 16, no. 2: 175–196.
Maghsodi, M. 2001. *Tahavolate Quomi dar Iran*. Tehran: Institute of National Studies.
Mahdi, Ali A. 2014. "Perceptions of Gender Roles Among Female Iranian Immigrants in the United States." In *Women, Religion and Culture in Iran*, edited by Sarah Ansari and Vanessa Martin, 189–214. London: Routledge.
Mann, Susan A., and Lori R. Kelley. 1997. "Standing at the Crossroads of Modernist Thought: Collins, Smith, and the New Feminist Epistemologies." *Gender and Society* 11, no. 4 (August): 391–408.
Manuello, Tessa. 2014. "Erbil Mission to Boost Canadian Business Opportunities in Kurdistan, Iraq." *Rudaw*. Accessed 20 January 2018. http://rudaw.net/english/kurdistan/11052014.
Marini, John, and Ken Masugi. 2005. *The Progressive Revolution in Politics and Political Science: Transforming the American Regime*. Lanham, MD: Rowman & Littlefield.

References

Maroufi, Nasser. 1968. "The Effect of Literacy and Employment on Age at First Marriage of Women in Various Parts of Tehran City." *Tenth International Seminar on Family Research, Institute for Social Studies and Research*. Tehran: University of Tehran.

Martin, Vanessa. 2005. *The Qajar Pact: Bargaining, Protest and the State in Nineteenth-Century Persia*. London: I.B. Tauris.

Mayring, Philipp. 1983. *Qualitative Inhaltsanalyse: Grundlagen und Techniken*. Basel: Beltz.

McDonald, Susan. 2001. "Kurdish Women and Self-Determination: A Feminist Approach to International Law." In *Women of a Non-State Nation: The Kurds*, edited by Shahrzad Mojab, 135–157. Costa Mesa, CA: Mazda Publishers.

McDowall, David. 2004. *A Modern History of the Kurds*. 3rd ed. London: I.B. Tauris.

McGregor, Heather Elizabeth. 2013. "Situating Nunavut Education With Indigenous Education in Canada." *Canadian Journal of Education/Revue Canadienne De l'éducation* 36, no. 2: 87–118.

Mehrpour, Hossein, ed. 1993. *Majmu'eh-ye nazariyāt-e shurā-ye negahbān [Collected opinions of the Guardian Council, vol. 1]*. Tehran: Center for the Islamic Revolution Documents.

Millbank, Jenni, and Catherine Dauvergne. 2010. "Forced Marriage and the Exoticization of Gendered Harms in United States Asylum Law." *Columbia Journal of Gender and Law* 19, no. 4. Accessed 20 February 2020. DOI: 10.7916/cjgl.v19i4.2612.

Mir-Hosseini, Ziba. 1993. *Marriage on Trial: A Study of Islamic Family Law: Iran and Morocco Compared*. London: I.B. Tauris.

Mir-Hosseini, Ziba. 1996. "Women and Politics in Post-Khomeini Iran: Divorce, Veiling and Emerging Feminist Voices." In *Women and Politics in the Third World*, edited by Haleh Afshar, 145–173. London and New York: Routledge.

Mir-Hosseini, Ziba. 2000. *Islam and Gender: The Religious Debate in Contemporary Iran*. London: I. B. Tauris.

Mir-Hosseini, Ziba. 2001. *Marriage on Trial: A Study of Islamic Family Law: Iran and Morocco Compared*. Rev. ed. London: I.B. Tauris.

Mohamadi, Mohamad Baqer. 1994. *"Esteedadhayeh Zan" [Woman's talents]*. Tehran: Islamic Propaganda Organisation's Research Centre.

Mohammadi, M. 2004. "Tamkin; Ghodrat-e Zanan ya Khooshunat-e Mardan" [Obedience; women's power or men's violence]. *Ketab Zanan in Women's Socio-Cultural Council Quarterly* 23: 12–20.

Mohammadpour, Ahmad, and Kamal Soleimani. 2020. "'Minoritisation' of the Other: The Iranian Ethno-theocratic State's Assimilatory Strategies." *Postcolonial Studies*. DOI: 10.1080/13688790.2020.1746157.

Mohammadpur, Ahmad, Jalil Karimi, and Mehdi Alizadeh. 2014. "Women and Culture of Poverty (A Qualitative Study of the Culture of Poverty among the Iranian Caretaker Women)." *Quality & Quantity: International Journal of Methodology* 48, no. 1 (January): 1–14.

Mojab, Shahrzad, and Nahla Abdo, eds. 2004. *Violence in the Name of Honour: Theoretical and Political Challenges*. Istanbul: Bilgi University Press.

Mojab, Shahrzad. 2001. "Women and Nationalism in the Kurdish Republic of 1946." In *Women of a Non-State Nation: The Kurds*, edited by Shahrzad Mojab, 71–93. Costa Mesa, CA: Mazda Publishers.

Molaverdi, Shahindokht. 2015. "Female Unemployment; This Is Not a Priority for the Government." *Deutsche Welle*. Accessed 15 November 2020. https://www.dw.com/fa-ir/بیکاری-زنان-معضلی-که-اولویت-اصلی-دولت-نیست/a-18507670.

Montazeri, Simin, Maryam Gharacheh, Nooredin Mohammadi, Javad Alaghband Rad, and Hassan Eftekhar Ardabili. 2016. "Determinants of Early Marriage from Married Girls' Perspectives in Iranian Setting: A Qualitative Study." *Journal of Environmental and Public Health*, 2016, article ID 8615929. DOI: 10.1155/2016/8615929.

Mora, Necla. 2009. "Violence as a Communication Action: Customary and Honor Killings." *International Journal of Human Sciences* 6, no. 2: 499–510.

Motavalli Haghighi, Yousef. 2010. "A Reflection on the Causes and How to Immigrate to Khorasan." *Specialized Journal of Jurisprudence and History of Civilization* 6, no. 21: 591–672.

Nanes, Stefanie Eileen. 2003. "Fighting Honor Crimes: Evidence of Civil Society in Jordan." *Middle East Journal* 57, no. 1 (Winter): 112–129.

Napikoski, Linda. 2020. "Patriarchal Society According to Feminism." Accessed 18 April 2020. https://www.thoughtco.com/patriarchal-society-feminism-definition-3528978.

Nawzad, Kosar. 2018. "Over 100 Kurds in Iran Commit Suicide in 6 Months, Many over Poverty." Kurdistan24. Accessed 1 November 2020. https://www.kurdistan24.net/en/news/078ad429-62bb-4ab7-b6d1-fcc0e53e4bab.

Nayyeri, Mohammad, and Iran Human Rights Documentation Center (IHRDC). 2013. *Gender Inequality and Discrimination: The Case of Iranian Women*. Accessed 16 March 2015. https://iranhrdc.org/gender-inequality-and-discrimination-the-case-of-iranian-women/.

Nisbett, Richard E., and Dov Cohen. 1996. *Culture of Honor: The Psychology of Violence in the South*. Boulder: Westview Press.

Nordt, Carlos, Ingeborg Warnke, Erich Seifritz, and Wolfram Kawohl. 2015. "Modelling Suicide and Unemployment: A Longitudinal Analysis Covering 63 Countries, 2000–11." *Lancet Psychiatry* 2, no. 3: 239–245.

O'Doherty, Mark. 2017. *Healing Pakistan – Improving Human Rights, Gender Mainstreaming and Religious Education in the Islamic Republic of Pakistan*. N.p.: Lulu.com.

Orywal, Erwin. 1996. "Krieg und Frieden in den Wissenschaften." In *Krieg und Kampf: Die Gewalt in unseren Köpfen*, edited by Erwin Orywal, Aparnar Rao, and Michael Bollig. Berlin: Reimer.

Otoo-Oyortey, Naana, and Sonita Pobi. 2003 "Early Marriage and Poverty: Exploring Links and Key Policy Issues." *Gender and Development* 11, no. 2: 42–51.

Pateman, Carole. 1988. *The Sexual Contract*. Cambridge: Polity Press.

Pervizat, Leyla. 2011. "Lack of Due Diligence: Judgement of Crimes of Honour in Turkey." In *Honour, Violence, Women and Islam*, edited by Mohammad Mazher Idriss and Tahir Abbas, 142–153. Abingdon, Oxon; New York: Routledge.

Petroni, Suzanne, Vikram Patel, and George Patton. 2015. "Why Is Suicide the Leading Killer of Older Adolescent Girls?" *Lancet* 386, no. 10008: 2031–2032.

Pickthall, Muhammad Marmaduke. 2017. *The Holy Qur'an, Arabic Transliteration - English*. India: Adam Publishers.

Pirnia, Bijan, Fariborz Pirnia, and Kambiz Pirnia. 2020. "Honour Killings and Violence against Women in Iran during the COVID-19 Pandemic." *Lancet Psychiatry* 7, no. 10: e60.

Pitt-Rivers, J. 1966. "Honour and Social Status." In *Honour and Shame: The Values of Mediterranean Society*, edited by John G. Peristiany, 19–77. Chicago: University of Chicago Press.

Pradel, Jean. 1991. *Histoire des doctrines pénales*. Paris: Presses Universitaires de France.

Qadir Shah, Hassam. 2002. *There Is No "Honour" in Killing: Don't Let Them Get Away with Murder* Lahore: Shirkat Gah Women's Resource Centre.

Qaeni, Mohsen. 1994. "Kotak zadan yeki az asar ryasat mard" [Beating is a symptom of the supremacy of man], *Zanan*, no. 18 (June–July).

Radio Farda. 2019. "Rights Organizations Urge UN Members To Condemn Iran Human Rights Violations." Accessed 17 April 2018. https://en.radiofarda.com/a/rights-organizations-urge-un-members-to-condemn-iran-human-rights-violations/30318461.html.

Rehman, Javaid. 2019. "Statement by Mr. Javaid Rehman, Special Rapporteur on the situation of human rights in the Islamic Republic of Iran at the 40th session of the Human Rights Council." Accessed 17 April 2018. https://www.ohchr.org/en/NewsEvents/Pages/DisplayNews.aspx?NewsID=24340&LangID=E.

Reinharz, Shulamit, and Lynn Davidman. 1992. *Feminist Methods in Social Research*. New York: Oxford University Press.

Report of Reforms of Crisis of Child Marriage in the Country. Accessed 17 April 2018. www.eslahat.news.

Rezaeian, Mohsen, and Gholamreza Sharifirad. 2012. "Case Fatality Rates of Different Suicide Methods within Ilam Province of Iran." *Journal of Education and Health Promotion* 1: n. pag.

Rezaeinasab, Zahra, Mohammad Taghi Sheikhi, and Fatemeh Jamilei Kohaneh Shahri. 2018. "Self-immolation of Women in Ilam City, Iran: A Descriptive Study." *Journal of School of Public Health and Institute of Public Health Research* 15, no. 4: 365–376. https://sjsph.tums.ac.ir/files/site1/user_files_edcd0e/admin-A-10-1-53-531e029.pdf.

Riessman, Catherine Kohler. 1987. "When Gender Is Not Enough: Women Interviewing Women." *Gender & Society* 1, no. 2 (June): 172–207.

2015 *Rights of the Child in Iran*. 2015. Retrieved from UN Treaty Body Database: https://tbinternet.ohchr.org/Treaties/CRC/Shared%20Documents/IRN/INT_CRC_NGO_IRN_19809_E.pdf.

Romm, Sharon, Heidi Combs, and Matthew B. Klein. 2008. "Self-Immolation: Cause and Culture." *Journal of Burn Care & Research* 29, no. 6 (November–December): 988–993.

Roosevelt, Archie Jr. 1947. "The Kurdish Republic of Mahabad." *Middle East Journal* 1, no. 3: 247–269.

Runciman, W. G. 1966. *Relative Deprivation and Social Justice: A Study of Attitudes to Social Inequality in Twentieth-century England*. Berkeley: University of California Press.

Ryazi, S. Abolhassan, and Banoudokht Najafianpour. 2016. "Comparison of Effective Socio-cultural and Psychological Factors in Women Suicide in Iran and Tajikistan." *Iranian Journal of Cultural Research* 8, no. 4: 143–167. Accessed 14 October 2019. https://www.sid.ir/en/Journal/ViewPaper.aspx?ID=508304.

Sadeghi, Mohammad Hadi. 2009. *Exclusive Criminal Law; Crimes against Persons*, 55–56. Tehran: Mizan, 8th, Spring, ISBN 964-5997-01.

Safilios-Rothschild, Constantina. 1969a. "'Honour' Crimes in Contemporary Greece." *British Journal of Sociology* 20: 205–218.

Safilios-Rothschild, Constantina. 1969b. "Sociopsychological Factors Affecting Fertility in Urban Greece: A Preliminary Report." *Journal of Marriage and Family* 31, no. 3: 595–606.

Saleh, Alam. 2013. *Ethnic Identity and the State in Iran*. New York: Palgrave Macmillan

Salih, Ruba. 2013. "From Bare Lives to Political Agents: Palestinian Refugees as Avant-Garde." *Refugee Survey Quarterly* 32, no. 2: 66–91.

Samadzadeh, Hassan. 2015. *The Book of the Kurdish Nomadic Community of Khalkhal (Kormanj)*. Tehran: Nokhbegan Publications.

Sanasarian, Eliz. 2000. *Religious Minorities in Iran*. Cambridge Middle East Studies. Cambridge: Cambridge University Press.

Sev'er, Aysan, and Gökçeçiçek Yurdakul. 2001. "Culture of Honor, Culture of Change: A Feminist Analysis of Honor Killings in Rural Turkey." *Violence Against Women* 7, no. 9: 964–998.

Shaddox, Colleen. 2007. "Years after Gas Attack, the Horror Lingers in an Iranian Town, EPH Alumna Finds." *Yale Medicine Magazine* (Winter): 6. Accessed 20 March 2017. https://medicine.yale.edu/news/yale-medicine-magazine/years-after-gas-attack-the-horror-lingers-in/.

Shakib, Shirin. 2017. "Child Marriage in Iran Forces Girls into a Life of Oppression." *Deutsche Welle*. Accessed 18 March 2020. https://tinyurl.com/yy35etl7.

Shalinsky, Audrey C. 1986. "Reason, Desire, and Sexuality: The Meaning of Gender in Northern Afghanistan." *Ethos: Journal of the Society for Psychological Anthropology* 14, no. 4 (December): 323–343.

Sheyholislami, Jaffer. 2011. "Kurdish Identity." In *Kurdish Identity, Discourse, and New Media*. The Palgrave Macmillan Series in International Political Communication. New York: Palgrave Macmillan. DOI: 10.1057/9780230119307_3.

Shin, Gi-Wook. 2006. *Ethnic Nationalism in Korea: Genealogy, Politics, and Legacy*. Stanford, CA: Stanford University Press.

Shojai, Mitra. 2013. "Honor Killing: Black Tradition that Does Not Know the Border." Accessed 20 March 2018. https://p.dw.com/p/183aR.

Shoro, Shahnaz. 2019. *The Real Stories behind Honour Killing*. Cambridge: Cambridge Scholars Publishing.

Siddiqui, Hannana. 2005. "'There is no "honour" in domestic violence, only shame!' Women's struggles against 'honour' crimes in the UK." In *"Honour": Crimes, Paradigms, and Violence against Women*, edited by Lynn Welchman and Sara Hossain, 263–281. London: Zed Books.

Silverman, David. 2005. *Doing Qualitative Research: A Practical Handbook*. London: SAGE Publications.

Small, Mario Luis, David J. Harding, and Michèle Lamont. 2010. "Reconsidering Culture and Poverty." *The ANNALS of the American Academy of Political and Social Science* 629, no. 1 (May): 6–27.

Smith, Rhona K. M., and Christien van den Anker. 2005. *The Essentials of Human Rights*. London: Hodder Arnold.

Smith, Joan. 1989. *Misogynies*. London: Faber and Faber.

Snow, David, Leon Anderson, John Lofland, and Lyn H. Lofland. 2005. *Analysing Social Settings: A Guide to Qualitative Observation and Analysis*. UK: Wadsworth Publishing.

Somerset, Carron. 2000. *Early Marriage: Whose Right to Choose?* London: Forum on Marriage and the Rights of Women and Girls.

Statistical Centre of Iran. *Statistical Yearbook (2017–2018)*. Accessed 18 March 2018. https://www.amar.org.ir/english/Iran-Statistical-Yearbook/Statistical-Yearbook-2017-2018.

Stone, Taraneh. 2019. "Child Brides in Iran: Tradition, Poverty and Resisting Change." *BBC Monitoring*. Accessed 21 March 2018. https://monitoring.bbc.co.uk/product/c200rxfl.

Sue, David, Derald Wing Sue, Stanley Sue, and Diane Sue. 2012. *Understanding Abnormal Behavior*. US: Cengage Learning.

Suhrabi, Zainab, Ali Delpisheh, and Hamid Taghinejad. 2012. "Tragedy of Women's Self-Immolation in Iran and Developing Communities: A Review." *International Journal of Burns and Trauma* 2: 93–104.

Syngellakis, Anna, and Gabriella Lazaridis. 1995. "Women's Status and Work in Contemporary Greece." *Journal of Area Studies* 3, no. 6: 96–107. DOI:10.1080/02613539508455740.

Taheri, Ahmad Reza. 2012. *The Baloch in Post Islamic Revolution Iran: A Political Study*. Morrisville: Lulu Press.

Takahashi, Yoshitomo. 2001. "Depression and Suicide." *Japan Medical Association Journal* 44, no. 8: 359–363.

Tartaro, Christine, and David Lester. 2010. *Suicide and Self-Harm in Prisons and Jails*. Lanham, MD: Lexington Books.

Tilly, Charles. 2003. *The Politics of Collective Violence*. Cambridge Studies in Contentious Politics. Cambridge: Cambridge University Press.

Tizro, Zahra. 2012. *Domestic Violence in Iran: Women, Marriage and Islam*. United Kingdom: Routledge.

Tizro, Zahra. 2014. "The Role of Orthodox Jurisprudence in Dealing with Domestic Violence against Women in Iran." *La Camera Blu*, no. 10 (September): 1–27. Accessed 18 March 2017. DOI:10.6092/1827-9198/2794.

Tope, Daniel, Lindsey Joyce Chamberlain, Martha Crowley, and Randy Hodson. 2005. "The Benefits of Being There: Evidence from the Literature on Work." *Journal of Contemporary Ethnography* 34, no. 4 (August): 470–493.

Tremayne, Soraya. 2006. "Modernity and Early Marriage in Iran: A View from Within." *Journal of Middle East Women's Studies* 2, no. 1: 65–94.

Triandis, Harry C. 1989. "The Self and Social Behavior in Differing Cultural Contexts." *Psychological Review* 96, no. 3: 506–520.

Tripathi, Anushree, and Supriya Yadav. 2004. "For the Sake of Honour: But Whose Honour? 'Honour Crimes' Against Women." *Asia-Pacific Journal on Human Rights and the Law* 5, no. 2: 63–78.

UNFPA (United Nations Population Fund). 2012. *Marrying Too Young: End Child Marriage*. New York: UNFPA. Accessed 14 March 2017. https://www.unfpa.org/sites/default/files/pub-pdf/MarryingTooYoung.pdf.

UNFPA (United Nations Population Fund). 2020. *Adapting to COVID-19: Pivoting the UNFPA–UNICEF Global Programme to End Child Marriage to Respond to the Pandemic*. New York: UNFPA. Accessed 17 December 2020. https://www.unfpa.org/sites/default/files/resource-pdf/Responding_to_COVID-19_Pivoting_the_GPECM_to_the_pandemic.pdf.

Vago, Steven. 2015. *Law and Society*. Abingdon: Routledge.

Vali, Abbas. 1998. "The Kurds and Their 'Others': Fragmented Identity and Fragmented Politics." *Comparative Studies of South Asia, Africa and the Middle East* 18, no. 2 (August): 82–95.

Vali, Abbas. 2003. *Essays on the Origins of Kurdish Nationalism*. Costa Mesa, CA: Mazda.

Vali, Abbas. 2014. *Kurds and the State in Iran: The Making of Kurdish Identity*. London: I.B. Tauris.

Vali, Abbas. 2015. *Modernity and the Stateless: The Kurdish Question in Iran*. London: I.B. Tauris.

Vali, Abbas. 2020. *The Forgotten Years of Kurdish Nationalism in Iran*. UK: Palgrave Macmillan.

Van den Haag, Ernest, and John P. Conrad. 1983. *The Death Penalty: A Debate*. New York: Plenum.

Vandello, Joseph A., and Dov Cohen. 2003. "Male Honor and Female Fidelity: Implicit Cultural Scripts that Perpetuate Domestic Violence." *Journal of Personal and Social Psychology* 84, no. 5: 997–1010. DOI:10.1037/0022-3514.84.5.997.

Vandello, Joseph A., and Dov Cohen. 2008. "Culture, Gender, and Men's Intimate Partner Violence." *Social and Personality Psychology Compass*, 2, no. 2: 652–667. DOI:10.1111/j.1751-9004.2008.00080.x.

Vandello, Joseph A., Jennifer K. Bosson, Dov Cohen, Rochelle M. Burnaford, and Jonathan R. Weaver. 2008. "Precarious Manhood." *Journal of Personality and Social Psychology* 95, no. 6: 1325–1339. DOI:10.1037/a0012453.

Vijayakumar, Lakshmi, Sujit John, Jane Pirkis, and Harvey Whiteford. 2005. "Suicide in Developing Countries (2): Risk Factors." *Crisis* 26, no. 3: 112–119.

Vogelstein, Rachel B. 2013. *Ending Child Marriage: How Elevating the Status of Girls Advances U.S. Foreign Policy Objectives*. USA: Council on Foreign Relations.

Von Hein, Shabnam. 2016. "Child Trafficking a Growing Problem in Iran." *Deutsche Welle*. https://p.dw.com/p/2T8uo.

Vreede-de Stuers, Cora. 1968. *Parda: A Study of Muslim Women's Life in Northern India*. Assen, Netherlands: Van Gorcum.

Warnock, Kitty. 1990. *Land Before Honour: Palestinian Women in the Occupied Territories*. London: Palgrave Macmillan.

Weber, Max, Hans Gerth, and C. Wright Mills. 1946. *From Max Weber: Essays in Sociology*. New York: Oxford University Press.

Weiss, Robert Stuart. 1994. *Learning from Strangers: The Art and Method of Qualitative Interview Studies*. New York: Free Press.

Weston, Kath. 2004. "Fieldwork in Lesbian and Gay Communities." In *Feminist Perspectives on Social Research*, edited by Sharlene Nagy Hesse-Biber and Michelle L. Yaiser, 198–205. New York: Oxford University Press.

Wilkinson, Richard G. 2005. *The Impact of Inequality: How to Make Sick Societies Healthier*. London: Routledge.

World Vision. 2013. *Untying the Knot: Exploring Early Marriage in Fragile States*. UK: World Vision.

Wyatt-Brown, Bertram. 1982. *Southern Honor: Ethics and Behavior in the Old South*. New York: Oxford University Press.

Yildiz, Kerim, and Tanyel B. Taysi. 2007. *The Kurds in Iran: The Past, Present and Future*. London: Pluto Press.

Zabih, Sepehr. 1982. *Iran since the Revolution*. Baltimore and London: Johns Hopkins University Press.

Index

activism 10, 52
activist 6, 8, 43, 46, 91
adultery: justification for honour crimes 14, 28–9, 38, 41–2, 48; permissibility for men 12; trial of husband after killing because of 45
Anti-Persian separatism 4
anxiety 13, 80
Article 23 of the Family Protection Act 1353 (1974) 71 Article 3 of the Amendment to the Law on Marriage 70 autonomy 12–3, 35, 64, 80

bayanah 45
beheading 11
bigamy 105
birth registration 66

capital punishment 29, 44
caretaker women 94–6
chauvinism 35
child custody 10, 53, 68, 98, 101
child marriage: cause of increased suicide rates 13; couples roles within 69; definition of 63; drug use in 79–80, 82; effects on women's health 66; firsthand experiences 73–5; historic causes of 64; international views on 65, 72; issues with consent 75–6; legislation about 70–2; promotion by Islam 89; regional instability's influence on 79; relationship to poverty 76–8, 95; statistics on 18, 63, 68, 70, 72, 81; violence women subjected to daily 10, 15
community education 55
consent: importance of guardian's 39; to infidelity or rape 41; to marriage 64–5, 72; people permitted to consent 75–6,

101; submission to government control 34; a wife's limitations without her husband's 37; with respect to age 67–70, 72
conservatism 22, 27, 109
Council of Elders 41 Covid-19 63, 98, 110
criminal injustice 21, 27
criminal law 21, 27, 37–8, 44–5
criminal responsibility 41–2;
cult of domesticity 47;
cultural rationalisation 63;
culture of poverty 93–5;
customary law 27

despair 99, 102, 110
discrimination: against the Kurds 5–7; against women 10–1, 13–4, 21–2, 35, 46, 72–3, 110; cause of suicide 18, 98; criminal injustices and 27, 55; economic 83; in the job market 90–2, 107; rooted in tribal culture 48–9, 101; through child marriage 63–6, 75
divorce: asking for 48; as a cause of suicide 98; causes for 89; changing attitudes towards 108; custody in 100; fears of 10; laws surrounding 69–70; life after 95; prevalence of divorce in early marriage 11, 78–9; as a result of child marriage 77; spousal rights in 37, 52–3; statistics on 68; threat of 30
diya 27, 39
domestic violence: encouragement for 90, escalation of 98–100; as a factor in child marriage 77, 80–81; as a factor in suicide 13, 108–109; lack of laws protecting women from 31; reduced punishment for 44; resources for victims of 51; statistics on 52

drug addict 79, 81, 92, 104
drug addiction 80
drug dealer 78, 103

early marriage *see* child marriage
education: child marriage's effect on girls 63–7, 69–70, 77–9; demand for Kurdish 4; as a factor in honour-based violence 29, 35–6, 46, 54–6; as a factor in misogyny 11; forced marriage's effect on 82–4; opposition to 76, 96, 107; poverty's effect on 91; women's access to 13, 31, 50
egalitarian families 47
ethnicists *see* nationalists

family: contributions of family pressure to suicide risk 13; divorce and 88–93; effects of child marriage 81–4; effect of honour on 29; effect on women's lives 31; family structures in Iran 30; hierarchy of family structure 15; honour of 47; human rights of 72–9; implementation of honour based violence 33–6; muslim views on 15; patriarchal 47; prosecution in honour killings 36–41, 48–54; reactions to honour based violence 44; rights 64–6; role of female family members in honour killings 14; traditional family roles among Kurds 8–11; views on honour killings 28; views on suicide 97–104
family pressure 13, 54, 100, 108
father: opposition to daughter's education 76; punishment for honour based crimes 40–4; role in child marriage 71, 75, 79; role in family 46–7; role in honour based culture 30, 34, 36, 100
feminist 15–7, 19–20
forced marriage 11; definition of 64; due to a child's lack of development 67; as a factor in increased suicide rates 99, 108; as a form of gender based harassment 65; as a motivation to not educate girls 76; punishment for resisting 101; as a repercussion of weak rule of law 54; as a result of poverty 74, 102; root causes of 72; in urban and rural environments 82

gender equality 81, 91, 96
gender inequality 27, 30, 46, 66, 107
gender roles 12, 95

gender-based discrimination 13, 46
gender-based harassment 65
gender-based violence 1, 22, 52, 81, 109
gêyrat 39

HBV *see* honour based violence
HDE *see* human development indices
hadd 38
hadith 39
honour 1, 11; definition of 34; as a factor in suicide 101; honour as a marker of status 32; masculinity and 52; modern role of honour 29; murder commited for 39; patriarchy and 13–15, 32–3; as a woman's asset 44
honour-based violence 10; criminal code on 55; factors in 29, 54; international response to 14; links with tradition 15; patriarchy as a factor in 29; as a result of men's stewardship 48; victims of 38
honour killings: definition of 13; extreme form of violence against women 11; factors in 36; history of 34; impact of family statutes on 15; laws applicable to 21, 27–30, 38–41; and Persian culture 48–9; punishment for 43–6; reforms needed 53–4, 55; role of women in 32; statistics on 14, 18
human development indices 96
human rights violation 8, 46, 64, 84

illiteracy 77, 84
Iranian Civil Code 70–1, 75
Iranian Constitution 27, 111
Iranian Kurdistan: geographical boundaries of 1; history of 4–5; patriarchy within 46; statistics on employment 91–2; suicide among women in 17, 99; traditional family structure in 14–5; traditional values of 22, 27; violence against women 52
Islamic law: criticism of 51; factors perpetuating child marriage 21, 69; formulation of 37–9; formation of laws in accordance with 43, 53; practice of 55
Islamic legal terms 39
Islamic Penal Code of Iran: Article 38 44; Article 43 44; Article 147 42; Article 179 41; Article 220 40, 42; Article 226, 42; Article 295 40, 43, 45; Article 301, 44–5; Article 630 41–3

Islamic Revolution 3, 5; changes made to law after the 27, 69, 89, 91

jealousy 11–22
judges role in injustice 49
 judiciary 36, 43, 45

kolbar 5–6, 92, 105
 kulbari *see* kolbar

language barrier 54, 76, 108
legal age of marriage 65–6, 68–9, 70–2
literacy 73, 83–4, 96

mahr 52
mahriye 30
marital abuse 30, 37, 81
marriage: abuse within 30, 37; consent to 75; as a factor in suicide 99–100; gender roles in marriage 11, 30; goals of marriage 88; international views on 65–7; Islam's views on 68, 89–90; minimum legal age of 69–72; rights within 37; as a shelter for women 96; statistics on 46; traditional practices of 9–10; women's position in society through 22, 103
masculinity 52
maternal health 79
maternal mortality 81, 98
mesl 30
misogyny 11
modernism 47
modernity 22
morality 48
mother: consideration as guardian 43; dangers for young 77, 83; determiner of blood money 40; inability to offer permission for daughter's marriage 74; participation in honour culture 100; roles of women in traditional communities 9–10, 47, 68–9, 91

nafage 30
nafaqa 69
nationalists 2–3
nomad 8–9, 34, 92
normative disorientation 52
nushuz 69

ojrat 30
orthodox jurisprudence 37
ownership 14, 46, 68

patriarchy 1, 20, 27; definition of honour through 32, 36; impact on female employment 91; impact on honour discourse 52; Islamic norms that support 39; in Kurdish society 46; Mohamadi thoughts on 12; suicide as a result of 97; in traditional society 29
Persian: as dominant Iranian culture 30; lack of honour killings among 48, language 2, 16, 76; as a sources 18, 98
Persian Aryanism 2
Persian nationalists 2
Persianisation 7
pardon 39, 44, 55
peshmerga 52
polygamy 54, 69, 100, 108
population control 9
poverty: cause for child marriage 64, 68–70, 72, 74, 82; cause for suicide 13, 89–95, 97–8, 102, 109–110; effects of child marriage 66; causes of 76–7; reform needs to fix 104–107; repercussion of economic instability 11; as a result of political oppression 4, 6
prejudice 48–9, 54
prostitution 39, 54, 77, 80, 91–2
protection of children 10
protest: cause for a woman to be punished 81, 101; after establishment of Kurdish governing body in Iraq 5; against fuel prices 8; suicide as 97–8; worldwide response to honour killings 50
puberty 41, 67, 69–71, 80
punishment: for child marriage 70–1; exemption from 75; necessary reforms to 53, 55; Qur'an's views on 39–44; received for honour killings 49–51; for sexual indiscretion 30; for women who resist tradition 101
purchase age 68

Qur'an 12, 38–40, 43, 90
qatl' amd 39
qisas 27, 39–43

reflexivity 20
regional instability 79, 84
remarriage 30, 95
reputation 13, 29, 32–3
resources for women threatened with

violence 50–1
retribution 39, 44–5
right of retribution 44
rule of law 36, 38–9, 54–5, 84

Sanandaj 1, 17, 41, 81
self-esteem 11, 13, 83
self-immolation 80, 98, 100–1, 105–107
sexual harassment in workplace 91
sexual maturity 67, 76
shame: effect on honour based crime 1, 11, 14, 22, 79; of sexual assault 52; women's experiences with 50, 54
social development 21, 64, 80, 94
substantive law 27
suicide: as an act of protest 74, 100; as a consequence of child marriage 80, 84; contributing factors of 11–3; epidemiology of 101; honour culture's effect on 35; lack of help to prevent 49–50; preventative community resources 108–109; rates in Sardasht after attack by Saddam Hussein 4; as social problem 97; statistics about 18, 88, 98

Sunni muslims 1, 7, 17, 48

tamkin 30, 69, 90
target-hardening 56
theory of planned behavior 33
theory of power control 47
TPB *see* theory of planned behavior

underage marriage *see* child marriage
unemployment: affect on suicide rates 89–94, 97–8; dependence on child labour due to 76; factors in the continuance of conservative values 54; implications on child marriage 80–1; as a result of state neglect 5–6; statistics on 2, 104–105

widow: children of 79–80; experiences of 22, 90, 104; financial situation of 5; rate of suicide 106; statistics about 68
widowhood 70
women's roles 22, 91

zina 39

CPSIA information can be obtained
at www.ICGtesting.com
Printed in the USA
LVHW080735080222
710389LV00026B/480